WHO SPEAKS

FOR THE RIVER?

WHO SPEAKS
FOR THE RIVER?

*The Oldman River Dam and
the Search for Justice*

Robert Girvan

**FIFTH
HOUSE**

Published in Canada by Fifth House Ltd., 195 Allstate Parkway, Markham, ON L3R 4T8
Published in the United States by Fifth House Ltd., 311 Washington Street,
Brighton, Massachusetts 02135
www.fifthhousepublishers.ca

Library and Archives Canada Cataloguing in Publication
Girvan, Robert
Who speaks for the river? : the Oldman River Dam and the search
for justice / Robert Girvan.
Includes bibliographical references.
ISBN 978-1-927083-01-7
1. Oldman River Dam (Alta.)--History. 2. Dams--Political aspects--
Alberta--History. 3. Alberta--Politics and government--1971-. 4. Piegan
Indians--Alberta--Government relations. 5. Piegan Indians--Land
tenure--Alberta. 6. Alberta--Ethnic relations--History. 7. Justice--
Alberta--Case studies. 8. Power (Social sciences)--Alberta--Case studies.
I. Title.
TC558.C32G57 2012   333.91′30971234   C2012-904810-0

Publisher Cataloging-in-Publication Data (U.S.)
Girvan, Robert.
Who speaks for the river : The Oldman River Dam and the search for justice / Robert Girvan.
[408] p. : photos., maps ; cm.
Includes bibliographical references.
Summary: A depiction of the clash between power and justice in the desperate final battle between
the Alberta government, Friends of the Oldman and members of the Piikani First Nation
over the building of Alberta's Oldman River Dam.
ISBN: 978-1-92708-301-7
1. Oldman River Dam (Alta.) – History. 2. Piegan Indians -- Government relations.
3. Environmental policy -- Alberta -- Oldman River Watershed.
I. Title.
333.913/0971234 dc23   TC558.C32G46 2012

Fifth House Ltd. acknowledges with thanks the Canada Council for the Arts, and the Ontario Arts
Council for their support of our publishing program. We acknowledge the financial support of the
Government of Canada through the Canada Book Fund (CBF) for our publishing activities.

Canada Council   Conseil des Arts
for the Arts   du Canada

ONTARIO ARTS COUNCIL
CONSEIL DES ARTS DE L'ONTARIO
50 YEARS OF ONTARIO GOVERNMENT SUPPORT OF THE ARTS
50 ANS DE SOUTIEN DU GOUVERNEMENT DE L'ONTARIO AUX ARTS

Text and cover design by Kerry Designs

Printed in Canada by Friesens Corporation
10 9 8 7 6 5 4 3 2 1

MIX
Paper from
responsible sources
FSC® C016245
www.fsc.org

To Christine, without whom this book, and much else
that I value, would not have been possible.

"Never judge a man until you have walked a mile in his
moccasins." – Native American proverb

"Human progress is neither automatic nor inevitable.…
Every step toward the goal of justice requires sacrifice, suffering,
and struggle; the tireless exertions and passionate concern of
dedicated individuals." – Martin Luther King, Jr.

"We abuse land because we regard it as a commodity belonging to
us. When we see land as a community to which we belong,
we may begin to use it with love and respect.… That land
is a community is a basic concept of ecology, but that land is
to be loved and respected is an extension of ethics."
– Aldo Leopold, *Sand County Almanac*

Contents

Preface

As a child growing up in New Brunswick I had a passion for maps. I loved the colours: green for lowlands, milky blue for shallow water, deep blue for deep water, and brown for mountains. The place names also enchanted me, particularly the unusual or evocative ones. Each name conjured up for me a world I did not know, a world to see one day. My favourite place name in Canada was "Rocky Mountain House," in Alberta. I did not imagine a house set in the mountains but a house built of mountain rock, a house that was somehow separate from, yet part of, the mountains. During my teen years, I saw photographs of the Rocky Mountains, with snowy peaks and blue sky above. I knew I had to visit them sometime, though they were a long way from my home. It became my dream to work for a summer in Alberta, among the mountains. Somehow life would be better there, of that I was sure. I never did work in the mountains. Yet, my dream of being near the mountains came true, in an unexpected way.

In early April 1982, when I was eighteen, my family travelled across Canada by train, from New Brunswick to Calgary, Alberta. Hour upon hour, in the calm clear light of the domed car at the back of the train, I watched my country slide by. For three days we travelled north and west across the vast, still-snowy landscape, past the wilds of Lake Superior, through western Ontario, then out under the big skies of the prairies. Finally, we arrived in Calgary. Then we took a hot, packed, Greyhound bus to Edmonton, along the relentlessly straight highway. It was in Edmonton where my father, then in his late fifties, had finally found a job. He was able to make a fresh start. We all were. Alberta was then, as it is now, a place of hope, a

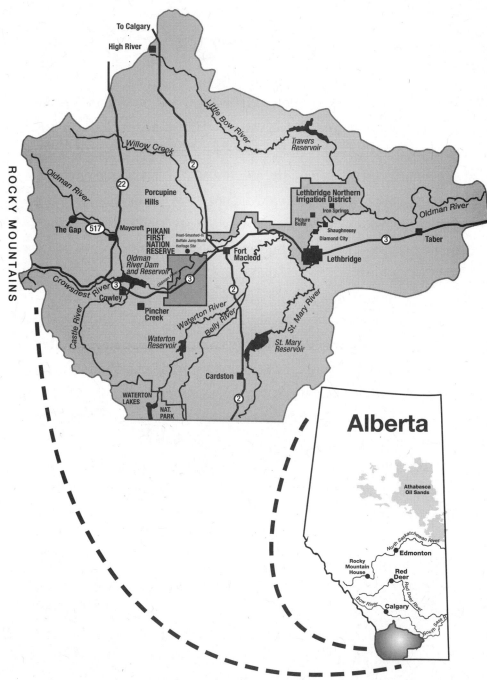

Map 1 - Alberta and the Oldman River Basin

last best hope to find a job, at least in Calgary, Edmonton, and in the North. The dry South is another, harder, story.

By 1988 my father was dead and my mother had survived a serious heart attack. And I, thanks to my time at the University of Alberta, had lit within me a passion to understand the world. University was wonderful. However, during short trips to the mountains I encountered something equally as great as school, perhaps even greater, but hard to name. When I had gas money, I would drive alone out to the Rocky Mountains for the day—almost an eight-hour round-trip from Edmonton—to see the mountains up close, to be among them. I was drawn to them for reasons I could not then understand. Looking back on it, I felt then something of what one feels looking at Cezanne's late paintings of Mont Sainte-Victoire: the power of nature and the longing for truth and permanence amid the transience of life.

I found the view of the mountains from the foothills, the way they cut into the sky, thrilling. Alone in the grandeur of the wide spaces, I felt that everything crooked was made straight, that everything broken was healed, that life was really something. I was free as the wind. On one trip, I remember running down a mountain brook, jumping from boulder to boulder under a flawless sky, surrounded by pines. It was exhilarating. I knew very little of this natural world around me—my parents knew nothing of such things—so I knew nothing of the history or the names of things beyond the names of the trees—yet, I felt part of it in a way I couldn't have explained at the time.

In 1986 I went to law school in Victoria, British Columbia. My lingering youthful idealism gave way to the desire to simply survive the amount of work, and the tedium. Law students are taught how to think like lawyers, to perfect a kind of razor-like thinking used to interpret laws and legal decisions. Provided the ruling government

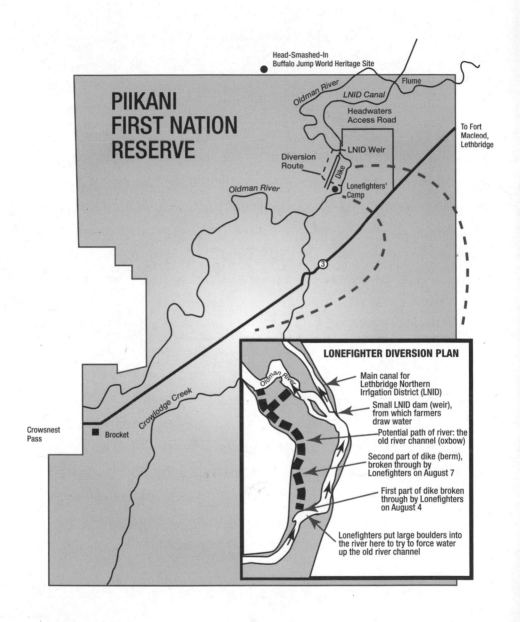

Head-Smashed-In
Buffalo Jump World Heritage Site

PIIKANI
FIRST NATION
RESERVE

Oldman River

LNID Canal

Flume

Headwaters
Access Road

To Fort
Macleod,
Lethbridge

LNID Weir

Diversion
Route

Dike

Oldman River

Lonefighters'
Camp

3

Crowlodge Creek

Crowsnest
Pass

Brocket

LONEFIGHTER DIVERSION PLAN

Oldman River

Main canal for
Lethbridge Northern
Irrigation District (LNID)

Small LNID dam (weir),
from which farmers
draw water

Potential path of river: the
old river channel (oxbow)

Second part of dike (berm),
broken through by
Lonefighters on August 7

First part of dike broken
through by Lonefighters
on August 4

Lonefighters put large boulders into
the river here to try to force water
up the old river channel

Piikani Reserve and Lonefighter River Diversion Plan

has not destroyed or weakened the credibility of the law through its own actions, an orderly system of laws provides a way to resolve disputes through consistent principles rather than through violence. Law school, at its best, is an introduction to how to understand and work within this system. I quickly realized, however, that to speak of "justice" within the confines of law school was considered, by many students, to be naive. The word was usually greeted with incomprehension, irritation, or, among the particularly clever, contempt, as if somehow the need for justice does not reside in the centre of our lives. As for the professors, they had little time for vague words.

I first learned about law school from a TV show I saw as a student, called *The Paper Chase*. It was about challenges faced by a group of law students. There was a certain Professor Kingsfield who told the students, "You come in here with a skull full of mush and you leave thinking like a lawyer." Oddly, this toughness appealed to me at the time. My later view of law school is captured nicely by a quote from Edmund Burke, "Law sharpens the mind by narrowing it." The danger of law school is that one comes to see the world as a lawyer instead of as a compassionate and moral human being with legal knowledge. One can only think within the rules and therefore within the established order. This amorality offers little protection when power comes calling later for arguments bought at a high price.

While I was trying to survive my legal education, unknown to me, in southwest Alberta, a great battle was taking place. The Alberta government was struggling—against the Piikani First Nation, environmentalists, public opinion (in Calgary and northwards), and the law itself—to dam the Oldman River in southwest Alberta. I call the battle "great" not because of its size or the amount of destruction wrought (compared, for example, to the oil sands in the northern part of the province), but because those who fought it cared so much about it, and the issues at stake were of universal importance.

In 1984 the Alberta government announced its final decision. It would dam the Oldman River at a location called Three-Rivers, near where the Crowsnest and Castle rivers join the Oldman River. The proposed dam would benefit farmers desperate for water in the dust-dry southern part of the province. The dam would also grow the economy and expand that government's electoral fortunes. Using its public relations, engineering, and political power, the Alberta government bulldozed ahead with its plan, despite stiff opposition and genuine questions about the economic merit, costs, and abuse of Native rights inherent to the project. As time passed, opposition to the dam, rather than disintegrating, strengthened. People felt strongly about the powerful and beautiful land that would be flooded to make the dam. The land that would soon be under water was the Piikani First Nation's ancestral home and sacred ground. People were prepared to fight the government. Environmentalists, ecologists, and the Piikani felt that the Oldman Dam plan represented another case of blind power rolling over whatever got in its way.

In 1990 the battle between the government and environmentalists was pushed toward its climax, led by activist Martha Kostuch. She used the law relentlessly to try to stop the Oldman Dam. Just as relentlessly, the Alberta government either broke or dodged the law to keep building it. When the law failed to stop the Oldman Dam, Piikani First Nation activist Milton Born With A Tooth entered the struggle in his inimitable way, and later went to jail for his actions. Both Martha and Milton were warriors: Martha operated within the law (usually), and Milton operated as Milton saw fit.

For the farmers in southern Alberta, the dam promised an escape from a hard present to a better future. Martha and Milton had a different vision of the future. Martha was determined to transform Alberta society based on a then (at least in Alberta) new idea called environmentalism. She looked to the future, to an ecologically literate society that would behave justly, not only to other humans but also to the earth. Milton Born With A Tooth believed that the answer to the situation for his people (and perhaps others), their land, and the river was buried in the past. He was determined to bring the buried understandings of his culture forward, try to stop the dam, and explain, if possible, to outsiders why the river was a vital part of who he was as a man.

Many years after the battle, it was through Milton Born With A Tooth, and a painting on a wall in Toronto, that I learned about this story.

–Robert Girvan, Winter 2012

Calgary Herald

75 CENTS MINIMUM   SATURDAY, SEPTEMBER 8, 1990

DAM STANDOFF

Lonefighter vows he won't give up

By Susan Mate,
Rick Molina
and Ashley Geddes

■ New road   A5

ANGRY: Milton and Lorna Born With a Tooth and Chris Buffalo defy RCMP in helicopter

Native rally first stage in war declaration

See NATIVES, Page A2

Judge OKs speed eye

By Kim Lunman

PART ONE

Gathering the Evidence

This painting by Aboriginal artist Doug Fox sparked my interest in the Oldman Dam story.

The Painting

The Oldman Dam story began for me in September 2004, when I saw a painting on a Toronto office-tower wall…

Let me back up a bit. In May of 2004, midway through the prosecution of a murder case in Toronto, I sent my boss an e-mail giving notice that I was resigning as a Crown prosecutor, once my case was finished. After twelve years of fighting cases in the trenches, I was wearied by the constant battling. I needed unstructured time to do crazy things, such as going for a walk in the sun. Resigning left me with the not inconsequential question of what I would do with the rest of my life, or at least the next year. I settled in to the idea of cleaning up a memoir I had begun years before; it was from a previous time I'd quit the law, sold almost all my possessions, and moved to Asia to teach English. To my surprise, however, I had no interest in re-living my own past, alone in my basement, staring at my computer screen. Perhaps my withdrawal from the social world made me long for something new, something that transcended my own life.

One day in September 2004, I got a phone call from Jim Vella, a headhunter for financial companies in Toronto. Would I like to go for lunch? He did business with my wife (who works in the financial industry), knew I had quit, and was curious to meet me and (I later realized) to help me, if possible. In a field in which slick headhunters wear fine suits, Jim approached his work as a counsellor, trying to get the right fit between company and person. He also volunteered as a counsellor for Native people at a Toronto-based hotline.

I met Jim at his office in a downtown tower. He had the deeply furrowed brow of a bulldog, but his eyes shone with a genuine desire to help others. He wanted to show me his paintings before lunch, he said. He had a strong interest in the plight of Native people in Canada and most of his paintings were by Aboriginal artists. Each painting constituted not only an individual aesthetic but also a story, told on many levels.

My eyes fell on the biggest painting. I could not take my eyes off it. It was almost two metres long, just over a metre high, and filled most of one wall. The upper part of the painting depicted a pure, deep, blue sky. The colours were clean and bright, the shapes clear and distinct. Stars twinkled in the upper sky. A moon loomed large, half of it lit, half in darkness. An orange, red, and blue bird with a sharp beak flew high in the sky. The bottom of the painting showed a river from the side. A bronzed man sat on a shimmering white horse that danced on the river's surface. A blue and brown bear, with orange flames climbing his body, was coming out of the river. Beneath the bear a coyote howled at a second moon.

A fish, a beaver, and some other creatures I did not recognize swam in the river. In the centre of the painting, a woman rested on her back in the river. Her stomach was swollen, as if she were pregnant. Instead of a baby, there were four people inside her, two men and two women, sitting in a circle. One person smoked a pipe. A yellow turtle floated above the woman's stomach. Inside the turtle was a world. Beneath a milky sky and pale sun, broken ridges of brown land rose out of blue water. The water surrounded a piece of land shaped like Alberta.

As I studied the painting, Jim told me how he came to buy it. Milton Born With A Tooth, from the Piikani Reserve in Alberta, had come to Toronto in the early 1990s to publicize his fight against the construction of a dam. Jim told me about Milton and the group he had formed—the Lonefighters—to protest the dam. He explained that the Lonefighters used a bulldozer and a backhoe to try to change the course of the Oldman River so it would bypass the place where farmers got their water for irrigation. Milton and the Lonefighters wanted to cut the farmers' water off to draw attention to their opposition both to the dam and to the historic injustices they had suffered. They set up a camp on their reserve, beside the Oldman River, near a parcel of land that had once been part of the reserve but had been expropriated and sold to the local farmers' irrigation district in 1922.

Jim said that eventually the police invaded the land and stopped the protest. Nearly a hundred police came one morning, along with a helicopter and heavy weapons. Milton ran toward the police carrying a gun. Later, the police put him in jail. "He was only trying to protect himself and his people," Jim explained. He added that Milton had an unfair trial and was sentenced to almost two years in jail. Even the Appeal Court concluded that the first trial was unfair. "It just shows the kind of things that happen every day to Native people in Canada," Jim said.

He added, "I don't know if the dam was ever built. After Milton came here, an Aboriginal artist named Doug Fox painted this to raise money for Milton's defence. I bought it to help. It is a powerful painting, isn't it?"

Jim showed me his other paintings, but I didn't see them. I stared at the painting depicting Milton's struggle. The brilliant colours, the elemental power of the forms, seemed to call one to a more essential, more powerful existence close to the earth. They seemed to symbolize a different world than the one I knew and lived with daily. It was not just the painting but also the story that captivated me. In my mind's eye I saw the blue of the sky and Milton with his backhoe and a misery of which I was ignorant, and the judge's stern face and the trial and the big dry land of the West, and the law and justice (or the lack of it) for the land and the people and the water and all that lived. I was drawn in, captured, blinded even, by the beauty of the painting.

After our meeting, I went home. I couldn't get the story out of my head. A few weeks after meeting Jim, I walked over to the Spadina branch of the Toronto Public Library and found a 1991 file of yellowing, well-worn, newspaper clippings about Milton Born With A Tooth. These articles were written during and after his first trial, and before his second. I read them all.

The June 2, 1991, edition of the *Toronto Star* has the following headline in thick black ink: "I Will Be Harassing the Enemy." Beneath it in big print are the following words: "Milton Born With A Tooth vows that a jail sentence won't halt his fight for the Oldman River." A large black-and-white photo of Milton is beneath these words. It is an outdoor shot, with the river to his right, darker land and trees above it. A strand of Milton's long black hair has strayed down to his eyebrow. His mouth is partly open, revealing bent teeth. He has a light mustache. He is looking toward a point above the camera. His cheekbones are high; his skin, one can tell by the grey ink, is deep bronze. The photo seems to have caught him speaking and moving, but it did not really catch him, or the moment.

The moment came and went, a fleeting truth tied to everything, a part of everything that was and is and will be. What is left now is interpretation, reconstruction, and rarely— perhaps in a work of literature—resurrection. Beneath the photo are the following words: "On every reserve there is somebody who thinks how I think and who wants to do what I did." The article quotes Milton: "The government doesn't understand what water is. It's the blood bank of this earth. If it was red and had the same structure and molecules as the stuff that runs in our veins, maybe people would look at it as something with more than an economic value."

I read the June 14, 1991, edition of a newspaper called Native-beat, which carried an article titled "Milton Born With A Tooth: Messenger of the River." The article explains that Milton Born With A Tooth is "very much a man of peace." The journalist tells of the evening he had seen Milton speak at a conference on Native people and the justice system. He writes that "the majority of the audience was non-Native and many openly wept," and that this was a "common response" to hearing Milton speak. The journalist writes that "Milton Born With A Tooth speaks from the heart with the voice of the River."

Milton told the newspaper that the justice system shows the woman with two scales—the Scales of Justice—yet Native people aren't represented by either scale. They are absent. He said he didn't want war; he wanted to preserve the culture. He added, "Our lifestyle is still there. The trees are still here, the water is still here, the roots and herbs are still here. But who knows how to connect with these things? That's where the extinction lies... We knew the real reason for them building the Oldman River Dam. It wasn't just about irrigation for farmers. It's more than that. Why are they building a dam without a license? Why are they willing to break their own justice system so blatantly?" Much later, I learned that when Milton spoke to journalists in 1991, his beloved Oldman valley—home to his people and their ancestors for thousands of years—was going under water.

I walked home from the library with Milton's words repeating in my head. Somehow, despite the wide cultural gulf that separates him from the English Romantic poets, such as Wordsworth, or the American essayist, Thoreau, Milton's words on nature reminded me of their works. Milton's vision is deeply rooted in the Native American vision, which includes both the ideas of his own people and those of many other peoples who once thrived in North America before the coming of white people, among them my ancestors. Of course, I read his words in light of my understanding, and ignorance.

As time passed, my busy city life intruded, and I forgot about the story—or so it seemed. In fact, the story lay hidden beneath the surface details of my life until one thing or another would release it to my conscious thoughts, revealing its surprising power to stay with me. Months passed. Daily I worked in the bad light of my Toronto basement, staring at electronic words on a computer screen, working on my memoir.

With irritating frequency, the big, bright, western sky appeared before me. In response, and without a plan, I gathered facts about the story. I returned to the Spadina library and found a thirty-year history of the Oldman Dam, *Once Upon an Oldman*, by Jack Glenn. Jack Glenn was a water resource expert who had worked in the Alberta government department that planned and built the dam, though he was not involved in the planning for the dam himself. After retiring, he spent years working in his own basement, conducting research and then writing his own book, purging his outrage (my educated guess, after I got to know him), setting forth a damning account of just what Alberta did to get its dam. The Oldman Dam was built and is in operation today.

The story was more complicated than I had imagined. One observer characterized Milton's first trial, held deep in southern Alberta, as showing "in a nutshell what Native people have faced in the past 120 years." I learned of two other Lonefighters, Evelyn Kelman, who was "camp mom," and Devalon Small Legs, the camp pipe man, in charge of spiritual matters. During the most critical part of the crisis, when the RCMP arrived at the Lonefighters' camp, Evelyn Kelman prayed for help to the Oldman River. Much later, I learned about Reg Crowshoe: Evelyn Kelman's brother, former RCMP officer, writer of a book on Blackfoot law, one of the leading ceremonialists in North America, and past chief of the Piikani. He opposed the Lonefighters, even his own sister.

I learned about environmentalist Martha Kostuch. I also learned about one of the leaders in the fight for the dam: Roy Jenson. He was a farmer and chairman of the Lethbridge Northern Irrigation District, which would benefit most from the dam. And I learned about Rick Ross, the engineer who was manager of the LNID, the man on the ground whose job it was to get water to the farmers.

Around Christmas 2004, I finally, reasonably, decided to put the story away forever. The events happened far away, some time ago, and my life was in Toronto, with my wife and two young children. I could not easily leave everyone for months of research. Looking back on what happened next, I am reminded of a quote on a bulletin board outside an Anglican Church: "The resurrection means that you can put the truth in a grave with a shovel, but you can't keep it there."

Though I had decided against doing the story, I could not stop my mind from brooding upon it, for reasons too deep to fathom at the time. Perhaps if I could have unriddled why the story attracted me so, it wouldn't have been necessary to write the book. During this time, I remembered some words I had read once in the book *The Desert Year,* by Joseph Krutch. They came back to me with pregnant power, hinting at a way forward in my life. One day in January 2005, I went to my bookshelf and found the passage that had begun to haunt me. Krutch discusses the pleasant feeling one has when visiting new places. He contrasts this with something altogether different:

More rarely, perhaps only once, perhaps two or three times, one experiences something more like love at first sight. The desire to stay, to enter in, is not a whim or a notion but a passion… If I never learned what it was that called out, what it was that was being offered, I shall feel all my life that I have missed something intended for me. If I do not, for a time at least, live here, I shall not have lived as fully as I had the capacity to live.

Not long after reading the Krutch quote, I knew that I could not escape or evade the Oldman story. Somehow, without really knowing how it happened, I had gathered the faith to begin. Perhaps most important, I would get out of my Toronto basement and go west, to the big western sky and the mountains, to be again in the West for the first time since I left Alberta in 1990, armed with the useful illusion that life had to be better somewhere else. I knew vaguely that my future ran through my past in Alberta.

This was the rare case in which I had to see for myself. I could not rely on the research of others in my investigation of the Oldman Dam story. Jack Glenn did not have access to the transcripts of Milton's trials, nor did he have the opportunity to speak to the Native people involved in the crisis. He did not see Martha Kostuch's journals. He had done a lot, but he couldn't do everything. I would add my part. I wanted to meet Martha Kostuch, to see what she would say about the story, and about the environment. As a lawyer and former Crown prosecutor, I wanted to look again into how the Alberta government had treated the law. I wanted to assess Milton's two trials. Had they been fair? I had other questions I wanted answered. What led the Lonefighters to do what they did? I wanted a deep understanding—if I could manage it—of past events, some of which may have contributed to the Lonefighters' action. I also wondered: Should the dam have been built? And, in the course of building the dam and fighting those who opposed it, had the Alberta government abused its own—and Canada's—laws as much as my sources suggested?

In January 2005, I began. None of the above ideas were as clear to me then as they are now. Rather than read all the history and form a definite picture of events first, I decided to interview as many of the key players as possible, to see what they had to say, in their own words. Then I would read the books and transcripts for context. I would return and ask more questions later. And so, over years of listening, reading, thinking, brooding, and writing, my conceptions of what constitutes the truth and meaning and relevant detail of this story have evolved. The more time passed, the more I realized that the shape of the story was also affected by who would, and would not, speak to me. I had to do the best I could with what I had, recognizing that truth is an ocean that cannot be completely captured in the net of words.

The Writer:
Jack Glenn

———

I knew I was coming to the Oldman Dam story as an outsider, which was both good and bad. The danger was in failing to grasp the subtle contexts of the struggle. On the other hand, as someone who had not taken part in the battle, and who did not have a preconceived certainty about where the truth would be found, I could at least try to look at events with an open mind. (Of course, no one is completely free of a guiding point of view.) I felt that the best way to start would be to speak to a writer who knew the story intimately: Jack Glenn.

Jack Glenn had spent years of his life researching his book on the Oldman Dam story. When I read Jack's book, I noticed that many of the chapters began with quotes from Lethbridge Herald columnist and editorial writer Joanne Helmer. I later collected over a hundred articles she wrote about the Oldman Dam and Native rights over a twenty-year period. As I read them, I was struck by her broad moral vision and her determination to ask necessary questions: Was a dam needed? Did building a dam make economic sense?

When I called Jack, I did not know what to expect. Would he be closed to me, desiring to protect his turf? Or, would he be open, even welcoming? Very quickly, with that raspy tough voice of his, he offered to do all he could to help me. He gave me access to all his research materials, which were then boxed up in his Calgary basement. He also invited me to stay with him and his wife while I looked through the boxes, an offer I accepted. Finally, he offered to pick me up at the airport.

———— • ————

As the plane rose in the blue evening sky, I looked back down at Toronto, through the brown film covering the city. I spent my first night in Calgary in a hotel, as I had arrived so late. Calgary is a city with money, energy, movement. Even the cab drivers seemed happy. I couldn't help but feel the sense of vigour, the mood of hope in the city. All this seemed an undiluted good, provided I didn't think too much about it.

Outside, there were no trees and no evidence of birds. I was just about to write this in my journal when I heard an unmistakable "cheep" in a gap in the traffic's hum. I went to the window and craned my head upward to see above the tall buildings. What I saw was that hard blue sky I remembered from my years living in Alberta. The flawless blue sky of the West, clear and bright, which had once consoled me, if only briefly, hinting of calm, of peace, of an end to restlessness. I was lucky that morning, as pollution, from time to time, now obscures that crystalline clarity.

The next day, I went to Jack's house, where I stayed for three days. Jack has a lean face, sharp eyes, and bristly white hair. He was in his early seventies at the time yet had retained the bearing of a tough colonel. In fact, he had served in the Canadian Army from 1956 to 1964, ending his career with the rank of lieutenant. Later, he became a geographer, first working in the Canadian civil service, then with Alberta's Department of the Environment. He did not suffer fools gladly. More than once, when I asked a stupid question

I received the comments the question deserved. I had the sense that as much as the injustice of the Alberta government's Oldman Dam bothered him, what he had even less tolerance for was the stupidity he had found everywhere in Alberta's Department of the Environment. During my stay with Jack, I spent many hours digging through his boxes of research materials and many more hours discussing his views on the Oldman Dam battle.

On my last day at Jack's house, I went to the office of the Alberta Court of Appeal. Over the telephone, a few weeks before I had left Toronto, one of the clerks at the court told me that she had found the entire trial transcripts from the second trial of Milton Born With A Tooth, in Calgary, but that she had not yet found the transcripts from the first trial, which took place in Fort Macleod. I told the clerk that I had heard that the judge in that case said some things that were inappropriate. She said to me, "That transcript will be full of howlers."

When I arrived at the Court of Appeal, the clerk had prepared both transcripts for me. As I lifted the heavy box of unexamined, verbatim, life, I was thrilled. People often criticize the justice system based on either inadequate understanding or inadequate knowledge of what actually happens in court. There are complicated rules about what evidence goes before the court and how the law is applied. These rules have been developed over many centuries to try to ensure a fair trial, and that issues are decided correctly. To know these rules and principles is the positive side of a legal education; to be trapped within them is always a danger. For example, what if some of the rules are unfair or worse? On the other hand, it is easy for a person untrained in the law to think that something unfair has happened

14

at court, even though the lawyers and judges involved have followed the rules and principles of court procedure, and where the rules and procedures are fair. With these transcripts in hand, I knew I now had a sound foundation from which to examine both of Milton's trials.

I ruminated on the fact that the court staff had found these documents for me. In some countries, inconvenient documents have a habit of going missing. I did not know then that this happened frequently within the Alberta government bureaucracy, but not in the courts, the guardians of the law and the constitution.

———— — ————

My final night at Jack's was hectic as I had many boxes of research materials to copy. Late in the afternoon, Jack drove me to a Kinko's. To my surprise, he stayed to help. I used one copy machine and Jack faced me on another. Given the height of the material to be copied, I realized that I would be there for many hours. After twenty minutes, I turned to Jack and said, "Look, when you are sick of this copying, just stop. It's not your headache."

Without looking up, he spoke, in his usual gruff tone, "I have been sick of it for some time now, but I guess I will see this through to the end." And he did. Four hours later, I bought Jack a late dinner. We spoke more about the story that he knew so well. We discussed again the battle between Martha Kostuch and the Alberta govern-ment, and how the Alberta government had treated the law. It made me want to meet Martha more than ever, to see what she was like in person. I knew that every person I met would teach me more about the story, and bring out the complexity of events.

The Guardians of the River: Lorne Fitch and Cheryl Bradley

For millions of years, water has flowed down the eastern slopes of the Rocky Mountains as the earth's climate slowly but relentlessly changed in a seemingly preordained unfolding. Some species became extinct; new ones evolved. Adaptation was crucial. Unlike in deep past time, our climate today is rapidly changing. It is no longer solely a natural process, but at least partially, human-created change.

For ten thousand years, long before it was separated from the earth in human understanding by the names "River" and "Oldman," water has flowed eastward in roughly the same channel as the Oldman River does today, cutting a path through the dry land. For millennia it was a wild river moving through a valley of wilderness, an unbroken link between the Rocky Mountains, the foothills, and the prairies. In the spring, fed by the melting of glaciers and winter snow, the river flooded its banks, regenerating the cottonwood tree forests. These forests anchored the vibrant concentration of life in this green valley, a place full of birdsong, deer, and wild paths; a place where nature smiled, or so it seemed, in contrast to the equally beautiful—but hard, dry, and treeless—prairie around it. Once the river leaves the mountains and heads out beyond the foothills,

16

the land turns dry as dust. Later, this land—now called southern Alberta—was labelled a semi-desert by human beings. The river flowed eastward, joining various other rivers on its long journey to the sea.

Soon after rolling down my window while driving through this area to interview people involved in this story, my throat felt dry, so parched that I picked up three one-litre bottles of water from a store near Turner Valley. As I kept going south the air became so parched that one felt like human civilization might just blow away in a hot dusty wind. I later learned that this was in fact what happened to some little towns during one of the area's periodic great droughts, which are a natural, though painful, part of trying to farm in a semi-desert.

A ridge of dark clouds crept over the mountains, heading northwest. Beneath the biggest clouds came dark streaks in the sky, which swept out onto the prairie—evidence of big storms and lots of rain. A powerful wind picked up from the same direction, which made me feel both exhilarated and vaguely uneasy. I knew I had a lot of outdoor work ahead of me, driving the stone and dirt backroads of the reserve of the once great Piikani First Nation, part of the Black-foot Confederation. The Oldman River meanders through the centre of their reserve, controlled by technology rather than nature, now that the Oldman Dam is in operation, several kilometres upstream from the reserve.

———————

For millennia the Blackfoot and their ancestors lived on the prairies and in the river valleys along the eastern slopes of the Rocky Mountains. For the Piikani, the Oldman River was the heart of their territory, an integral part of their relationship to the earth and eternity. As one old-timer put it, the Oldman River and its valley is "where the Piikani became Piikani."

I later learned from Devalon Small Legs that in Blackfoot the Oldman River is called *Napi-Niitahtaa*, (which also means "Oldman River.") The relationship between the Blackfoot and the Oldman looms large in the Napi, or "old man," stories of the Blackfoot people. It is said that Napi's home was at the headwaters of the river. There are many ways to tell Napi stories. The variety of the stories is proof of the creative human response to ultimate questions. Percy Bullchild tells many traditional Blackfoot stories in his book *The Sun Came Down: The History of the World as My Blackfeet Elders Told It*. He tells how Napi was created. The story goes like this.

In the beginning was Creator Sun. And he will live forever. He lived alone in a spiritual place. He was lonely, so he put his spit and space dust together to make muddy clay. Much later, this became Earth. One day he put an exact image of himself on Mother Earth—and he called it Napi. He wanted the people to lead a good life, so he sent them a disciple to lead them out of corruption. He was to teach, by words, and by example, the good life. Napi had almost as much power as Creator Sun himself. Napi travelled far and wide, giving advice on good living from camp to camp. Napi had a magic power, to put things into the heads of people—which he used for good. He even had a miracle power. It was clear to the minds of the people. He was a great one. The people looked up to him. He was their saviour.

Time passed. People continued calling him a great one. "Well, things kind of went to his head… The power that was entrusted to him got the better of him." He started to take more and more power, doing more and more mischief. He went a little crazy. He lost more and more respect for Creator Sun. He had too much respect for himself and his own power. As more time passed, Napi completely broke away from his duty to lead the people into righteousness. "He was the great one in his own mind. He could do anything with the power he had been given." There are many versions of how Napi's exploits ended. In one version, he vanished up by the Oldman River. In another, he was turned into a pine tree and still stands on a bank of the Highwood River, in Alberta.

The Blackfoot peoples comprise four nations: the Aputosi Piikani (previously known to English speakers as North Peigan), the Kainai (Blood), and Siksika (Blackfoot). These nations are all in Alberta. A fourth nation, the Amaskapi Piikani (South Peigan, or Blackfeet) is in the United States. This book deals mainly with the North Peigan. For simplicity, I call them the Piikani. For millennia, the Blackfoot peoples lived on the prairie. Life out on the prairie was hard, yet the Piikani and other Blackfoot tribes lived intimately with the river, land, buffalo, and all that lived and died with them. Their way of life, the harshness and joy, is almost impossible for an outsider to grasp in our age. For a long time, the Piikani had only dogs to help them move camp and hunt the buffalo. Later, with rifles and horses, the Piikani greatly expanded their territory against other tribes in armed battles. Some tribes, fearing extermination, fled over the Rocky Mountains. With horses and guns the Blackfoot became the great power of the region. They had immense respect for the buffalo but nonetheless took part in its destruction through overhunting. When millions of buffalo were wiped out by white, Métis, and First Nations men with rifles, the Piikani and other Blackfoot tribes were devastated.

———— • ————

When I spoke to Jack Glenn about my proposed book, I told him that I had to meet someone who knew the Oldman River intimately, someone who cared about the river. Jack didn't hesitate: "Talk to Cheryl and Lorne." So I drove to Fort Macleod, a small town named after the respected North-West Mounted Police Colonel James Macleod, who had helped negotiate the treaty between the Blackfoot peoples and Canada in 1877. In the west part of town I found the A&W, where I had planned to meet biologists Lorne Fitch and Cheryl Bradley. As I got to know them better, they seemed to me to be guardians—not just of the Oldman River but also, with their knowledge of the ecosystems of river valleys, of the earth in its natural state. Theirs is a knowledge that many of us in the cities must carefully learn or we will not realize—"like wanton boys to flies" as Shakespeare said—just what we are destroying.

Lorne had worked as a fish biologist for the Alberta government on most of the rivers up and down the eastern slopes of the Rockies for more than twenty years; he had a special interest in the Oldman River. Cheryl's expertise was in cottonwood trees, especially the impact of dams on them. Both had a deep knowledge of the Oldman River valley ecosystem. Above all, they knew, lived with, and cared for the Oldman River. Lorne and Cheryl were married, so I could meet them both at once.

As I was drinking root beer from a frosted glass, a woman with dark-brown, slightly greying hair, dark-rimmed glasses, and no make-up walked toward me. It was Cheryl. Lorne was in the parking lot, waiting in their beat-up Toyota Four Runner. The truck was dusty, and the front windshield had many cracks, suggesting many hours on rocky backroads. We got into the truck and turned west to see the Oldman River. Both Lorne and Cheryl looked to be in their mid-fifties.

As we drove, Cheryl mentioned that Alberta had recently sent out an advisory that pregnant women should not eat fish from the Oldman River due to the high mercury levels. She said she would send me a copy of the advisory by e-mail, which she later did.

I called the Piikani health officer myself to see if they knew about the advisory. The person I spoke to had heard about such an advisory, too, but had never seen a copy of it, so I sent it on to her by e-mail. As I continued research for this book, I noticed that the same advisory seemed to have been issued about the fish in many of Alberta's rivers.

That day, Lorne, Cheryl, and I visited several areas along the Oldman. Lorne told me, "The crucial thing is how to look at the land. We must learn to see. If you see it first as a 'resource'—comparing fish to wheat—wheat will always win. But if you see the land and river as an ecosystem—one that is broken—you can then try to find a way to fix it. How you frame the issue is vitally important."

At one point, Cheryl turned to me and said, "It makes me mad that I can no longer read the river. I have no idea what is happening upstream, in the headwaters. What I see and hear means nothing; it is all man-controlled."

"Now we read nature by roads," Lorne said.

We spoke many times over their wooden dining-room table. Our conversations were painful for them, but they were, at times, saved by laughter. One day Cheryl said, "We are still wrapped up in it, all these years later."

During one of our conversations I saw a copy of a book on their table, *Collapse*, in which the author, Jared Diamond, discusses why past civilizations have collapsed. We talked about the book. Cheryl said, "One day the Pueblo peoples just ran out of water; that ended their civilization."

"It is like here," Lorne said. "Native people thought buffalo would keep coming out of the ground. We keep thinking oil will keep coming out of the ground."

Late in the evening, on my final day speaking with them on that trip, Lorne told me the story of the sparrow and the horsemen:

A horseman rides down the road. He finds a little sparrow

lying on his back, his two little feet extended skyward.

"What are you doing?" the horseman asks.

"I am holding up the sky so it doesn't crash into the earth," the sparrow says.

"These spindly little feet? How much can you do?" the horseman scoffs.

"You do what you can; you do what you can," replies the sparrow.

Treaty 7:
Sharing the Land?

The Blackfoot lived on and with their land for millennia. In 1690 Charles II of England presumed to grant a large portion of North America, called Rupert's Land, to the Hudson's Bay Company. In 1869 Canada bought the land from the company. In 1874 the then NorthWest Mounted Police came west, asserting the power of the Queen's law. The Blackfoot had a "dread of the white man's intentions to cheat them." They feared that the police were in the country not only to enforce the law, but "to protect white people against them, and that this country will be gradually taken from them without any ceremony." In 1877 the Blackfoot petitioned Canada, asking the government to stop the "invasion of our country." In the 1870s the Government of Canada negotiated seven treaties with First Nations people in the west. Other numbered treaties were later negotiated for land in the north—a total of eleven numbered treaties in all.

By 1877 eastern Canada wanted to build a transcontinental railway. "Settlers were eyeing the rich grasslands." The Canadian government knew about the Indian Wars in the United States. The pursuit of legality and fairness in their dealings with First Nations people would hopefully buy peace. Furthermore, Canada was bound in spirit, and perhaps legally, to the words of the Royal Proclamation issued in 1763, which recognized First Nations people as "rightful occupiers" of their land unless and until their rights to the land were ceded to government.

Canada and the Blackfoot "signed" a treaty—called Treaty 7—at Blackfoot Crossing, in September 1877, after many days of negotiations. It is clear now that neither side understood the other; how much true communication there was remains an open question. For many years, in the English language, what passed for a history of the treaty was based on newspaper accounts, the written treaty itself, and the report of Canada's chief negotiator, David Laird. The Blackfoot point of view did not exist in English until such scholars as Hugh Dempsey tried to bring it forward. When I asked Piikani ceremonialist Reg Crowshoe about the treaty, he said that the Piikani had not even intended to go to the negotiations, until the police found them at a place called O'Agency—where the Oldman and the Crow Lodge rivers meet—pointed a cannon at their camp, and told them to "get up to the treaty, or we're going to blow the whole camp right out of the Oldman River valley."

When the treaty negotiations began, it took the Canadian government three tries to find someone who at least seemed like he could negotiate the Queen's English into Blackfoot, and then back into English. Since words cannot be divorced from the vision of the world they articulate, the treaty negotiations between English and Blackfoot would be an attempt not only to translate words but also to cross the chasm between vastly different cultures. A man who knew the Blackfoot peoples, Father Scollen, who had been present at the signing of the treaty, later wrote that "the interpreters were incapable of explaining the terms of the Treaty, and could not deal with such things as land surrenders and reserves." He wrote in the same letter, "Did these Indians, or do they now, understand the real nature of the Treaty between the Government and themselves in 1877? My answer to this question is unhesitatingly in the negative…"

24

David Laird told the Blackfoot that the Queen "wishes you to allow her white children to come and live on your land..." He also promised that a reserve of land would be set aside for each tribe, "upon which none others will be permitted to encroach." The Piikani and the other tribes agreed to the treaty, though what, in their own minds, they were assenting to is a hotly debated question. The written words of the treaty do not speak of sharing the land with the white people, but that the Piikani would "hereby cede, release, surrender, and yield up to the Government of Canada for her Majesty the Queen and her successors forever, all their rights, titles, privileges whatsoever to the lands..."

The Blackfoot could neither read nor write English. So their names were written down, and then they each touched the pen. The pen would then be used to mark Xs beside their names. With this touch of the pen, they were purporting to give up ownership of the land they had lived on for millennia.

There is no written record of how words like "cede, release, surrender, yield up, and reserve" were interpreted into Blackfoot. According to a recent book by Treaty 7 Elders, *The True Spirit and Original Intent of Treaty 7*, the First Nations chiefs who signed Treaty 7 thought they were signing a peace treaty, not agreeing to land surrender. "There was no [Blackfoot] word for surrendering or relinquishing of title to land. We are one with the land. Is it possible to relinquish or give away part of oneself?" Treaty 7 Elders today see the treaties between First Nations and Canada as "Magna Cartas," "as the place where we articulated just how we would live with the newcomers and just how we would share the land with them."

When I asked Devalon Small Legs about the treaty, he seemed frustrated, not with me, but that such foundational facts, self-evident to him, were not better known off the reserve.

"Treaty 7— that's when the swindle started. We did not

fight. It was an ideal situation to make peace. So we made a treaty. It did not say we would be put on a reservation. It said we would live together. Nowhere does anybody say there is going to be an *Indian Act*—even though the *Indian Act* already existed at the time in other parts of Canada. In 1884 we were forced onto the reserve. Nobody had ever said, 'You are going to live inside this fenced place.' Nobody ever said that."

According to historian Hugh Dempsey, the Blackfoot remembered the winter after the treaty as *Itsa-estoyi*, "the year of the mild winter." It was unusually warm; little snow covered the ground. The Blackfoot waited for the snow to "drive the buffalo herds towards the foothills. But instead of snow, prairie fires roared across the land, leaving behind a black barren waste." Some historians believe this was a deliberate attempt to keep the buffalo to the south and east for slaughter there. "By the time the Blackfoot realized their predicament, many of them were already starving." By the spring, "the dwindling herds returned," but the days in which the "country had been black with buffalo" were over.

The Blackfoot realized that the buffalo, and their way of life, were almost gone. In the early winter of 1878, "not enough meat could be found in the area to feed the Blackfoot camps." In the spring, many were starving. They hunted anything—gophers, rabbits, mice, moles, porcupines, badgers, "no matter how rank." As winter turned to spring, then to summer, they were forced to eat their dogs, then moccasins and pieces of rawhide were "boiled in water to bring out any nourishment they might contain."

The country had no game left. Nature's bounty had been exhausted. The tribes of the Blackfoot "waited patiently in the daily line-ups for beef and flour." The Canadian Indian Department employees, many of whom were "rough frontiersmen," showed little respect for these proud, now helpless, people. "They often were rude and belligerent, even to the chiefs, and treated the Blackfeet as though they were little better than the dirt under their feet. The warriors looked on helplessly while their women turned to prostitution to obtain extra rations." The flour was often "spoiled"; even unspoiled flour was so bad "it could only find a market at the Indian Agency." Contractors kept the best parts of the meat and sold them to the highest bidder. The Blackfoot felt that they should be treated fairly. "But who would listen?"

They had been a fierce and great people, with a vibrant and powerful culture. Now, the buffalo were dead. The old world was gone. Now they were ravaged and defeated, not by the Government of Canada, but by brutal necessity—by the death of the buffalo.

They had one place left that had not been taken away: the reserve of land. They also had their treaty, their contract with the Great Mother, Queen Victoria, containing legally binding and morally powerful promises made by the Great Mother, for which she had received, at least in her eyes, almost all their land. They realized they would need to depend on the Queen, to test the strength of her promises, of her laws, her fairness and justice, her compassion, her decency, and even her understanding. In this time of suffering and desolation, at least they had their dignity, their stories, their sense of themselves as a people in time and in eternity, their sense of past and destiny, and their relationship with Father Sun and Mother Earth, as renewed in their rituals and lives. Soon, these things, too, would be nearly destroyed.

The Farmer:
Roy Jenson

———⁘———

Some people retire to Florida, or to the Okanagan Valley in British Columbia, to play golf. Roy Jenson's version of retirement from farming in southern Alberta was buying and working another farm in central Alberta, where he expected to have enough water for his crops. When I spoke to him on the telephone in the summer of 2006, he told me they were having an awful drought. "We need a dam up here, too," he told me, jokingly. He spoke slowly and quietly.

In 2006, Roy was in his mid-seventies. I had listened to his voice on a tape made thirteen years previous and heard the moral certainty, the vigorous fight in the man to defend what he thought was right. When we finally spoke on the telephone, it only took a few minutes to hear the fight come back into his voice as he told me what was right and what was wrong. He told me, with that raspy but newly enthusiastic voice, that he had boxes and boxes of stuff to show me. Later, when we spoke at his farm, the thunder returned to his demeanour. He pounded the kitchen table, shaking the dishes and cups, to make his point about what he felt was an injustice.

Roy was not only a farmer but also chairman of the LNID for over twenty years, one of the leaders in the fight for the dam. I knew it was easy for an outsider to romanticize not only the lives of Native people but also the beauty of the land, and miss the harshness and the sheer struggle to survive.

Roy's farm is set amidst gently rolling hills and yellowing fields, edged by groves of trees here and there. Roy came out of the house when I arrived. He was over six foot two, and this was at seventy-five years old. His back was ruler-straight, so he seemed every inch he was tall. His face was deeply tanned, his eyes clear.

As we spoke, he got lunch for us: cherries and sandwiches. We sat at right angles to one another across his kitchen table, in his big kitchen, with bright afternoon sunlight coming through the windows. I put my tape recorder between us and turned it on. Over a few hours as we recalled some of the events and battles in his life, Roy, by turns, grew animated then passionate, angry, outraged, and, at times, as he reflected on the future, very quiet. He had offered to make dinner for me when we arranged our meeting. I had offered to bring a bottle of wine to thank him.

"No, thanks. I'm a teetotaler," he said with a quiet laugh.

Roy told me that he had moved up to central Alberta ten years before, when he was sixty-five. Before that, he had lived on that one irrigation farm northwest of Lethbridge for his whole life. It was tough to leave his farm, but it was time to retire. He didn't need to make a large income. Now he makes enough to cover his expenses, plus a little bit more. He likes central Alberta. "It is a picturesque place; it's Alberta's parkland, with little trees running up and down the fence-lines."

Roy said that they had some bad years of drought in central Alberta. During those years, he hardly made any money, but crop insurance had helped them out, as had the savings he and his wife had put away. As we spoke he spontaneously remembered his life on his irrigation farm: "A lot of hard work. A lot of times when there was drought, we didn't have water on the hills. And the water that was down below the level where we could irrigate by hand was in the low areas, and you would wash the side of the hill down and get too much on the bottom. It was a pretty rough way to make a living. And, yet it was better than not having that irrigation."

Roy Jenson was born in 1932 on his family's irrigation farm northwest of Lethbridge. His mother died when he was three and a half from complications of childbirth. As he grew, he didn't remember her at all. His father raised him, as well as his brother and three sisters, alone. When his mom died, his older sister was nine, and she helped around the house. It was tough on her and her younger sister—trying to run the house, cooking, putting the meat in brine, and making cheese. Roy told me, "It wasn't easy—but everybody else had the same problem."

At three or four, Roy was working under the hot sun in the fields. He remembers that it "wasn't too bad for kids, because you couldn't do the heavy work." As he got bigger, work and life amounted to much the same thing. They did everything by hand in the 1930s. In the long hot days of summer, they began work at 5:30 a.m. and worked as long as the horses could stand it, or the light held out, which was around 10:00 p.m. The bigger kids would be in the fields with shovels, trying to irrigate, trying to get a little bit more crop. "It was a pretty rough way to make a living, and yet it was better than not having irrigation, it gave us some crop all the time," Roy told me. The farm's produce brought in the total income for his family. They thought they were doing poorly all the time, but when Roy looked back on it he realized they weren't doing too badly. Nobody else had it any better.

Roy explained: "When I got my kids in school and I got elected chairman of the Home and School Association, I learned a few things there, and people thought I was pretty good, and the next thing they wanted me to run for was the Lethbridge Northern

[Irrigation District]. And that was in 1967. And so I ran for the board of directors every year and won for twenty-six years." After he had been on the board for ten years, he was elected by the board to be chairman and was re-elected chairman for the next sixteen years. Roy told me he thought the reason he had been re-elected so often was that he explained things honestly to the farmers. He had seen so many people "beat around the bush while trying to explain something, saying you need to know this or you need to know that." The farmers got frustrated by that. He was able to speak clearly with the farmers, so that they knew the LNID was doing the best it could. When Roy told me this, I remembered what Rick Ross, the manager of the LNID, had told me about Roy, about his honesty in dealing with the farmers.

When I met with Rick in Lethbridge, he had told me a story about how Roy treated his fellow farmers. Rick explained that it had become evident that there was not enough water for farmers during dry years. According to Rick, there wasn't a water shortage; it was a question of timing, of having the right amount of water at the right time. Up until that time, if farmers needed extra water, they could simply take it. One day, Roy Jenson brought forward a motion at a meeting of the LNID board, proposing that from that time forward, farmers would have to apply for any extra water they needed. Roy explained that the change was necessary because of the water problems they were having. He added that he would put a paper up on the wall that day; anyone who wanted more than their allotment of water could sign their name to request more water. After the meeting, Roy went outside and signed his name on the paper. As Rick said, "Roy would have known he was going to bring the motion forward at the meeting. He could have just taken more water before the meeting. But he didn't. He waited until after the meeting, when he would have to sign up for water as everyone else did."

During our interview, Roy left the table now and then to bring back various records for me to see. He showed me his record of expenses for his various jobs, including what was spent, what day, and the date, all in perfect order.

After we had spoken for awhile, I asked Roy, "Why did the farmers need a dam?"

"We needed the dam to make the whole irrigation system more economical. We had lots of drought years in a row. At the same time, in the 1970s and 1980s, people said the world is going to be short of food. The issue of a global food crisis was out there very strong. Prices were going up in the early 1970s. That was a good reason to say: 'There is no reason to wait. We need the dam now for the sake of the farmers, and southern Alberta economics. So, get it now. Why wait?'" He added that with then-new sprinkler systems you could put water on all your land, which made irrigation more economical, but you still needed more water.

At one point I asked him about economic development across the world. "Do you think that development can keep going at the same pace, or is something going to have to give somewhere?"

He paused and looked beyond his kitchen window for a long time. Then he let out his breath slowly. Finally, he spoke, "Yeah, something's going to have to give, I guess." He was silent a few moments then continued, very quietly, very slowly, "I don't, don't know how you can stop it. Money seems to be the controlling factor wherever you look. Factories going in everywhere. I sold a quarter-section next to me to a guy, and it had a corner with trees and bushes, and I really appreciated those trees. What did he do? He took everything out, flattened it all, right away. He even took the trees down between the garden and my house—great big trees that I had grown and were then thirty feet tall. They are all gone. They are all gone." He shook his head slowly and looked away.

I asked Roy why he had moved away from southern Alberta. He said, "Down there it was being farmed corner to corner and there wasn't much wildlife. We came up here because there is parkland, trees, water spots. It was more appealing to me ... Irrigation was a lot of work, and I wasn't so young anymore. The sprinklers we had— three or four—you had to move each one of them three times. It is a real hard day. Sometimes you're through at midnight, and you have to start again at 5:00 a.m. They are long days."

After a few hours, I had to go. He had more to say, so he kept talking as I went outside to my car, and he shook my hand a few times more at the car. He told me that he and his wife were likely going to do missionary work abroad the next year. He told me how the media were often not interested in the truth; how they would often make the story more dramatic to blow it up. As we were leaving his house, he added, "I know you have to make a story, too." I got in my car and we spoke more through my open car window. He didn't want me to go; he had more to say, to help me understand what it was like. Finally, I pulled away. He turned, waved goodbye, and slowly walked back toward his silent house, set amid the darkening trees, as the sky above had turned dark. A big thunderstorm would soon be arriving. I hoped for him that the rain would come.

PART TWO

The Players

The Farmers and the Lethbridge Northern Irrigation District (LNID)

In the middle of the nineteenth century John Palliser led an expedition through this land. He called the area a desert and said there was a certain part of southern Alberta—later called the Palliser Triangle—that was too dry for farming, which should never be settled. In the decades after 1900, immigrants from Europe and the East had been lured west by the Canadian government through pamphlets promising free land and sunny skies. The brochures did not mention "the loneliness, the grasshoppers, prairie fires, bad roads, long cold winters, or lack of trees and water." Millions of settlers came west. During the immigrant influx, a writer for *Canada West Magazine* called southern Alberta "a land blessed of the Gods—a land over which bending nature ever smiles and into whose cradle she emptied her golden horn..."

The problem is, blue skies don't produce rain. Between 1916 and 1926, hardly any rain fell. The land turned dry and hard. Crops shrivelled and died. Dust storms howled across the prairie. Towns died; yes, ceased to exist. There were too many people, too many farms, for what the land and climate could tolerate. In his book *Empire of Dust*, David C. Jones told how "frothy boosterism, lightning expansion, and utter miscalculation" led to the death of towns and to an empire of dust, when the rain stopped falling. "Buildings and equipment were smothered and buried... Relief for farmers was instituted. Banks were told to stop foreclosures."

In 1919, after years of effort trying to convince governments of the plight of farmers and the economic viability of irrigation, the farmers formed the Lethbridge Northern Irrigation District (LNID) to take water from the Oldman River to irrigate their lands. The book *Just Add Water*, published by the LNID, tells the story of the making and partial destruction of the irrigation works on the Oldman River. In May of 1923, after years of construction, the irrigation system on the Oldman River opened. The official opening of the new irrigation system was scheduled for June 1923. The June opening was cancelled, however, when a great flood severely damaged the irrigation works built with such effort.

In late May 1923, "several days of thunderstorms occurred" in the Rocky Mountains. On the night of May 31, the Oldman River "rose at an unprecedented rate." The LNID used all the men they had to try to protect the irrigation works. But a powerful thunderstorm pounded the area "most of the night." The Oldman River "rose quickly" and the LNID irrigation works were overwhelmed. The canal system was opened again in October of 1923, after many months of work to repair the damage. During the storm, the Oldman River had formed a new channel, around the farmers' weir. (In 1990 the Lonefighters intended to send the water down the old channel, the one that existed before the storm.)

Time passed, yet the farmers, and the semi-desert they worked so hard to farm, remained. Roy Jenson—and others—had a living memory of what it was like during the terrible droughts of the Dirty Thirties. Nature seemed to be, and was, to those farming a semi-desert, the enemy: the towering dust, the barren sun. In the West, 50,000 farmers went bankrupt. The desert was "menacing"; one had to make a "conquest" against it. The engineers were the heroes of the story, according to writer James Gray in his book *Men Against the Desert*. This was not the wonderful Nature of the Romantic poets, but a kind of living, waiting, dusty hell. Southern Alberta poet and farmer's wife Edna Jacques gives a feel for the time in this stanza from a poem written during the Dirty Thirties:

> The Crop has failed again, the wind and sun
> dried out the stubble first, then one by one
> the strips of summer fallow, seared with heat,
> crunched, like old fallen leaves, our lovely wheat,
> the Garden is a dreary, blighted waste,
> the very air is gritty to my taste.

On August 1, 1931, Canada "discovered that there had been a series of crop failures in the Palliser Triangle." The Canadian Red Cross asked Canadians for "food and clothing for 125,000 destitute farm families." "Relief trains kept many farmers alive." In 1936 an area east of Lethbridge became a "zone of disaster." In late May, the wind "began to blow the soil off the land." This was followed by great dust storms in July. It was the driest it had been in twenty years in the Palliser Triangle. "Sand dunes drifted high around abandoned buildings." Such was the landscape into which Roy Jenson was born.

———————

July 17, 1984, had been another day of relentless sun, blue sky, and waiting. Roy Jenson was running late for the meeting. Years later, he remembered this as the day he gave his greatest speech. In his book, *Once Upon an Oldman,* Jack Glenn tells just how dry it was that year. The whole summer had been hot and dry—the eighth year in a row of drought—the worst drought since 1916. Day after day, from late June to late July, no rain fell in Lethbridge. The farmers without irrigation had been watching their crops—and hopes—die under the relentless sun. Soon, water restrictions would begin again for the city of Lethbridge and the other towns in southern Alberta. Even farmers with irrigation from the Oldman River worried that the LNID might have to shut off its canals for the fifth time since 1977 to allow water to refill in their main water reservoir. One member of the Legislature passed "idle irrigation equipment" on open fields, and observed, "in frustration," that "it was like a sea of silence." Church congregations prayed for rain. Reverend Mayberry of Fort Macleod said, "Our faith in God is such that if we shout enough, we'll get rain." Near Lethbridge, the Oldman River had become a pitiful rivulet of water in a wide riverbed. By late July, the town of Fort Macleod had initiated water restrictions due to the "dwindling flow of the Oldman."

Drought was natural in the semi-desert of southern Alberta, but knowing this was not much comfort for those who lived through it. From 1977 and all through the 1980s, the farmers of the LNID were running out of water almost every year, but not just because of the drought. Because developments in irrigation meant farmers could irrigate more of their land, the total amount of irrigated land had increased. In 1977, for example, at the height of summer—late July into early August—the LNID ran out of water completely. Nothing. The irrigation district shut down the system for five days then put it on a few days, then shut it down five days more. By shutting the system down, the district's management hoped there would be

40

enough water coming down the river to refill the reservoir.

In 1977 about 350 farm families—about 1,200 to 1,500 people—depended on water directly from the river. They had no water. Other farm families, who received water from a reservoir fed by the river, also had no water. As well, water was not reaching 40,469 hectares of irrigation land. Since the whole system was shut down, water stopped coming to many small communities, such as Iron Springs, Picture Butte, Shaughnessy, Diamond City, and, indirectly, Lethbridge. People could not water their lawns. What little water they had, they needed to keep for possible fires and drinking. Without water, the farmers and their families had nothing. Industry suffered. Lethbridge was in danger of not having enough water to treat its sewage. There was so little water in August that one could walk across the Oldman River as it flowed through Lethbridge.

The year 1984 was not as bad as 1977, but it was bad. The area was "literally running out of water." And so, the farmers had organized a meeting for the night of July 17 in a high-school auditorium in the town of Picture Butte to "demand a commitment" from the Alberta government to build the Oldman River Dam. Five hundred people, mostly farmers, squeezed into the auditorium.

Rick Ross was at that July 17, 1984, meeting in the high school at Picture Butte. His job was to make sure farmers had the right amount of water at the right time. "During nights in dry seasons I didn't sleep sometimes," he explained to me. "People would call me up personally and say, 'I ran out of water yesterday; I talked to the ditch rider and I still don't have it.' I knew where most of the people lived so I could say, 'You don't have it yet?' Or, 'It will take twelve hours to get to you.'"

Rick told me that people knew the dam wasn't just about politics. He said, long before that meeting, irrigators were good at using vivid examples to influence politicians. "We had the premier, and some of the ministers come down when it was really dry here. On one side of the road, there is irrigation, and there are flourishing crops. On the other side of the road, there is grass that is brown and burned up. We also showed them satellite photos to show them the actual areas of irrigation, and the actual area of the brown stuff. Then we reminded them of lots of economic studies done in the 1950s, then redone in the 1970s. We made a rational case."

When we spoke, Rick still vividly remembered the anger farmers felt at the meeting. "They weren't angry at nature, they were angry at the government for not proceeding and angry at me for not having water for them. They knew that because they were not irrigating they were not getting crops; that it was going to hit them all in the pocketbook. They were just really upset. The message to the ministers was: 'Get those reports moving.' They felt their very survival depended on it. I felt sick. We had improved the infrastructure over the years, but it wasn't enough." There had been plans to dam the river since the 1950s, but nothing had yet been done about it.

——— — ———

When Roy Jenson finally arrived at the high-school gym, he was lucky to find a place to sit at the back. Normally, as chairman of the board, he would organize such meetings. But this time, the farmers wanted to do it themselves, as the farmers. They didn't want the politicians to organize the meeting; and, as Roy later told me, he was "sort of a politician." They didn't even invite Roy and the other members of the board to take part. Late in the meeting, Roy asked if he could speak. They said, "Sure," so Roy stood up and began to speak.

When Roy told me about this meeting, he looked over my head, pounded his kitchen table, and was back there again, speaking in the present tense: "We're running out of water too often here. You're letting all that water go down the river and just dumping it in the ocean. We can use that water and not have any negative impacts. You've talked about this way too long, about this positive thing, this thing that should be done, and now is the time it needs to be done. We want that decision now. We've already done all the studying; the best possible decision has already been made, and now is the time to do it."

Far from the desperation of the gym, the Oldman River flowed quietly in its valley, supporting cottonwood trees and an ecosystem; a sanctuary for abundant life in a dry overdeveloped land. Far away in geography, and in spirit, were the Piikani. The Piikani were not merely far away, they were also competitors for the same water. There were no Piikani in the gym that night. They were living—the ones on the reserve at least—as they had for a long time, in fenced-in desperate poverty.

A few weeks after the farmers met in 1984 in Picture Butte, the town of Fort Macleod "instituted water restrictions on residents and businesses." Alberta's agriculture minister promised a decision on the dam that summer.

In August 1984, less than a month after the farmers' meeting, Alberta's Premier Peter Lougheed announced that the Alberta government would dam the Oldman River at a location known as Three-Rivers. The farmers felt that the government had finally listened and done the right thing. It wasn't just about money; it was about survival and hope for the future. As one old farmer, Leonard Haney, said to me, the dam "would give us some water to look after us." The majority of people in southern Alberta felt they needed the dam at any cost.

Controversy and Mitigation

Not everyone agreed with the government's decision to dam the Oldman River. Lorne Fitch was in his truck that August day in 1984 when he heard the news. He wasn't very far from the Oldman River; he was never very far from the river. At the time, Lorne was the regional habitat biologist for southern Alberta for the Alberta government. By 1984 he had worked in government for many years.

I met Lorne in 2005; he was over six feet tall, had green eyes, sandy-brown hair, and a full beard, greying in the front. He wore a red checkered shirt and jeans. Lorne spoke in a baritone voice about his years as a fish biologist with the Alberta government; he was nearing retirement. He could—more than that, he *needed* to—speak freely. Lorne spoke slowly, precisely, elegantly, taking time to find the right words. He had studied both English literature and biology for his first degree, before biology won out for his graduate work. He told one story after another of his experiences with the Alberta government, for whom the land was merely "black spots on maps." The emotion underlying his words wavered between anger and lamentation. Now and then he would laugh—a great releasing laugh—at a particularly stupid or horrible action of the government.

Lorne was born and raised on a farm in west-central Alberta. As a child, he could walk out off the back step of his farmhouse and within ten minutes be in the midst of an aspen and willow forest. Lorne described it to me like this: "That land had never been cleared, never cultivated and no trails or roads through it; a paradise of aspen groves, willow thickets, wetlands, and space. It was an incredible piece of wild country for a kid to roam around in, watch wildlife, get wet from wading in wetlands, and learn about connections in the natural world. One of the wetlands was large enough to be the focus of skating parties. I learned to skate on that wetland when I was four or five." He added that the land was "filled with little nooks and crannies, little sloughs—it was like living on the edge of a wilderness." He went there all the time.

One day, all that changed. The land was sold and cleared for use as farmland. The land was cleared with a new type of machinery, the Caterpillar tractor, which took its design from military tanks. Thousands of hectares were cleared in just a few years in the late 1950s and early 1960s. Lorne later remembered, "It was stunning to me as a kid. I mean, all those nooks and crannies and sloughs... Every day was a new opportunity, and now it was just a big flat plain of stumps; and the next year it was grain."

Lorne later became a biologist. For years he walked up and down creeks and rivers, doing inventories, catching fish, and doing biological sampling. He completed fish inventories of all the Eastern Slopes' streams, from the Montana border up past the Oldman River at its headwaters, to west of Rocky Mountain House. By the time he retired from the Alberta civil service, he had been through seven government departments and fifteen reorganizations. For years he wrote briefing notes for the minister. Lorne's notes provided the bones for the speeches the minister would later give in the Legislature. At some point he realized that the minister often did not even read his notes in advance and that nobody else did, either. For years, Lorne drafted all kinds of commitments for the minister to make.

In 1981 the government formed a regional habitat branch for southern Alberta, and Lorne became a regional habitat biologist for the area. He explained to me that it was his chance to move beyond simply cataloguing information and actually do something to protect the area's precious habitat. Since most of the land in southern Alberta was used for ranching and farming, almost the only wild spots left were the river valleys. Unfortunately, he and others in his department were not allowed to say no to development; they always had to find creative ways to say yes. He added, "In 1993 the habitat branch was axed by politicians who thought we were being too effective, industry captains who felt we were impeding economic progress. Timorous bureaucrats didn't stand up for us. I was functionally demoted."

When the noon news came on CBC radio that August day in 1984, the news that the dam would be built almost made Lorne physically ill. He knew that the Alberta government's own arm's-length environmental assessment body, the Environmental Council of Alberta (ECA), had concluded that a dam wasn't needed. And yet, the government had announced that the Oldman Dam would go ahead. He couldn't quite believe it. In spite of all the scientific advice, Lorne said, "all that hype of drought and low water flows, it had all been pumped up, tarted up, to rationalize the dam, and there it was, they were making the announcement. I was surprised at the decision." Looking back on that moment, he later said, "I guess I was somewhat naive, thinking that reason would prevail, that reason would trump politics."

A photo taken a few years later of Lorne at a protest against the Oldman Dam in Maycroft gives a sense of Lorne at that time: a man in his thirties, with anxious eyes; someone who is committed to a cause beyond himself, and deeply worried. In one of our conversations, Lorne quoted Aldo Leopold, who wrote the great book about

46

ecology, *The Sand County Almanac*: "Having an ecological educa-tion opens you up to a world of wounds." Lorne went on to tell me: "You can't avoid them. They are always there. Every day, nature is simply being destroyed." And the Oldman Dam, that was one big wound for Lorne. Lorne was the guardian of the river, at least from the perspective of the white world. It was his job, in theory, to protect it, its fish, and the habitat it nurtured. When the government announced it would build the dam, Lorne knew he would have to preside over the destruction of over forty kilometres of river valley, the dissolution of a corridor that stretched from the mountains to the prairie, which would endanger the cottonwood forests.

What made things worse, perhaps, was that he knew that the link between not enough water and drought was a "contrived story," as he explained to me. He knew that the main reason there was not enough water for the city of Lethbridge during August was not only because not enough rain was falling but also because the LNID was taking almost half the river away upstream. But of course, being a government employee, he couldn't say that out loud.

———————

Since the 1950s, there had been talk of a dam on the river. And, in the 1970s, the LNID (with support from the Alberta government) had expanded beyond the natural water-carrying capacity of the land. By that time, the government knew that a big project showing a commitment to water development in southern Alberta would buy votes. In the late 1970s, an Alberta government committee chaired by civil servant and engineer Peter Melnychuk concluded that the Oldman River should be dammed. The dam would create a forty-two-kilometre reservoir of water upstream. The committee's report did not assess if the land affected by the dam was important to the

Piikani or if the dam would have negative effects on the reserve, nor did it mention human costs to the farmers and ranchers and their families who owned houses on land to be flooded by the proposed dam. The report did not review the importance of the Oldman River ecosystem, or the economic costs of the project.

Even within the Alberta government bureaucracy, not everyone agreed with the plan to dam the Oldman River, at least not at the location known as Three-Rivers, which is where the dam was ultimately built. The deputy minister from Alberta's Department of Recreation and Wildlife, T.A. Drinkwater, set out his concerns about the project in a letter to Peter Melnychuk, dated September 1976. In the letter, Drinkwater explains: "[T]he recreation value of the Oldman River would not be enhanced by the construction of the [dam] reservoir." The land would have a "greater recreational value if left in its unaltered state." He gives several reasons for this, including the fact that the reservoir would create "high wind velocities" making boat use "unsafe." He also notes that Alberta's Department of Environment seemed to prefer the Three-Rivers site as a dam location for economic reasons alone. Drinkwater suggests, "while economics are very important," his department believed that choosing the Three-Rivers location would be a "serious mistake" as the "social and environmental impact of a reservoir at this site is far greater than at alternative dam sites…" He goes on to note that if economics were to be "a major factor" in the decision, the economic analysis done up to that time "may be misleading" as that economic analysis was "very preliminary" and only considered the costs to build the dam, with disregard to related costs.

The Environmental Council of Alberta, the third-party assessment group Lorne told me about, reviewed the idea of damming the Oldman River and concluded in 1979 that a "dam is not required at this time, or in the foreseeable future." The ECA felt that there could be some expansion of irrigation—though less than what the farmers and government wanted—by simply creating reservoirs of water off-stream (away from the river), at a fraction of the cost of a dam. The ECA concluded that this was the only way expansion of irrigation in southern Alberta made economic sense. Later, when the Alberta government decided to build the dam anyway, one member of the ECA called the decision "indefensible." Jack Glenn later concluded: "Alberta's studies in relation to the Oldman Dam lent an aura of scientific respectability to what was essentially a political decision."

In the book *The Oldman River Dam: Building a Future for Southern Alberta,* published by the Alberta government, Peter Melnychuk is quoted as saying why he disagreed with the ECA decision: "It was simply a different vision for the south… Government felt there had to be some vision for the south beyond a no-growth scenario."

As the ECA was holding democratic public hearings about the dam, a secret committee formed by Premier Lougheed—known as the Water Advisory Committee—was meeting to discuss, among other things, the possible transfer of water from basin to basin within Alberta. Peter Melnychuk, in a letter dated October 25, 1979, to the chairman of the Water Advisory Committee and Cabinet Minister Henry Kroeger, sets out a radical plan to dramatically re-engineer Alberta's ecosystems to move northern water south by transferring water from basin to basin. He notes in his letter that his plan "is in response to your request." This plan included twenty-four dams and diversion canals, encompassing most of Alberta, and was to be built in several stages. Stage One included the "Three-Rivers Dam (Oldman River)." (See Appendix, page 359.) There is no mention in Melnychuk's report about the monetary, ecological, or human costs of such a massive series of dams. Perhaps as an engineering report, it need not have this information; the question was: did the government have this kind of information from any source?

While Melnychuk worked on this plan, the Alberta government was also developing plans to implement a comprehensive and sophisticated public relations initiative to "create a demand" for water development in the province. One element in the plan was to create two kinds of pamphlets: one aimed at elementary school children and a second at the general adult public to convince Albertans of the importance of developing water resources. The purpose of the water transfer was not just for irrigation but also for economic development. In one Water Advisory Committee executive meeting on July 22, 1981, Premier Peter Lougheed purportedly said, "water… is controversial… because it is crucial."

From time to time, Martha Kostuch and other environmentalists woke up in the morning to find manila envelopes on their doorsteps, stuffed with secret documents from within the Alberta government bureaucracy. These packages were given to them by opponents of the government within the bureaucracy. When I met Martha in the spring of 2005, she gave me a number of Alberta government memos she received in this fashion, including Peter Melnychuk's water-transfer memo. When Melnychuk's memo and others on this issue were eventually released to the public, the Alberta government said it was not going to go through with the planned diversions. Was the Oldman Dam built only for farmers, or was it also built as part of a radical engineering plan that was not killed, only delayed a few decades? If so, then the Oldman Dam—as part of Stage One—was important not just to farmers but to the government itself.

Decades later, in 2005, Peter Lougheed wrote an article for the *Globe and Mail* titled "A Thirsty Uncle Looks North," warning Canadians to protect their water from the United States. In this article, Lougheed describes how Henry Kroeger "convinced me that we should transfer water from Alberta's more northerly rivers to the

50

dry areas in the southern and eastern parts of our province. When we took the proposal to caucus (we held almost every seat) we were shocked by the aggressively negative reaction. I learned then that water is an emotional political issue; I was usually able to get support from the caucus—but not when it came to fresh water."

In 1980 the government announced that it would build a dam on the Oldman River at one of three locations, including one location on the Piikani Reserve. In November 1983, the chief of the Piikani, Peter Yellowhorn, forwarded a plan to have a dam on the Piikani Reserve, jointly managed by the Piikani and the government.

Powerful forces worked tirelessly to promote the dam. The issue wasn't just water but also big money. Water has a tendency, at least in human society, to flow toward power and money, until the power and money wane. Hundreds of millions of dollars in contracts and water-fuelled money were to be made; and political careers would advance by landing the water and money. Of course, more noble motivations—having jobs and a thriving community for the next generation—must also have been present.

Against this vision of engineered development —and the collective power of the Alberta government, farmers, local politicians and businesses, engineering, and construction companies—leaned a few lonely voices. These few wanted to tell a different truth, one that was independent of power and money. *Lethbridge Herald* writer Joanne Helmer was one of those voices. Joanne asked her fellow citizens unpopular questions about the need for the dam, and about Native rights.

As time passed, Alberta government officials stopped speaking to Joanne. Rick Ross also stopped speaking to her. He felt her articles were not fact but disguised opinions. Roy Jenson continued to speak to her, but, as Joanne later told me, "It seemed hard for him." I later asked Roy about this, and he laughed good-naturedly and said, "No, it wasn't hard. Joanne just didn't understand the importance of irrigation because she didn't grow up here like we did. Joanne felt that many of those in southern Alberta were not bad people but were simply 'caught up in their own sense of righteousness' and would not listen to opposing points of view."

Joanne later told me what it was like to oppose the dam, or at least ask hard and necessary questions about it: "Here, those in authority said, 'We need water, therefore we build a dam.' Many in the community thought they were pro-dam because they were pro-water. These people were just, they were just—appalled by me. They were appalled by my questions. They were honestly disgusted because they couldn't understand why anyone would ask these questions about such a basic need in society. It didn't matter how many times you told people there are alternatives, there are better ways to provide this water."

When I spoke on the phone to Joanne in the spring of 2005, she told me that she had been "downsized" from the *Herald* after working there over two decades and had moved back to southern Saskatchewan, where she had grown up. Joanne, who loved being a journalist, whose articles could easily have been in the *New York Times,* was no longer working as a journalist.

We spoke many times on the telephone about the Oldman Dam. Joanne warned me: "when you get to the reserve, forget what you think you know. Listen. Look. Try to see with your own eyes." She told me that I must try to speak to Devalon Small Legs, one of the leaders of the Lonefighters. We also spoke about the price she paid in her personal life because of her opinions on the dam and Native rights. I was surprised—though I now know I should not have been—by how traumatic the Oldman Dam battle had been for her. At the time, very few people wanted to hear her questions. Most people hated her opinions. She said that only now, years later, has she been able to put together the pieces of that experience, to begin to understand just how hard that period of her life had been.

Joanne no longer has the articles she wrote then. She explains that many were purged from the newspaper's database when she was told she was no longer needed at the *Lethbridge Herald*. But they are still available in old-fashioned paper, a testament to the time and her struggle.

In Joanne's opinion, the Government of Alberta constantly made things worse instead of being reasonable. The government kept saying, "The dam or nothing." In addition, as time passed, Joanne began to feel that she, or her children, might be in danger. One day an irrigation farmer who enjoyed debating said, "You had better not run into my wife because she'll shoot you." Joanne knew that he was joking, but as she was living alone, raising two children, that was not the kind of joking she wanted to hear. At one public event, an announcer from one of the radio stations was so angry with Joanne that he was going to punch her. A lawyer intervened to stop him, saying, "She is just doing her job."

She did not find the atmosphere at her newspaper any better. The newsroom was extremely tense. People didn't understand that one must explore both sides of a problem, that journalists are supposed to ask hard questions. They couldn't or wouldn't understand the water issue. They had no concept of Native rights, so they didn't understand that reserve land is different. People did not understand that the reserve of the Piikani existed before Alberta existed, that there was a strong argument that the Piikani had special rights to the water of the Oldman, and even land off the reserve, due to their treaty with Canada. It was not a simple case of Piikani land being equivalent to that of a rancher who happened to own the same amount of land. The Piikani were closer to another order of government than any other landowner.

Joanne added, "There was such an anti-Native feeling in the newsroom at that time that they forgot about humanity when it came to Native people, Native issues. But the water issue had already inflamed everybody."

One man who had been a city councillor at the time kept telling her, "You don't understand these people. They went through the Depression. They know what it is like not to have water—not to even be able to grow a potato in their yards." Despite everything, however, she still had support in the community, more than she ever had at work.

During the Oldman Dam battle, on more than one occasion, the newspaper tried to have the editorial position changed. In an article dated March 27, 1990, the paper's headline read: "Editorial Opposition to Oldman River Dam Slammed." Roy Jenson was quoted in the newspaper as being "disappointed" in the newspaper's editorials since the beginning of the Oldman Dam project. "We have had numerous discussions with the editor in an effort to change the *Herald's* opposition, but there has been no progress. We have tried to identify where it (the *Herald's* position) comes from. The *Lethbridge Herald* should not be so negative on growth in southern Alberta." Lethbridge Councillor Don Lebarron also met with Don Doram, the publisher of the newspaper. He opposed a "boycott" of the newspaper. He added that the editorials made people "more environmentally aware." But he also wanted the editorial position changed. In the meantime, while Joanne struggled to educate the public about alternatives to the Oldman Dam, the Alberta government moved forward on all fronts to implement its decision.

———— • ————

When Alberta's Premier Peter Lougheed announced that the Alberta government would dam the Oldman River in the summer of 1984, neither the Piikani nor the landowners who would lose their homes in the river valley areas to be flooded were told of the decision before the public announcement. The decision to build the dam horrified environmentalists. Not only would forty-two kilometres of a irreplaceable river-valley ecosystem be drowned by the reservoir—all living things either drowned or cut off from the rest of the river valley—but the cottonwood forests downstream from the dam were also at risk, and the river's fish were in danger of not having a long enough reach of river in which to spawn. The Alberta government said that any damage to the environment would be "mitigated" and explained that it would spend a great deal of money to ensure this. The government suggested that the many kilometres of drowned river valley would be mitigated by enhancing fishing in other parts of the river, to create something called "no net loss of recreational fishing opportunities."

When I spoke to Lorne Fitch, he told me that he quickly realized that the government didn't really "give a damn" about mitigation, that theirs was going to be an exercise in "window-dressing." Lorne was concerned that there was no way to measure if the government mitigation effort had reached its targets. One high-up civil servant explained, "When the budget is spent, we will have made our targets." Lorne was determined to make sure the government's efforts were more than just public relations.

Lorne told me that the government didn't want to know the truth. He remembered one time when a biologist's report containing unpleasant truths vanished into government and never surfaced. When he began working for the government, the political portion of the civil service was at the very senior levels of government. As time passed, the political dimension began to creep down. More and more employees' jobs and output were directly related to political leanings, which meant that Alberta's was not a dispassionate, disaffected, stand-alone civil service. As time passed, the number of people employed by the communications division of Alberta's Ministry of the Environment made that ministry the largest in the Alberta government. As Lorne later said, "So anything that comes out of government, even a status report on species at risk, is vetted through that Ministry of Truth."

Lorne says that reservoirs and dams are never good at the site. "If we fail in our attempts to tell an honest story about these projects, I think we are inclined to continue to do them, because we never toll up what their impacts are in a real sense, and sooner or later the impacts start to eat us up."

Part of the government's "mitigation plan" involved a huge excavation by archaeologists of the area to be flooded by the dam reservoir upstream from the Piikani First Nation, in their ancestral valley. Had the Alberta government done nothing, all of the artefacts found would have been buried. So, the government hired archaeologists to dig up and move these items. In its book about the Oldman Dam, the government states, "Another benefit from the dam came on the historical resources side…" Between 1985 and 1991, archaeologists excavated and found many things, including "tee pee rings, buffalo drive sites, campsites." Despite the obvious link between these artefacts and the Piikani and their ancestors, no one asked permission from the Piikani to excavate the area upstream from their reserve, "nor did they seek consultation" with them. They just took the artefacts, almost certainly because they had been given authority and direction to do so from the Alberta government.

In 1986 the recently elected Piikani Chief Peter Yellowhorn, who once worked as an executive for an oil company, told the press that his people were in a struggle for their survival. He said, "[T]he proposed dam is the most recent threat in a history of trespass, confiscation and suppression that will destroy the Peigan people economically, culturally and spiritually." He warned that while he would like to resolve these issues using the law, some of the Piikani "might not have the patience to wait out lengthy court battles." He and the Piikani band council issued a water "proclamation," stating that the Piikani had water and land rights to the Oldman River and the water channel, based on their treaty with Canada. Furthermore, the Piikani hired noted Native rights lawyer Louise Mandell and former Justice Thomas Berger to file a lawsuit in April 1986 against Alberta, claiming rights to the water of the river as it flowed through their reserve, and to the riverbed on the reserve, and seeking damages for harm done by the Oldman Dam; as well as a second lawsuit against Canada on similar grounds, with the addition that the court should order Canada to act on its fiduciary duty to protect the Piikani.

In the spring of 1986, Albert Yellowhorn, the chief research officer for the Piikani, warned the LNID that their water would "soon be cut off unless the provincial government acknowledges that the Piikani have sole ownership rights to the Oldman River while it flows through the Indian Reserve." He added that the Piikani were "trying to be fair, and everyone should realize that our actions are the result of the government's unwillingness to settle this longstanding matter." Yellowhorn explained that the plan involves "digging a 600 metre long trench through the Oldman's floodplain, near the heart of the reserve, and sending the river's flow around the LNID diversion weir, leaving the structure high and dry." He told the press: "[W]e don't want to sound militant. We're not militant. We just want everyone to know that we're not pushovers. We've been sitting here for two years, trying to negotiate a deal, while water that generates millions of dollars a year in crops has been slipping through our fingers."

In February 1986, the Alberta government received a report

from Brian Reeves, a leading expert on plains archaeology, who concluded that the area of the proposed dam should be "designated a Provincial Historic Resource, and the Oldman River Dam should not be constructed." He said that Native people had occupied the area to be flooded behind the dam for eight thousand years. This area was "one of the two most important river valley settlement areas in the foothills of Alberta." He concluded flooding this area would be a loss of "international" magnitude. This report was not released to the public. When the *Edmonton Journal* made reference to it as "yet-to-be-released" archaeological study that "had recommended against construction of the dam," one government spokesman said that all the reports would be released when they were "finalized." A second spokesman said, "We don't know which report is being referred to."

Construction on the Oldman River Dam began in the fall of 1986. To build the dam, a small temporary dam had to be built to block the river. Tunnels were constructed under the river. Once these tunnels were finished, the river flowed through underground pipes for a kilometre, allowing for a dry construction site where the river once flowed. In the summer of 1987, the Alberta government issued itself a license to build the dam, without giving notice to the public.

For the government, things were proceeding as they always had. Decisions made at high levels were implemented without too much fuss. Native people suffered in silence, as did the earth. No one challenged the inevitability of development, as it was then defined. However, though it was not yet evident, things had changed. New ideas about both the land and the rights of Native people had been quietly and slowly gaining momentum in human society generally. But leaders were needed to bring these ideas forward and try to translate them into action, into a new vision of life and justice for the present and the future. One such person had moved from a small town in Minnesota to the town of Rocky Mountain House in Alberta. Her name was Martha Kostuch. She brought with her the radical idea—at least for Canada—that the government really must serve the people and must be held accountable. She also harboured the equally radical idea that the earth—the land and the rivers, all life—mattered. The earth's bounty did not merely represent raw products for human beings but they also had their own intrinsic worth.

The Crusader:
Martha Kostuch

For a long time, environmentalists outside of southern Alberta stayed out of the battle against the dam. The locals had said, "We want to do this ourselves. We don't want you coming in." Farmers and ranchers who owned houses on land to be flooded by the proposed dam formed the Committee for the Preservation of Three-Rivers to fight the dam. But in 1987, they realized they had lost when the Alberta government came to get their land, with the threat of expropriation hanging about them. That same year, Martha Kostuch got a phone call from a naturalist in southern Alberta: "We have given up. Come down and have at it. Will you facilitate for us? Can you plan some strategy sessions?" Martha Kostuch did not need to be asked twice.

One old farmer in southern Alberta known for his wisdom once said that in the early twentieth century all the great innovations in farming came from the United States and moved north at a rate of a hundred miles a year. The same could be said of great innovations in relation to ecology. This old farmer couldn't stand Kostuch, but his words could apply equally to her. She was an environmentalist in a time and place when it was not an easy or fashionable thing to be. Now she is ashes scattered to the winds on her beloved Kootenay Plains. But once she had long, straight, brown hair, piercing blue-green eyes—eyes that laughed merrily when she heard a good joke. She was blunt, unsentimental, and caring. Later, during her relentless campaign to stop the Oldman Dam, she had no time for southern Alberta's claim that it was desperate for water.

Martha Kostuch was born and raised on a farm near Moose Lake, Minnesota. As a child she hated town; she particularly hated shopping. The woods were her passion. Her house was noisy. She explained, "We were an aggressive ....r assertive family." When she needed to be away from everybody, to find solace, she went into the woods. She went for long walks in the forest. She built stone houses in the rocky north woods. She climbed—and hugged—trees. She practiced clarinet in the branches of her backyard apple tree.

Her dad taught agriculture and biology at a nearby school. When she was older, he took her for long walks in the forest, showing her the living world around her, explaining the symbiotic relation-ships between all life forms. Her love for the woods never died. She later explained, "All my life when something major happened—like grieving when my parents died, or when my ex left me—it was the woods I turned to. I love the smell of the woods, it always takes me back. Especially in the fall, when the leaves are falling. I love the woods in all seasons—each season has its own wonders."

Her dad was her hero. "He was outgoing," she recalled. "We often had political discussions and debates in the house. Both my parents were union supporters. They saw themselves as union workers and strong Democrats." Martha became an organizer at a young age when she directed a play in high school. She later said, "It was quite a challenge, especially getting the football players to learn their lines. I had to make them come in and learn lines during lunch period." In Grade 8, she decided to be veterinarian because she loved animals as much as trees.

As a child, she was educated about the American Revolution. "We were taught that it was not only our right but also our responsibility to object if we did not agree to what authorities were doing," she said, "even to the degree of overthrowing the authorities if they did not represent us. We don't want to be anarchists. If you don't accept some authority—if you challenge everything—that is not good, either. There are a lot of activists in leadership positions in Canada who came from the United States."

One of the things that got her started in environmental work was, as a vet, seeing the effect of sour gas emissions on animal health, particularly the post-partum health of cows. When she came to Alberta, she found that after they had calves, almost 100 per cent of cows, even in well-managed herds, developed an infection called uterine metritis. The cows showed other signs that their reproductive cycles were compromised, too. When she was still working in Minnesota, Martha routinely saw this same infection in only 3 per cent of the cows. She called on Alberta government vets to come out, and while they agreed that what they were seeing was abnormal, they could not find the cause. She did her own reading and research and noted that other problems in livestock had been found in areas affected by sour gas emissions. She raised her concerns with the companies and government; everybody said the emissions met the requirements. So she went to the media; she made a lot of noise. She intervened in hearings. After that, her activist work was nonstop.

In May of 2005, on a gloriously bright spring day, I drove to Rocky Mountain House to meet Martha Kostuch. In this part of Alberta, just shy of the foothills, well north of Calgary, the woods are thick and plentiful, and the trees and grass very green. There is lots of water here. The only issue for growing things is the cold; one doesn't go more than a few weeks even in the summer without the temperature dipping below zero at night.

On the edge of town, I found Martha Kostuch's combined

home and workplace. The wooden house has a sharply angled roof and is shaded by trees beside her house. The smell downstairs was pungent and announced clearly that this was a vet's place of work. Up a narrow winding stairway was Martha's house. I don't think there was one part of the building that was exactly square. The house was full of light, angled rooms, and hidden spaces that housed old documents and Martha's journals.

I met Martha and most of her family at the same time. Martha was fifty-eight at the time and there were lots of laughing, screaming, playing grandchildren about. I don't think I ever counted them up. Before I arrived she had said, "You can interview me when I am operating." I didn't say anything in response to this but hoped other arrangements might be made. Martha never did sit down for an interview. She was too busy. We spoke when walking in the woods, when she was cleaning the kitchen, between her appointments at the clinic and phone calls in the car related to her environmental work. Between her clinic phone and her other phone, she was on the phone a lot.

I had first met Martha earlier that spring, when we did several interviews over the phone. Martha didn't need any convincing to speak to me. I told her that maybe this book would make her better known and therefore better able to protect the earth she so loves. "I hope there is something left to deal with," she replied.

———— • ————

That first day at her house she showed me where her files were: back behind a set of stairs. She mentioned in passing that she also kept journals from that time, and that she still kept a journal. She showed me where they were: stuffed in the corner of a closet, falling out of old plastic bags. I rummaged through them. They were little books, fifteen by eight centimetres, coiled at one side. The collection of little books, filled with notes, went back to the early 1980s. I could see her clear, precise, almost terse, style in the entries.

"They are like police notebooks," I said.

"Yes," she said. Police officers keep notebooks to record key events and details in their investigations, while the events are fresh in their minds. This way, years later, after one's memory has faded, the details and events will be there. Of course, one can still lie in notes in the first place, but it is less likely during or immediately after something has happened for someone to invent details about it. People—even whole countries or peoples—often use the past to serve present needs; writing down notes about what happened soon after it happened constrains this urge.

I flipped through the books. Martha's notes were as succinct as any police officer's. Unlike notes made by police, however, Martha's entries wove together the details of her environmental work with her life as a vet, and her personal life.

I spent three days with Martha and her family. The second day, Martha laughed more. She told me the story of her access to information request. Martha had filed the request regarding a development authorized by Alberta Environment. Alberta Environment granted the request but told Martha she had to pay more than $5,000.00 for copying the pages. Martha said she did not have to pay because the law said those acting in the public interest did not have to pay for photocopying. So Martha went to the Information and Privacy Commissioner—rather like a mini-judge for these kinds of questions—and asked for a fee waiver. The Information and Privacy Commissioner wrote that Martha: "serves a public education function" and that she "serves an environmental watchdog function and is well known in that role. The applicant's watchdog function has special significance, given the cutbacks to Alberta Environment's monitoring ability."

Martha got her fee waiver. "I have less trouble from them now," she said. "When they see me coming, they ask, 'What do you want?'"

In the evening we spoke more. At last, the busy house was quiet. Her grandkids had either left or gone to bed. Though it was almost 9:00 p.m., the northern sky remained clear blue, and sunlight streamed through her window. I asked how her view of the dam was different from that of the farmers. She said she understood their position but did not agree with it. As she spoke, invariably in sharp bursts, her eyes lit up. "For farmers, everything is produce for mankind." She suggested that for some farmers, and others, a tree dying of old age is a waste, even if that dead tree provides nutrients to the ecosystem in which it falls—to birds, moss, organisms that aid in decomposition and returning nutrients to the soil. For these people, she said, "there is no value to a tree or a bird or a river unless it can be used by people to further their aims." She added, "I understand that point of view; what I do not understand are the personal attacks that were made against me during the battle." She said she does not mind arguing with people on the issues. "People have different views on things. That's what makes the world interesting. I don't think that people should attack personally. Most lawyers understand—they can argue both sides. I can do that. In fact, I find that helps my thinking to be able to argue the other point of view. It helps me clarify the issues. It strengthens my arguments."

Martha added, "You have to put yourselves in their heads. I cannot say definitely that one point of view is right and the other is wrong. I want to have public knowledge, and a public debate." She told me she would always tell the press, "'You must talk to my opponent.' I may not agree with the point of view of the irrigation farmer, who sees dams as creating a better environment—I may not agree, but I will support to the end his right to say it."

———————

After Martha Kostuch answered the call from southern Alberta in the summer of 1987, she planned a strategy session. Her journal entries show that with each passing day, more and more representatives from environmental groups said they were coming to the meeting—so her estimate of how many people would be present grew and grew. She met with southern Alberta naturalists on August 28, 1987, in a library in Lethbridge, to create an organization dedicated to one purpose: stopping the Oldman Dam. Seventeen people attended the meeting, including representatives of most of the main wilderness and naturalist groups in the province. At the time of the first meeting, there was little environmental legislation in place and few interest groups dedicated to protecting the land. Many Albertans at the time saw water solely as an economic resource. Others were prepared to go along with the Oldman Dam. However, there was a small group of people who knew about the land and rivers and was prepared to stand up to the government. In this sense, they were leaders.

Martha set the agenda for the meeting. She later said, "We wanted to be for something, not against things. That's how we chose the name: Friends of Oldman River. We were for the river."

Everyone arrived and the meeting began. The room was tense, even despondent, but there was hope. Martha looked around the room and spoke, "I think we only have a 20 per cent chance of stopping it. But we've got to try—otherwise, we are condoning it." Everyone agreed they had to try. Martha laid out her strategy, which she later explained to me: "We used a lateral, not a linear, strategy. I don't believe in linear strategies. I always have actions in different fields: legal, political, public awareness through education and media, organizational, information and research, and others. You have to have actions in a number of areas that complement each other. You do not know which will have the most success when you start out. Having legal actions, for example, puts more pressure on government—they get media attention, which generates public awareness. But you need also to have a political strategy. After all, if you just win in court, they can just change the law. You have to have a broad strategy to be successful."

As Martha discussed the strategy at the meeting, the room became more hopeful. They hoped they could at least implement the strategy. Martha decided to take charge of the legal strategy herself. Going after the Alberta government's treatment of the rule of law was like—as the saying goes—shooting fish in a barrel.

By the end of the meeting, Martha Kostuch was vice-president of the new organization, and southern Alberta biologist Cliff Wallis was president.

Cliff told me that as a child he had camped and fished all over southwestern Alberta. As a teenager he drank, smoked, and played lots of pool, but he always loved the land. Later, he got a job working for Alberta Parks. His job was to go out and watch birds and plants in beautiful places in Alberta. He later left Parks to become a consultant. In the mid-1980s, after the site for the dam had been chosen, he was hired by the Alberta government to work as a consultant on environmentally significant areas of Alberta—including the Oldman River valley. Everyone knew the area would be flooded by the dam reservoir. Government representatives explicitly told Cliff not to look in the Oldman valley, even though it was a significant area.

Cliff said, "Here is this nationally significant area, and it's all going to vanish, and I wasn't even allowed to look in there to assess it. It was a triangle of land. We went in there anyway. It was like Glen Canyon in Colorado that was flooded—all those wonderful things that disappeared. I wondered: what is going to happen here in the Oldman valley? I knew it was a place of national significance for fish, nesting birds, and the variety of rare plants and plant communities. The landscape of the valley to me is one of the power spots on the planet. You can understand why the Peigan care so much about the land there. It speaks to you in ways that you can hardly put into words. It is something you've got to try to hold on to."

———•—

Martha didn't take long to begin her attack. She knew that the Alberta government would have to give itself a permit or license to dig in the river as it began to build the dam. That August she went to a government office in Edmonton and discovered that the Alberta government had not yet issued itself a permit. She returned in September and found out that by that time Alberta had issued itself a permit without, apparently, following the law.

The law said that the government must "give notice," it must tell people, towns, and certain government bodies what it is planning to do so that these people and organizations can give the government their views on those plans. Of course, everyone knew about the dam, but the law about giving notice allowed people to respond to the government's plan. No notice, no chance to respond. Giving notice may not seem important, but it is woven into the law, which makes it important. Martha discovered that a government official had issued the Alberta government a permit without giving notice to anybody, due to the "urgency" of the situation. The official did not explain the "urgency," given that the permit application had been made almost a year and a half before and nothing had been done. As well, everyone knew that Alberta wanted to build the dam mainly for irrigation. However, when Alberta asked itself for a permit, it said it wanted to build a dam to control floods and for other reasons, such as conservation. The Alberta government did not ask for a permit for the irrigation. If it had asked to build a dam for irrigation, it would have had to file more paperwork and complete more studies.

Martha Kostuch and the Friends of Oldman River launched a legal action against the Alberta government decision to give itself a permit, arguing that Alberta had clearly broken the law by failing to give notice. Joanne Helmer felt that the court challenge was helpful, since "the Alberta government has never offered a satisfactory explanation of its decision to build the dam." Minister of the Environment Ken Kowalski, who was the government minister responsible for the dam, called some environmentalists "social anarchists" and described the legal challenge to the permit to build the dam as "absurd, nonsensical, and to the point of being ridiculous."

On December 8, 1987, Chief Justice Moore of the Court of Queen's Bench ruled that due to the "clear noncompliance" of the law by Alberta Environment, the permit to build the dam would be quashed. Because Alberta had not followed the law, the permit was no good, no longer valid. With this ruling, Alberta no longer had a permit to build the dam.

The judge did not go further, however, and say the building of the dam should stop. There is a tradition in Canadian law—rooted in British law - that governments are not ordered to follow the law. Instead, they are presumed to follow the law. In a society in which the government does not follow the law, then the rule of law, and democracy itself, is in danger. If a judge says something is wrong, government is presumed to correct the situation.

Martha and the environmentalists were exhilarated with this ruling. Alberta, however, kept building the dam without a permit.

"Construction is continuing. There is no change in status," said an Alberta Environment spokesperson. Alberta said it had an independent legal opinion that construction could continue while it applied for new permits, though it did not release the kind of reasoning that would allow it to break the law with impunity. Alberta appealed the decision.

Shortly after the decision, Joanne Helmer wrote in the *Herald*: "The Court decision may force a review of the government's decision to build the dam. That review is not unimportant and it is not too late… Governments are not above the law or the implementation of the law in their own procedures, as Justice Moore pointed out. Why should that be a surprise to anybody?"

The Attorney General of Alberta claimed that since the judge had not ordered Alberta to stop building, it could keep building without a permit. While the courts prefer to simply make a ruling on the law, and are reluctant to attempt to order governments to act, if the government continues to disobey the law after a clear decision of the court, the court will consider whether the government should be ordered to obey the law. In this case, Friends of Oldman River took the Alberta government to court again to try to enforce the first ruling. In a further court decision, Chief Justice Moore said, in effect, the government could "keep building the dam" until an appeal of his decision was heard.

Alberta Report, a popular magazine in southern Alberta at the time, quoted Roy Jenson's reaction to the first ruling, which cancelled Alberta's permit to build the dam. "This isn't justice," Jenson "thundered." The mayor of Pincher Creek, a town counting on the dam to provide much-needed local employment, said, "I think the judge is nuts. He gave the tree-huggers a victory and personally I don't like the SOBs. He should be sued."

When Roy Jenson had heard that the permit to dam the river

had been cancelled, he called his lawyer. Roy explained to me that he called his lawyer because, "It didn't seem to be going right. It seemed unfair." He told me that he was really frustrated. So he asked his lawyer about it: "Where the blazes is the justice in that?"

"Listen buddy. Don't ever compare the justice with the law," his lawyer answered. According to Roy, this lawyer was appointed judge a month later.

Shortly before the appeal of the case was to be heard, the Alberta government cancelled its appeal and gave itself a new permit. Again, the government did not give notice to the public. This was unusual. From time to time, courts rule that the federal or provincial governments have overstepped, or flagrantly broken, the law. Usually, the government will act to correct the error, retracing its steps carefully, so as not to break the law a second time. In this case, the Alberta government again didn't formally give notice, despite the ruling of the court. Soon, Martha Kostuch was back in court. This time, the Court of Queen's Bench ruled that Alberta didn't have to give notice to the public because Alberta had filed a lot more information than it had the first time, including information about how expensive any delay in building the dam would be.

———— • ————

In his book, Jack Glenn explains that Martha Kostuch's success in having the dam's permit cancelled "ignited" the pro-dam lobby. The irrigation farmers formed a new organization called the Southern Alberta Water Management Committee, to, as Roy Jenson told me later, "correct the falsehoods about the dam."

Roy told me that people not from the South "did not get it." "It" was the reality of life in the South, how the dam was desperately needed. Martha Kostuch did not comprehend it. "It was very difficult to tell her so she would comprehend it. We found it exasper-ating when we had media coming back and forth saying Martha said this or that. Cliff Wallis was the same. He did not pretend to know agriculture; he put an environmental spin on everything." Cliff Wallis wore a pin whose message was "No Dam Way." Roy continued, "You don't want a dam? Hey, we don't either, unless it's really needed, unless it's really economically feasible, and we can show this."

According to Roy, the environmentalists had the ear of the press. What they said was taken as fact by the press. Southerners had a very difficult time convincing the press after the fact that what they heard and perceived to be right was not right at all. They could give the press all kinds of facts, and the next day the reporters would retreat to their original thinking. This environmental "spin" was new and strange, particularly to those who might suffer economically due to it. Roy felt and still feels that most people are more prepared to protect precious land that will limit somebody else's economic devel-opment than will limit their own. He told me, "Martha Kostuch: she works really hard for that side of it. But a lot of her arguments are off the mark. She loses her credibility the way she argues, too many issues. But it seems that in order to be well heard, and for the press to accept you, you got to be making statements all the time; and they can't all be good ones."

———— • ————

I wanted to hear the strongest possible defence of the dam from an engineering perspective on nature. The person I spoke to was the former manager of the LNID, Rick Ross. I read in the newspaper that when he learned that there would be a full environmental assess-ment of the Oldman Dam, he said "that would be a good idea." He only wished it had been done sooner.

I had trouble finding Rick at first as he had retired from the LNID and started his own management company specializing in water resources. Early on, during one of our many conversations, he told me that he went into engineering because he had the aptitude and because he wanted to help people. He was the general manager of the LNID for over twenty-seven years. Rick's role also included explaining to the public, and defending where necessary, the interests of the LNID. In an earlier water crisis with the Piikani, back in 1978, Rick went on television to explain the LNID members' point of view. Later, during the Oldman Dam battle, Rick presented the LNID position in the media and attended various hearings in relation to the dam in order to explain why the dam was needed.

I first met Rick at his doorstep in a quiet residential street in Lethbridge on a sunny day in August 2005. He brought me into his immaculately clean and organized kitchen and offered me a coffee before sitting down across from me to answer my questions. Rick is tall, big-boned, and lean. He was calm, at least outwardly. His breathing was measured; now and then, it quickened. His face was angular, his hair sandy brown, and he wore square dark-rimmed glasses. The day I met him, he wore jeans and a checkered shirt. He was cautiously friendly. He did not laugh at my jokes, even the few that might have been funny. When he did smile, it seemed genuine.

Rick listened carefully to my questions and he always gave direct answers—but slowly, methodically, choosing his words precisely—in logical and clear sentences. I had the sense that he was telling me the truth, as he understood it.

Rick was born in Alberta, in the town of Lamont just west of Edmonton. His family lived on a farm until he was six, then they moved into the town of Grand Prairie where his parents ran a motel, service station, and coffee shop rolled into one. They sold the farm because his dad had a heart condition, and the farm involved hard physical labour. When it came time to go to university, he decided to take engineering. He knew he was good at logic, and he liked mechanics.

Rick particularly liked studying water flow and bridges, to calculate the bearing strength of bridges. He wanted to make sure that bridges were safe. His broader goal was to improve the lives of others. Instead of wading a stream, he reasoned, people could walk over a safe bridge.

We spoke at Rick's house, later on the telephone, about the history of the LNID and the history of irrigation in Alberta. Rick knew a lot. He explained that before irrigation, there was very little farming in the area. Alberta's agriculture was mostly grasslands ranching. They had all the right ingredients for good crops in southern Alberta, except enough water. Rick explained that the region's history was replete with stories of farmers who developed the land then left it during dry years. They had worked hard to develop the land, but they couldn't live on it.

I asked him if the Oldman Dam was needed. Emphatically, he said, "Yes." He said that the dam provides not more water but more stability for the water. Normally there is much water in the river in spring, little in the fall. With the dam, there is water all year, as its reservoir stores water during the spring then releases it at a steady rate as needed by irrigators. He felt the dam was good for the health of the river, too.

Rick explained that he found it difficult to talk to the environmentalists who opposed the dam, and it wasn't for lack of trying. He said he was dumbfounded because he could usually talk to just about anybody. He was simply unable to communicate with Martha Kostuch and another environmentalist who worked with Martha, biologist Cliff Wallis. Rick explained that the only way to really communicate with someone with a different background is to have a common understanding of something and then build from that. Without that understanding, that connection, there is no communication, only words.

While many people I spoke to, and much that I read, elaborated on misleading statements put forth by the Government of Alberta during the dam battle, Rick told me that some environmentalists had also been misleading. For example, LNID farmers once invited an environmentalist to one of their conferences as a speaker. He said that this environmentalist spoke of a wonderful chemical farmers could use that would save water. Rick explained that some farmers came to the next meeting angry. It was at this point in his telling of this story that Rick switched to the present tense, as if the event he was describing had happened only yesterday and not twenty years ago. His voice became harsh as he imitated one of the angry farmers: "The chemical didn't work. That guy lied." Rick said he didn't know if the environmentalist really lied or if there had been some kind of honest misunderstanding, but it was a bad experience, nonetheless. He said that he had heard similar misleading statements from some environmentalists throughout the dam battle.

I said that some environmentalists might see him as evil. He agreed and laughed good-naturedly. I asked him who the farmers saw, if anybody, as evil. "To some of the uninformed farmers, Martha Kostuch," he said.

At one point I asked Rick why he was speaking to me. He said, "Because I think what I did was right." He said he kept a diary of the events from that time because he thought the battle was interesting. I told him Martha Kostuch had done the same thing.

When I spoke to Rick about the Friends of the Oldman River and Martha Kostuch, he told me he felt that he was an environmentalist, too. I asked him to explain how he saw the Oldman Dam issue, as compared to those who tried to stop the dam. He told me that environmentalists always thought that the Oldman Dam was part of a secret plan to transfer Canadian water to the United States. He added that he doubted there was any plan to do this but said that the Oldman Dam "might be a step in water transfer, but not to the United States. Eventually, water will be transferred from one basin to another within Canada. A series of dams properly utilized will allow water to be moved to the South, where the dry areas are in Canada, and away from the surplus water areas such as the North. Six days of flow of the Peace River is the entire year's flow of the Oldman River. That's all you would need for the entire South. I don't think the ecological consequences will be as significant as some people think. There will be some."

He added that the environmentalists who fought against the farmers knew the headlines, but they didn't know what impact the dam would have on individuals from the South, and they weren't directly affected one way or another. "They did not have to choose not to water their lawn or not to take a shower because they were out of water. There is an emotional attachment to water in Canada. We have lots of water, but we also·have most of the world's land ....on a per capita basis we have huge amounts of water, but when we fill up our population to match our land, we need our water. I think we in the South have less emotional attachment to the environment and more physical attachment."

He told me that the biggest thing that separates him from most environmentalists is that they see the biological world as it is today as what they want to preserve. They have forgotten about evolution. "Evolution includes man-made evolution, and that includes dams. Drastic radical change on a massive scale is bad for the ecology of all, and we are directly affected by that. We want to re-engineer nature so that the basic ecological structure will survive mostly intact—

76 ·

but there will be minor glitches in it, and I will guarantee that will happen."

I asked Rick, "Why should human beings be deciding that all these fish and animals are going to die for us? Shouldn't we think of these other living creatures?"

"The question reminds me of a bumper sticker prepared by a chemical company I saw one time," said Rick. "It went, 'Boycott Food Manufacturers—Stop Eating.' We are carnivores. We need to eat living things for protein. Either we are going to shoot two billion people or we are going to continue to change the surface of the earth."

———— •– ————

As Friends of Oldman River made progress in the courts, the air war intensified. In his book, Jack Glenn explains that the Alberta government's "chief weapon was the control, spin, and dissemination of information." Alberta used its various communications agencies "staffed by people trained and experienced in advertising, public relations, or the media . . . to cast the decisions and actions of Alberta in the most favourable light." Alberta news releases "accentuated the positive, and eliminated the negative" about the social and environmental costs of the dam.

To defend the dam, Alberta's communications department launched a sustained and sophisticated attack in the media. Its employees "wrote to newspapers and periodicals offering hair-splitting arguments" in response to any perceived criticism of the dam. They even wrote back against letters to the editor. The Alberta government "authored articles favourable to the dam" and sent them to local newspapers. These articles were published without readers knowing that they were authored by the government. In 1989 the

Government of Alberta "sent an 'information package' to schools in southern Alberta that included a letter and government-produced videos explaining why the Oldman Dam was needed, extolling the benefits it would provide, and arguing that the environmental impacts would be minimal." Alberta Environment launched its own Oldman Dam newsletter called Update, accentuating the positive and eliminating the negative. "When bad news could not be avoided, it was presented as good news." Jack Glenn gives vivid examples. The fact that a priceless archaeological heritage would be flooded out by the dam became "our past coming to life" and "a unique opportunity for amateur archaeologists." He suggests that the "most ambitious and shameless of Alberta's information projects" was the publication in 1992 of *The Oldman River Dam: Building a Future for Southern Alberta*. The theme of the book is the "triumph of man… over nature, in the form of an 'erratic' and 'unpredictable' river." The "heroes" of the story were "provincial politicians, civil servants, and irrigation farmers."

Martha Kostuch tried to counter the Government of Alberta point of view with a "steady stream of news releases" focusing on the position of the Friends of Oldman River and "ignored or put a negative spin on information that favoured the dam or the government." Others fought against the Alberta government in their own fashion. Martha was a warrior for the earth. For her and the Alberta government, facts were fodder in the battle: words became swords.

Environment Canada (Parks) naturalist Kevin Van Tighem, who lived in Jasper at the time, had a different way of approaching the media spin. In response to criticisms that anti-dam people were inaccurate with the facts, he wrote: "I did my own research before forming my opinions; I did not rely on either Friends of Oldman River or the Alberta Irrigation Projects Association to tell me what to think."

Kevin Van Tighem's family has lived in the West since the late nineteenth century. He studied plant ecology at the University of Calgary. Later, he studied wildlife and worked in various parks for thirty-four years, retiring in 2011 from his job as superintendent of Banff National Park. Van Tighem is not only a naturalist but also a gifted writer who has won many writing awards. He has written books, stories, and articles on issues relating to understanding and conservation of the natural world. He has also served in leadership positions within wilderness associations in Alberta.

Perhaps putting his own job at risk, Van Tighem put his knowledge and love of the earth and its rivers into many dozens of reasoned articles and letters to editors all over Alberta. He learned about irrigation and agriculture in order to fight against the dam. Above all, he wished to show the public—as best as one could with the limited possibilities of black words on white paper—the living earth and its rivers, to place it directly before the readers' eyes.

When he came to battle against the Oldman Dam, no newspaper was too small to receive a carefully reasoned *"essay"* under the guise of letter to the editor from Kevin Van Tighem. He wrote these words to the *Edson Report* under the headline "Environmental Issues Keep Blowing Up":

> ....W]e who live in Alberta have always taken a lot of things for granted. We've always assumed our rivers would be clean and productive, the wild places of our foothills and the north would be there for us to visit and enjoy, wildlife would be common, and the air would be clean. These are part of our myth... These things used to be true—but time stands still for nobody. Today we see our rivers sucked dry for irrigation, our northern rivers becoming industrial sewers, our northern forests given away to logging companies, the air smelling like

sour gas or pulp mill emissions… stress points are everywhere.

In some articles, this knowledgeable, reasonable man can barely restrain his anger. On October 14, 1987, he sent this letter to the *Lethbridge Herald*, among other newspapers:

Environment Minister Ken Kowalski complains that the discussion of the three-rivers [sic] dam has been clouded with "inaccurate or incomplete information." His letter is proof of that—but the misinformation emanates from Alberta Environment! The [ECA] specifically stated: "An onstream dam is not required at this time or in the foreseeable future."

Kowalski's letter says that Alberta Environment is following the recommendations of the ECA report. If that is how it follows recommendations, no wonder it's noted for irrational and expensive decisions.

Kowalski promises us "no net loss of recreational fishing opportunities." What this means is that he will flood more than 40 kilometers of top wild trout streams, then try to replace them by stocking hatchery fish in the reservoir and adding artificial enhancements to other streams…

If nobody in his department understands the difference between a wild river and a stock pond, perhaps it should change its name.

At a conference on the Oldman Dam in the spring of 1988, Van Tighem "told the crowd that the river is a complex, inter-related living system, and all means of water conservation should be exhausted before any damming is considered." He added that damming is not "progress… as the ecological as well as economic costs are simply too high. The beauty of an entire region of Alberta will be lost. Damming should be an act of desperation, like burning the furniture to keep warm."

Roy Jenson later told me that none of those environmentalists knew anything about irrigation "except that Dutch guy."

Martha v. Alberta and Canada

On August 2, 1988, at 7:00 a.m., Martha Kostuch went to meet her lawyer, Clayton Rice. When she arrived, everything was ready. Martha looked through the affidavit prepared by Rice and signed it. Next, they drove to Pincher Creek to file the papers. In some circumstances, Canadian law allows private citizens to prosecute others when the government refuses to launch a prosecution. This power is often used in minor assaults, or thefts. In this case, Martha intended to prosecute the Government of Alberta itself, as well as some of its ministers and the construction companies building the dam. She alleged that they committed crimes against nature in breach of Canadian law by building the Oldman Dam without a federal permit.

On the way to Pincher Creek, Martha and Rice stopped at the Oldman River downstream from the partly constructed dam. Big terraces, row on row, had been cut into the valley sides where trees once stood. During the previous two winters, men with chainsaws had cut the trees at the higher levels, and backhoes had knocked them down at lower levels where the dam was to be. The trees had been burned on the floodplain, spirals of smoke heading up into the cold winter sky. For forty-two kilometres, a living ecosystem had become a pile of stumps.

Lorne Fitch saw the burning and later tried not to remember it. He had asked the dam builders to hold off on cutting down all the trees to give the animals one more year of life. The construction companies said no—not because they were necessarily bad or unkind men, but because they were following a contractual timetable set long before.

What did the dam site look like to those who really know how to look? A few months after Martha and her lawyer were there, Cheryl Bradley visited the site. Cheryl is a cottonwood tree expert, with expertise in the devastating downstream impact on the trees wrought by dams. She later told me what she felt and how the area looked that day. What to farmers looked like a helping hand that would guarantee their future looked rather different to her. That day, Cheryl had spoken at an irrigation conference and part of the conference included a tour of the dam site. Along with the irrigation farmers, she took a bus to the edge of the valley. Cheryl knew the valley well and had canoed it that spring from the upper Oldman down. She remembered the valley as it had been. It was beautiful. The river was broad and meandering, with cliffs and point bars. The north-facing part of the valley had dense woodlands of spruce, fir, cottonwood, and willow. It was a rich environment, replete with birds and fish and other animals, seen and unseen.

When she arrived at the site, Cheryl looked down. The whole valley was a brown barren hole with no water in it because the river had been captured and run through a pipe. In front of her was a pit where a river had once flowed. In this pit, scurrying everywhere, were tractors, Caterpillars, and backhoes. "It was like a bomb had hit the valley. People were running around, excited about it, completely remoulding the whole thing." It ripped her apart. All those trees, all the vegetation, all that life, everything had been cleared away. "They had ripped the guts out of the river—they killed it." It was such a powerful shock, she thought, "I don't ever want to be in this place again."

The others on the bus didn't see the site in the same way Cheryl did. They thought it represented great progress, that this was a great advance. The dam was going to do wonderful things for the economy of southern Alberta. She spoke a little bit about her concerns to individuals on the bus. One guy was rude to her. Another kept saying, "You're not getting it. The dam is going to be great." They were defending what they thought was the right thing to do, and Cheryl was suggesting that their right thing was wrong. Cheryl couldn't relate to the others on the tour nor could she communicate what she thought was an atrocity. For the farmers, the dam was just another thing one did to advance the economy and society. In the end, Cheryl became speechless. A reporter wanted to interview her about her response.

"I can't talk about this," Cheryl said.

When I met her, Cheryl was calm, quiet, but at the same time tenacious in discussion. If she had a point, she was determined to make it, and she would make it, quietly, insistently. She lacked any of the self-righteousness I feared I might find, based on my experience with some city environmentalists.

Cheryl was living in Calgary when she learned that the Oldman Dam was going to be built. She was aghast and decided immediately to put her scientific knowledge to the service of the Friends of Oldman River. Cheryl had grown up on a dairy farm in Ontario. As a child, she read books about wild places. When Cheryl was twenty, she went to the Yukon and got to see real wilderness. After that, she knew she wanted to live in the West. When we talked about this, Cheryl spoke very softly, as one might in church, "I wanted to be where those wild places were." Cheryl told me about her experience of studying cottonwood trees. She told me that during one study she "was laughed at, working on my silly trees." Few people had really thought about the cottonwood trees. Yet, when people contemplated not having cottonwood trees any longer, they realized the trees were important.

Around the time the government announced the dam, Cheryl was reading a book by John Eisenhauer, *Rivers on Borrowed Time*. In the book, Eisenhauer writes that the Oldman River was one of the very important wild rivers in Alberta. Cheryl told me that her academic studies showed that there were very negative effects of dams downstream; the cottonwood forests would be at risk. From the moment of the announcement onward, as the Oldman River Dam battle began to take shape, Cheryl carried with her a feeling of dread: she wanted to protect the "very significant ecological environmental spaces in Alberta."

Finally, that day when she saw the valley in ruins, on the verge of tears, she told the journalist, "'This is horrible, absolute destruction—fish have died, wildlife has died, plants have died. We have completely destroyed a segment of a living river. We've cut off this river from downstream. We stand a chance of completely altering it.' To me it was just wrong, wrong, no matter what kind of justification you try to put on it."

———

That morning in August 1988, Martha and Rice looked down at where the Oldman River used to be. Rice turned to Martha, and said, "Where is the river?"

"It was gone. The damage was obvious," Martha later wrote of this moment.

After visiting the river, Martha and Rice drove to the courthouse in Pincher Creek. They went inside and told the justice of the peace that Alberta and the dam builders had broken the law—the *Canadian Fisheries Act*—in building the dam, and she was there to prosecute Alberta and the dam builders for their crime. Federal law stated that "no person shall carry on any work or undertaking that results in the harmful alteration, disruption, or destruction of fish habitat"—unless they have permission from Canada to do so. The law applied to provincial governments. Martha said that Alberta had no permission from Canada to build the dam, and it was destroying fish habitat during the dam construction. Therefore, Alberta was guilty of breaking the law. Martha had gathered the evidence like a police officer; now, with the help of her lawyer, she would conduct the prosecution as a private citizen. One couldn't expect the Alberta government to prosecute itself, so she was going to do it.

The law at the time was clear—if you destroy fish habitat without authorization from the federal government, you are guilty. The only possible defence to this crime would be if you had tried—had used due diligence—to find out the law but had somehow not known that you had nevertheless broken the law. Needless to say, this kind of defence might be easy to make for an unsophisticated person, but it would be very hard to believe such a defence put forth by a government that employs dozens of constitutional and criminal lawyers. Unfortunately for Alberta, that defence was its only chance to avoid a successful prosecution by Martha Kostuch.

The Alberta government had a big problem, bigger even than Martha knew. Alberta was never happy with the federal law because it intruded on what it felt was its jurisdiction. As a result, Alberta never applied for authorizations; at the time it was one of only two provinces that refused to seek authorizations. If Alberta was successfully prosecuted for not getting an authorization in this case, dozens of projects could be imperiled. In this case, not only did the Alberta government not apply but also when it later asked the federal government for a retroactive exemption from the law, it had been refused.

When I spoke to Martha, she described the consequences of a successful prosecution for Alberta: "The cost would have been huge. We were up in the millions of dollars of maximum fines, and potential jail sentences. There was also the risk to the dam. Under the *Fisheries Act*, we would have gone for tearing down the dam. We could have stopped it and ordered them to fully reclaim the land— and that is what we would have asked for. The implications were enormous, and they were in a real conflict of interest. After all, they were the dam builders, and they were the people with the power to stop the prosecution."

Martha and Rice gave the legal papers to the justice of the peace, who swore an Information, charging the Alberta government of crimes against nature—destroying fish habitat. Martha later filed many other Informations. For various legal reasons that are unimportant to this story, Martha at times named various government ministers, and also the two construction companies working on the dam with the same charges. Put at its simplest and clearest, Martha was going after the Alberta government. Now, the government would have to come to court and defend itself.

The lawyer with the Government of Alberta who had the unenviable task of dealing with this issue was Bruce Fraser, director of the Special Prosecutions Branch of the Alberta government's Attorney General's office. The Attorney General's office in every government has a unique role. On the one hand, their lawyers are supposed to prosecute cases independent of political power and influence. Usually in Canada, in my opinion, prosecutions are conducted in this fashion. This is a true achievement of our legal system, though of course it is not perfect, and we must always be vigilant. On the other hand, the Attorney General's office is run by the Attorney General, in this case, part of the ruling Conservative Government of Alberta. Needless to say, the tension inherent in enduring a prosecution on an important project must have filtered down to the lawyers within the Attorney General's office. (This is my educated speculation, rather than the product of inside knowledge.)

Martha did not believe that the Alberta government lawyers she dealt with in her struggle behaved improperly; they were simply following orders. Nor do I think they acted improperly, in the sense that they acted according to the law or policy as it existed. One must remember that lawyers do not necessarily agree with the actions of their clients. It is their job to represent them, whether they agree or not, provided they are not being asked to lie or to do dishonourable or improper things. Did Fraser have doubts and anxieties about his role? Was he a "true believer" in this cause? Or was he simply an honest advocate in a tight spot? Fraser was later appointed as judge of the Provincial Court in Alberta. As a result, he is not at liberty to speak about events of that time on the record, and extra care must be taken to bring out the equities that may exist on his side of this story. In December 2011, I tried to speak to Fraser in an off-the-record interview, in order to better understand his point of view. I was unsuccessful.

A few weeks after the charges were laid, Rice got a letter from Fraser. He explained that he was going to "stay"—to stop or kill—Martha's prosecution. He said that before any matter can be prosecuted, an investigation must be done "by the appropriate enforcement agency." Since Martha had done the investigation herself, he would stay the charges immediately. Much later, Judge Fradsham of the Provincial Court of Alberta, reviewing the history of Martha's attempts to prosecute Alberta, explained that Fraser's statement that an "appropriate enforcement agency" must do the investigation was "as erroneous as it is patronizing and paternalistic." Judge Fradsham continued: "At this point, Dr Kostuch, who had followed properly the procedure set forth in the Criminal Code, found herself in a situation where a government functionary had overridden the Code, decided that no complaint was 'formal' unless made to a Government agency, and nothing would proceed without his Department's blessing."

In a later decision, Judge Harvie looked at the same issue from a different angle. It seems that the Alberta government had a "blanket policy" of intervening in private prosecutions and requiring that there be a police investigation first. Judge Harvie stated that he considered this blanket policy "contrary to law." He was also concerned that, in this case, the blanket policy could lead to "a risk of the perception that justice may not appear to be done when the Attorney General of a province undertakes to show that either another minister of the provincial Crown, or the provincial Crown itself has committed an offence." It turns out that the prosecutor, Fraser, was applying government policy that was itself against the Criminal Code, and thus, contrary to law.

It is common for prosecutors to adjourn matters, sometimes for many months, while further investigation is done. Unless the prosecutor says there is not enough evidence to continue the case, there is no reason why a prosecution cannot be delayed while information is gathered. In this case, in conformity to a policy that was contrary to Canadian law, Fraser didn't delay, but rather killed, the prosecution.

Later that September, Fraser asked the Royal Canadian Mounted Police (RCMP) to investigate the matter. Whether he had strategic or moral reasons, this was a sound decision, as the investigation would be separate from the Alberta government. As time passed, Martha returned again and again to the courthouse to file new Informations to "update the crimes" alleged against the Alberta government. Between August 2, 1988, and July 24, 1990, Martha launched seven Informations.

In the meantime, the RCMP thoroughly investigated the matter. In a series of reports, Inspector S.A. Duncan of the Commercial Crime Section of the RCMP concluded that proof that the Alberta government destroyed fish habitat without authorization from Canada "is fairly straightforward and all documents, studies and experts are available to present this evidence without any further police investigation." Inspector Duncan added that whether there is a legal defence for Alberta is "technical" and "will have to involve a legal decision by the courts. From a police review of this matter, the investigative part of this case has been done by the society." Inspector Duncan's opinion is straightforward; there was clearly a solid case against the Government of Alberta, with possible technical defences. The final decision about whether there should be a prosecution was left with the prosecutor. For some reason, however, Duncan's report did not end the matter but instead was only the beginning of a series of reports in which the question of whether or not Alberta had a defence against the charge was explored. This is rather like homicide officers deciding that there is a sound case to prosecute somebody and then deciding to investigate, in great detail, all the possible defences the accused might possibly advance at trial. This is normally the job of the defence lawyer, provided the case has enough evidence to proceed.

Did Alberta have to get authorization from Canada to destroy fish habitat? Could Canada delegate that authority? Inspector Duncan refers to speaking to two senior Alberta civil servants in his report dated January 29, 1990: "We also discussed the blanket agreement between the Federal and Provincial Government involving fisheries and concluded that the legislative responsibility under the Fisheries Act—s. 35—could not be delegated. Each time permission to violate Section 35 is required it should be authorized by the Minister or under regulations made by the Governor in Council under the Fisheries Act."

Based on this, the last element of the charges against Alberta seemed to be present—Canada did not delegate any power to Alberta to destroy fish habitat. And, as a matter of law, such power cannot be delegated. It is unclear, however, if Duncan's "We" means that the two Alberta civil servants knew that Canada's power could not be delegated to Alberta. If so, then it weakened any claim later by Alberta that it "didn't know" what the law really was. What these men knew or did not know would have to be discovered in a trial, if there had been one.

Did Alberta simply refuse to follow a federal law it felt was treading on its power? Did Canada let Alberta get away with it? And then, to spoil this little deal—this "cooperative understanding" to ignore the law, side-step the Constitution, and avoid protecting the environment—along came an angry bee, Martha Kostuch. Did the politicians really not know the law?

———

On the morning of August 9, 1988—a week after Martha met with her lawyer and filed the affidavit in Pincher Creek—she woke up very early. It was going to be a big day; perhaps the beginning of a transformed era. With the help of Martha's organization skills, the Piikani people had planned an act of non-violent civil disobedience for that morning. They were to blockade Highway 3 on their reserve—the main highway passing through the prairies to the Rocky Mountains in that area of Alberta—to protest a relentless history of unfair treatment by the governments of Canada and Alberta, and, in particular, to voice their opposition to the Oldman River Dam being constructed several kilometres upstream from their reserve.

On July 15, 1988, the Piikani had called for an immediate halt to the Oldman River Dam. Nelbert Little Mustache, a band councillor, told the press, "There are people who are ready to lay down their lives for this cause. I don't think the young people are going to sit back and take what we are getting from the Province on the Oldman River." He explained that the Oldman Dam and the forty-two-kilometre reservoir of water upstream from the dam would "flood out sacred burial grounds, ceremony sites, and inscriptions carved in stone. It would destroy a way of life… All they need is the green light and you are going to see a cadre of young people out there," said Little Mustache. A few days later, on July 19, the Oldman River was diverted from its valley by the engineers building the Oldman Dam.

The blockade was scheduled for August 9 at 6:00 a.m. A few days before, Martha had met with the Piikani. She later wrote the following in her journal about her meeting: "Meet with the Piikani. The split in Council is evident. Albert Yellowhorn said: 'We don't need culture, we need money.'"

The night before the blockade, Martha called Andy Russell, a fellow Friends of Oldman River activist. Russell a writer and lover of wild places, wrote a book in defence of the Oldman River called, *The Life of a River.* It is a wonderful book, a delightful description of the river, its history, and Russell's own life. When I read it, it made me feel nostalgic for *his* life. He died not long after I first became interested in this story. Cheryl Bradley told me that there had been heavy rains in the mountains for several days after Russell's death. One of the eulogists at the funeral said that it was as if "the mountains wept" at his death.

The night before the blockade, Russell told Martha, "I figure the police will be waiting for us."

"So what?" Martha said. Moments later, she added, "I have never been more hopeful."

That night, she wrote in her journal:

I feel that major new steps for Alberta will be taken for this coming week and months and will probably change the direction of the environmental movement in Alberta. I don't know what effect it will have on me and my future, but I look forward to it almost eagerly but not totally without reservation since I have always tried to be a law-abiding citizen and work within the system to change it. It gives me courage and hope to know that there are so many deeply committed people willing to sacrifice so much to save the three rivers, although it makes me feel a little guilty that I am not prepared to do more.

The next morning Martha left her house in central Alberta, where the trees and grass were green and water is plentiful, and drove south, to where the land is brown and yellow and only the river valleys are green.

To plan this blockade, environmentalists worked together with the Piikani. Each had a role in the overall strategy. The Piikani Youth were to stop the cars from travelling down the highway. Prior to that day, Martha had brought some experts to the reserve to train both the Friends of Oldman River and the Piikani in non-violent civil disobedience. Martha explained to me that in non-violent protest one must both have protesters (Native people in this case) and observers (the environmentalists), who report what happens and later are witnesses. She added, "To be effective, your protest really has to be non-violent; violence weakens you. In non-violence training people learn how to organize the event: Who will bring food? Who will call the media? Who will act as witnesses? People also learn how not to react if taunted."

Martha repeatedly emphasized to me that "civil disobedience is a powerful tool, provided it remains non-violent ....here are times when civil disobedience is the only way to challenge a bad law, particularly when there are no other mechanisms to challenge the law, such as during apartheid in South Africa, or when women could not vote here in North America." Martha said, "There are other times when the law is not necessarily bad, but you believe in your own principle. You are willing to break the law, using non-violence, and suffer the consequences. In the case of the Oldman Dam, you had the lawmakers breaking the law, and we had First Nations people and the environment suffering the consequences."

Martha had called the media in preparation for that morning. When she arrived at the site, the media was there, but hardly anyone else. No police officers were there. At first, Martha only saw her friend Buff Perry. (Perry later began a hunger strike to try to stop the dam. However, if the law couldn't stop the Oldman Dam, a hunger strike did not have much chance). Later that morning, others arrived, including Andy Russell and archaeologist Brian Reeves. Martha and the others, along with an increasingly impatient press, waited quietly for the Piikani to arrive. The silence was broken by occasional cars whizzing by on the highway. No one arrived. The waiting continued.

A photo in Jack Glenn's book from those moments shows Russell and Reeves staring over the land, facing different directions, as if the force of their strong wills alone could summon up the Piikani from past to present greatness; or, at the very least, summon them to the blockade. Russell is wearing a black hat, his jaw of granite set in a look of anxiety. Beside him, Reeves has his arms folded, left hand digging into his bare right upper arm. Behind them are dirt, gravel, low shrubs, and hard brown land under a milky sky, with no water in view.

At last a young Piikani man became visible on the horizon, running. He arrived with a message from the Piikani Youth. He told Martha that the blockade had been called off at the last moment. Martha told me that she had been told by a member of the Piikani that during the night, ceremonialist Joe Crowshoe had a dream that the Oldman Dam would be finished and that at some point in the future it would be destroyed. Joe understood that dream to mean that the dam had to be finished and that it would fail. So that was how it had to be. The Piikani could no longer do the demonstration, because, spiritually, the dam was meant to be.

Martha's journals do not reveal who told her about the dream. Was it Joe Crowshoe? Later in her journals, she wrote that she spoke to Joe. However, there was no mention of his telling her why the blockade was called off. What is confusing is that Joe's dream, while apparently enough to stop the blockade, did not stop him later from taking further steps against the dam. There is also the possibility that something was lost in translation between Joe and whoever spoke to Martha that morning. When I later asked Joe's daughter, Evelyn Kelman, about such a dream, she said that her father never told her about any dream like that. But, in 1991, Milton Born With A Tooth told the magazine *Nativebeat* about a prophecy that "came a long time ago. It talks of two dams, the first one built in 1922, the second they're building now. Prophecy says the second dam is going to break, but it does not say how it is going to break, but it's going to be culture that will break it."

Though the blockade brigade did not show up, other Piikani did: the drummers who were to accompany the blockade. Martha asked them to drum for the media. One of her friends told Martha, "The media are going to crucify us."

Martha was terribly disappointed. She later wrote in her journal, "We did our best to mitigate the damage" with the press. Martha and the others went over to a nearby restaurant to discuss what had happened and figure out what could happen next. They decided that the next steps had to be organized by the Piikani themselves. Buff Perry tried to convince Martha to go and see Joe Crowshoe, but she was so upset she didn't want to see anyone. She later wrote in her journal that she "just wanted to cry."

The day after the failed blockade an article in the *Lethbridge Herald* commented on the event. In "A Dam Blockade that Fizzled," reporter Al Beeber wrote that the role of the media is sometimes "exploited" by groups wanting media attention. He characterized the blockade as a "non-event," cancelled at the last moment by Joe Crowshoe for reasons which remain "vague." After being told about the cancellation of the protest, "with the media gathered around this group of seven protesters which resembled an early-morning picnic of grey-haired flower children, FOR [Friends of the Oldman River] took the opportunity to reiterate its opposition to the dam and the irreparable damage it will create." The article dismissed them as a "bunch of hippies."

Martha was disheartened. However, Martha, being Martha, would not give in to fate. She would try to overthrow it. A little less than two years later, she would meet a Piikani man named Milton Born With A Tooth—someone who was also prepared to challenge the inevitable.

———

The RCMP investigation was being conducted in secret, but few government secrets managed to remain hidden from Martha Kostuch. She had learned that the initial investigation had been

96

completed and a report forwarded to the federal Department of Justice. Martha wrote to the minister herself on October 31, 1989, almost fifteen months after she had laid her charges against Alberta, and explained that the "RCMP investigation was completed in December 1988. I am very concerned about the length of time it is taking your department to decide whether or not they are going to prosecute this case. Justice is certainly not being done."

On January 8, 1990, the office of the Minister of Justice wrote Martha: "You may appreciate that the decision to prosecute can only be made after a thorough and prudent study of the matter has been conducted and concluded." The letter did not explain why the legal issues seemed to be taking so long to be understood and assessed, particularly since such issues were fairly straightforward and could, if necessary, be answered within a week by any one of an entire team of constitutional and criminal lawyers at the disposal of the Government of Canada. One wonders—why *did* the matter take so long?

By January 11, 1990, Martha's rather limited patience was used up. She went back to court and tried to charge Alberta and the two construction companies with the same crime under the *Fisheries Act*, updating the allegations to include the more recent alleged crimes. Fraser, for the Government of Alberta, opposed the new charges. They argued their case before Provincial Court Judge Harvie, and the arguments continued on February 28, 1990. Canada, though having been "invited" to attend by Martha's lawyer, refused to send a lawyer. During the entire battle, the Government of Canada never showed up in court, though, on occasion, it sent letters. Clearly, the Government of Canada wanted to have nothing to do with prosecuting another level of government. Canada did not oppose the Oldman Dam and was prepared to let Alberta proceed.

Fraser explained that the RCMP investigation was not finished and, in any event, the Crown could not be charged. He explained that it would be "a rather ludicrous situation" to have "Her Majesty the Queen charging her Majesty the Queen." He noted that historically, the Queen cannot be charged. He continued, "And, in fact, the reasoning behind that, as I understand it, is that the King or the Queen, Her Majesty, the sovereign, is incapable of doing wrong." People within government can do wrong and be charged for it, but "the King or the Queen or the sovereign, that body itself, cannot." Martha's lawyer responded that this old doctrine should not apply in our modern age.

Judge Harvie decided that Martha could begin a new prosecution of Alberta. Once the court allowed the prosecution to begin, a further dispute developed, because the Alberta Attorney General's office wanted to take over Martha Kostuch's new prosecution. Martha, on the other hand, was sure the Attorney General's office would simply stay it again. Unless Martha could show that Alberta's purpose was "flagrantly improper," she could not stop Alberta's lawyers from taking over the prosecution. Justice Harvie concluded that since the RCMP were still assessing the matter, there was no proof of flagrant impropriety at this time, so the Alberta Attorney General's office was given control of Martha's new prosecution.

At the end of Judge Harvie's decision, he raised a point that only radicals mention, and even then quietly (at least in Canada). He wondered if the Provincial Court of Alberta was independent enough of the political power of Alberta to even decide the case: "Counsel for Mrs. Kostuch appears to assume that the Provincial Court of Alberta is a statutory tribunal that is sufficiently independent of the executive of Alberta, and in particular, for it, as an institution, to deal with issues relating to the duties and powers of the Attorney General such as arise in this case... [One can make] serious contention to the effect that the Provincial Court of Alberta may *not* be an independent tribunal as required."

Finally, on July 10, 1990, almost two years after Martha had started her prosecution, Kim Campbell, the Minister of the Department of Justice for Canada, issued a press release, noting that Alberta had implemented a program to mitigate the environmental "consequences" of the project, and that the Government of Canada had reviewed the project. She concluded: "I do not believe that any proceedings by way of prosecution would serve the interests of the proper administration of justice." Nowhere in this press release does she suggest that Alberta in fact had the necessary authorization under the *Fisheries Act*.

On July 11, Bruce Fraser wrote to the clerk of the court and announced that Martha's second prosecution had been stayed. Alberta kept building the dam.

Undaunted, Martha commenced her third prosecution on July 24, 1990. She charged Alberta and the construction companies with more alleged crimes in relation to destroying fish habitat, updating the Information to include the new accusations. Not long after, the construction companies brought Martha to court, claiming she was abusing the court's process—in effect, abusing the justice system—with yet another prosecution. They also wanted the court to stop this new prosecution and stop Martha from launching any other prosecutions against the dam. Alberta decided to join this application. The Alberta government, which had the power to stay Martha's charges, was asking a court to do it for them.

Judge Fradsham, in the judgement I referred to above, found in Martha's favour, concluding:

Dr. Kostuch has not attempted to abuse the process of this

court. On the evidence before me she has, through her counsel, attempted to utilize, in the most proper and professional manner, those rights given to her under our legacy of the common law and the provisions of the Criminal Code. On two occasions she has convinced judicial officers that a prosecution has been warranted; on two occasions that prosecution has been thwarted by the Attorney General. In both cases, the reasons behind the actions of the Attorney General, though not on the evidence before me motivated by *mala fides* [bad faith], were faulty. She again seeks the assistance of this court—that is not abuse of process, but a very proper use of the process.

The Alberta government and the construction companies appealed this decision. Their appeal was refused. Justice Miller, of the Court of Queen's Bench, noted: "In most instances, allegations of abuse of process are made against the Crown by the Accused. In the matter before this court, the Crown joined forces with the named accused, all of whom allege abuse by the private prosecutor. This is highly unusual, since the Crown had at its own disposal the right to stay proceedings on its own discretion."

The Alberta government and the construction companies appealed again, to the Court of Appeal. The Court of Appeal refused to overturn the decision, saying, "We do not think that the fact that the Attorney General had on two previous occasions entered stays can be taken as an indication that he will do so in this case. His failure to intervene suggests the contrary." I agree with Jack Glenn, who wondered if the Court of Appeal—the chief guardian of the law in Alberta, outranked only by the Supreme Court of Canada—was giving the Alberta government a clear hint not to abuse its own justice system.

The Alberta government asked George Dangerfield, a senior prosecutor from Manitoba, to look at the case and decide if it should be prosecuted. This was also a sound decision. It could also be considered a tacit acknowledgement that the Alberta Attorney General's office would be in a conflict of interest if it had tried to decide the issue on its own, as it had done the previous two times when it stayed Martha's charges. Dangerfield told the court, "[S]imply because a crime may have been committed is not necessarily a reason to prosecute if it isn't in the public interest to do so."

Next, Dangerfield told the court about several letters Alberta received from Canada suggesting that Alberta would be applying the *Canadian Fisheries Act*. In the very next sentence, Dangerfield explained: "Now, irrespective of whether that delegation of authority was lawful," Alberta "would get" from that correspondence that it could "manage this resource as if it were the federal government." With these words Dangerfield told the court, indirectly but clearly, that according to the Constitution and law, Canada could not delegate such power. One Alberta civil servant tried again to clarify the law. The Government of Canada did not respond to his letter. Dangerfield looked at other letters from Canada, in which it is clear that Canada does not object to the dam. Then, he states the law: "If you build a dam in the middle of the river and you haven't got the proper authority to do so, you are guilty, so the section reads." He continues that the only defence is due diligence. Again, did the accused try their best to ascertain the law?

In conclusion, Dangerfield said: "[I]t is clear that the province exercised due diligence in attempting to decide whether it could go ahead with this plan." They had "acted in good faith." Alberta built a dam not following the law but thinking it had followed the law because of certain letters it received. Finally, Dangerfield said that prosecutions must have "some likelihood" or a "real possibility" of

JUNE 11, 1989

THIS OLD MAN
"A Celebration of Its Life, Its Land, and Its People"

Join us for this historic Wilderness Concert
as

IAN TYSON
presents
CHINOOK ARCH RIDERS & "FRIENDS"

GORDON LIGHTFOOT
MURRAY McLAUCHLAN
MARK KOENIG

With Special Guests

DAVID SUZUKI
ANDY RUSSELL
PEIGAN TRIBAL ELDER JOE CROWSHOE

In Support of "Friends of the Oldman River"

Site opens 11:00 AM   Concert 2-5 PM   Free Admission

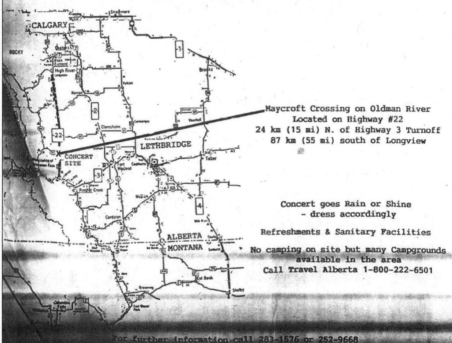

Maycroft Crossing on Oldman River
Located on Highway #22
24 km (15 mi) N. of Highway 3 Turnoff
87 km (55 mi) south of Longview

Concert goes Rain or Shine
- dress accordingly

Refreshments & Sanitary Facilities

No camping on site but many Campgrounds
available in the area
Call Travel Alberta 1-800-222-6501

For further information call 283-1576 or 252-9668

MANAGED BY EVENTS UNLIMITED

conviction, but "in this particular case I say there is none.' And so Martha's third prosecution was dead.

There is a doctrine in criminal law called willful blindness. It is often used to convict drug traffickers but rarely governments. When a person ignores suspicious circumstances because they do not want to discover the truth, they are practicing willful blindness. Such a person is as guilty of a crime as the person who intentionally commits it. Had this case come to trial, a vigorous defence counsel would have been curious about how Dangerfield could so easily and clearly discover that the Alberta government did not have the right to build the dam without federal consent, yet Alberta, with many constitutional and criminal lawyers, could not do so. Such an enterprising defence lawyer would also, no doubt, ferret out Alberta employees who might shed further light on the issue. None of this happened, because there wasn't a trial. The enduring legacy of Martha's attempts to prosecute Alberta is not so much whether the prosecution could have succeeded, but how the rule of law fared during the battle.

Despite these defeats, Martha Kostuch was just getting started. So was Bruce Fraser, who in 1991 would speak eloquently about the rule of law while prosecuting Milton Born With Λ Tooth in the deep south of Alberta.

Maycroft:
The Happening

On a gloriously bright July morning in 2006, I drove west on Highway 3, toward the Rockies. I was going to a tiny recreation area called Maycroft, beside the Oldman River, in the beginning of the high country. I drove to Maycroft with something in mind. On June 11, 1989, others had converged on this same spot—environmentalists, Piikani spokespersons, musicians, ranchers, and other concerned Albertans—to try to stop the Oldman Dam; it is a day that shines in the memory of people like Cliff Wallis, Dianne Pachal, Cheryl Bradley, and Lorne Fitch. At Highway 22, I turned north. East of me was green grass and cultivated land. To the west, near the road, was cultivated land, and above it, brown pastureland with patches of trees. Here and there were hay bales. Farther to the west, in the foothills, the land began to roll like a choppy sea, mostly without trees, up and up, in ever-lengthening yellow and brown waves. Jutting behind these brown hills were the peaks of the front ranges of the Rocky Mountains, lit grey and blue in the morning light, clear as a knife against the blue sky. To the south, a line of peaks swept across the horizon southward to Montana.

After a while, I noticed a dirt road heading into the mountains. Nestled between the dirt road and Highway 22, beside the Oldman River, was the recreation area at Maycroft. There was space for only a few tents. I stopped and got out of the car. Two tents were there, but nobody was around. I walked over to a picnic table a few feet from the river and sat down. A cool wind blew from the northeast. The silence was beautiful. I closed my eyes and tried to feel what it was like there on the day they thought they would stop the dam.

I opened my eyes, calmed by the eloquent silence given substance by the sound of the river and the gusts of wind in the grass. I looked around, ready to see whatever my eyes landed on. A lone tree stood on the south ridge of the river, set against the sky. On the south side of the river there was a slab of concrete. I couldn't figure out what it was until my eyes trailed northward and I saw another slab on the north side, as well as a bent and rusting guard-rail. There had been another bridge here, but no more; its existence was but an instant in geological time.

It was now 8:00 a.m. A sharply incised cliff was on the north side of the river. Rocks beside the river had gold and yellow moss growing on them. In the river were brown rocks shining white in the bright sunlight. Water flowing over the rocks made a kind of perma-nent whitewater—stationary yet always moving—in the perpetual unfolding of things. The sun was warm on my face. Occasionally, a car passed behind me, after which the air rang with the long, steadily receding whine of the car engine and sound of tires on asphalt.

I took a last look at the rooted tents then got back into my car to head west, to see the site from higher up the gravel road into the mountains. A peeling sign to my right read: "Caution: Logging Trucks Next 15 Kilometres." Wire fences lined both sides of the road. I stopped the car, got out, and looked back at Maycroft and the river. It was the river as it was back in 1989, yet it was not. A white moon sank in the pure blue sky. I looked longingly north; the dirt road curled toward a place of spectacular beauty and power, known as the Gap. I had been there once, in August of 2005. It was a place where there were no fences, for now. But there were logging trucks. When I talked about the logging trucks I had seen up by Maycroft, one old farmer told me, "Without those logging trucks you wouldn't have any houses." I looked back south one last time and saw the few tents that were Maycroft.

On June 11, 1989, it was not so quiet at Maycroft. The tiny campground beside the river was busy with musicians getting ready to perform and speakers ready to tell their stories. Up above the campground, on the plateau that slopes gently upward forming a natural amphitheatre, a growing crowd was waiting expectantly.

———— ——— ————

On Friday, June 9, 1989, people began to arrive. They had to make camp in the rain. One woman asked the locals, "Is this where the rally's going to be?" Sandra Petrich, spokesperson for two hundred workers at the Oldman River Dam worksite said she "doubt[ed] the men w[ould] attend the concert." She added, "They'd like to go, but they think there might be some trouble and they don't want to be involved—they might lose their jobs." A journalist asked local rancher Buster Davis what he thought when he was "busy driving cattle to summer pasture." Davis said, "We need more dams, not less. It took five dry years to open my eyes— without water, this country is nothing." The co-owner of the Rangeview Confectionary and Gas Bar, located in a nearby town, told journalists, "There wasn't much advertising" for the concert." It is just a "waste of time." He added that "this dam can't be stopped. It's half-finished and a half-finished dam doesn't do anybody any good."

Why were people coming to Maycroft?

Months before, musician Ian Tyson and some of his friends went to see Cliff Wallis and said they would like to support the work being done by the Friends of Oldman River. Tyson was concerned about what was happening to the Oldman River, so he called up his former music partner and wife, Sylvia Tyson, as well as Gordon Lightfoot and others. Soon the event began to take shape. Cliff helped Tyson organize the concert.

Years later, Cliff told me the purpose of the concert: "We were just trying to raise awareness, get a few people out, get the media out, have a good time, break even, not lose too much money, pass the hat around kind of thing." There was a lot of planning: getting the port-a-potties, the musical equipment, the generators. Cliff got there the Saturday night and worked late. He was coordinating everything. "It was peeing down with rain the night before. And we thought, oh, geez, oh, Christ. People who had come over the Porcupine Hills said it was almost impassible, a section of mud. We were thinking, how are people going to get here? We were concerned about this."

Cheryl Bradley and Lorne Fitch arrived on Saturday. They were to help set up the camp on Saturday night and early Sunday morning. Cheryl and Lorne had been assigned the role of back-stage security. On Saturday, they helped to build the stage, which was little more than a flatbed truck.

Dianne Pachal also arrived at Maycroft on Saturday night to help out. Cliff and Martha set the directions for the Friends of Oldman River, but it was Dianne who "kept the boilers running," as she put it, from the organization's headquarters in an old heritage house in Calgary. Dianne made everything happen—from answering calls to publishing a newsletter. She had grown up on a farm. Her family moved to Calgary when she was a child and eased their collective dislike of living in a city by going on long camping trips to southwestern Alberta. During these excursions, she got to know First Nations people.

Dianne's job at Maycroft was to make sure there were

plenty of pamphlets and posters ready for the people who came. The night before the event she camped beside the Oldman River at the Maycroft site. She got up very early Sunday morning to help with set up. That morning she looked around and saw that it wasn't raining at Maycroft, but she heard that it had rained in Calgary. She wondered: how many people are going to come out in this weather? She thought, "Surely we will get two to three hundred; it would be great if we will get five hundred."

Sunday, June 11, was cool and grey, with low heavy clouds just above the juniper pines. The forecast for the day: heavy rain and thundershowers. That morning, cars were parked as far as the eye could see along Highway 22, both east and west of Maycroft Crossing. When I spoke with her, Cheryl remembered seeing the cars that morning and her feeling of awe: "I have never seen anything like it. It hardly had any publicity. It just kept expanding. Cars were parked on a narrow road, for miles. It was a two-mile walk to the site."

Lorne remembered it this way: "On Sunday, we walked to the top of a hilltop, which was south of where the concert was, and as you looked north, here is the big tent that the performers were playing in, and even from that distance it was a sea of people; and Highway 22, as it stretched north, it was a line of parked cars on both sides of the road as far as the eye could see. It was profound."

When I spoke to him, Cliff told me about that morning: "Got up in the morning and the clouds parted. It was cloudy all the way around; it was raining everywhere else, except in our power spot. The sun was coming down, it was calm. It was usually windy as hell down there. Everything was perfect. We couldn't believe it. It was a great day. Then Ian Tyson and Gordon Lightfoot came, and then the people started coming. And we were expecting a few hundred, and they were coming by the thousands—cars lined up for four miles. We had somewhere between eight thousand and fifteen thousand people."

"They came by car, camper, truck, bus, jeep, and even horseback," Cliff remembered. People were excited; as the size of the crowd grew, it seemed that this event had become something more—a happening. It was an expression of something that was building, though precisely what was not exactly clear. People were hungry—and many for more than music.

As the people arrived on Sunday morning, Dianne gave out information. She was busy during the entire concert having people sign petitions, passing out posters. Years later, Dianne told me that she felt more hope that day than she had in a long time. She explained, "That whole area of the Oldman is not just beautiful. It is a spiritually significant area. I am sure that it was not just me, but others knew. That morning when the people kept coming we just knew that something really magical was happening here. And I was just on a high all day, because it was just, 'This is great!' We knew we weren't alone. I told people that there are southern Albertans who are also against this dam, having seen the donations come in. Having all those people there vindicated all the hard struggle people were having to try and stop the dam. So, it was very uplifting; you felt you weren't alone. And you knew you weren't wrong. It was hopeful. It was people-power. We thought we were going to stop it." Her voice quavered as she said these words to me over twenty years after the event, as if she were going to cry.

The magical and nostalgic word "Woodstock" was on the lips of some, even if it was to recognize that this was different than that famous concert. One participant said: "It may not be Woodstock, but we're still stardust and we're still golden. Our fight for the garden must continue." Journalist Wendy Dudley, who filed a number of articles from Maycroft for the *Calgary Herald*, noted, "While some fans said they felt like they were heading for Woodstock—and then taken a wrong turn, most were pleased with the event's serious tone."

Though the clouds looked bleak, the journalists were plentiful. "Reg Crowshoe, son of Piikani leader Joe Crowshoe, talked about the prospect of traditional Indian land going under water: 'This river was the life source of our people... It's like putting your church under water and then putting on your diving gear and going down to pray.'" "Ben Gross, a Pincher Creek farmer said he really was here just for the music and he supported the dam. 'Oh, irrigation. For everybody, all of southern Alberta. That's just life. Things like that happen, you know.'"

According to press reports, the environmentalists said that the dam would "drown" three rivers. Cliff was quoted as saying: "There will be severe upstream and downstream effects, particularly below the dam, for 100–150 km, which would result in the loss of an entire ecosystem." Musician Murray McLauchlan, "agrees that such concerts don't solve environmental problems, but stresses they expose the public to these important and underexposed issues. 'Then it's the people themselves, in the long run, who have to want to do something.'"

The Oldman Dam had a public relations spokesperson. She told that press that she had "'some concern' the show will fortify the anti-dam movement and give the project a poor public image. 'I am sure it will have some effect on us, but we'll keep putting out facts on the dam and hope people will listen to those facts.'" An Alberta government communications director, Jan Berkowski, told the press that the Oldman Dam will "enhance the environment in the area."

The program began. Tipis had been set up in the valley. Piikani "drumming and dancing took place all day." Piikani traditionalist Joe Crowshoe went up on the "small canopied stage on the back of a flatbed truck." In front of him thousands of spectators clapped enthusiastically. Many wore "No Dam Way" T-shirts and caps. Joe Crowshoe told the crowd, "Politicians have already taken away our land, now they want to take our holy river." Next, something happened that would look contrived had it happened in a Hollywood movie. As Joe Crowshoe spoke, the clouds opened, and sun fell on the stage and the crowd. Not only that, an eagle swooped down then flew away. Martha's critics might have secretly wondered if she let a caged eagle go at just the right time for the crowd; but even they did not think Martha controlled the weather.

Much later, during one of our interviews, Martha remembered the moment, trying to speak through her laughter, "It was fairly cloudy—the clouds parted, and an eagle circled overhead… we did not plan this—it really did happen like this… you couldn't plan something like that." As the eagle circled up and vanished, Joe Crowshoe continued, blessing the four winds and the event that the spectators were to see.

Folk singer Ian Tyson sang many songs that afternoon, some with his ex-wife Sylvia. The crowd cheered. The atmosphere was festive, hopeful. Nearby, "Frisbees flew with kites, and dogs played catch." Many of Ian Tyson's songs are about the "foothills ranch country." In one of his songs "he reached a line about people who do not understand its magic—'They never seen the northern lights, they never seen the hawk on the wing; they never seen spring on the great divide, they never heard ol' camp cookie sing.'" Murray McLauchlan sang, as well, including "The Farmers Song," which he dedicated to farmers. The crowd clapped. All afternoon volunteers in the crowd collected money for the cause in hats, garbage bags, and cardboard boxes.

Andy Russell also spoke to the crowd. Anyone who has read Russell's book on the Oldman River can feel the power of his experiences in the foothills and of the river. Andy spoke of the "timelessness" of the area and its importance to Native spirituality. Then he continued, "Our heritage is here in this valley being buried under concrete. It is an absolutely essential winter range for deer and home to cottonwood groves." He spoke next about "sustainable development" and "man's capacity for self-correction." Then he spoke about human beings in general and what the battle for the Oldman River might mean: "Some of us have revolted against the killer beast that man has become. A step forward to save the Oldman is a step forward to save the world itself. I join my long-time friend Joe Crowshoe in praying this will not happen."

David Suzuki took the stage, too. "While fans clapped enthusiastically for" the musicians, "it was Suzuki's emotion-packed speech that brought them to their feet." The crowd stood, clapped, and cheered. David Suzuki's public profile, and his words, brought hope that the course of history might actually be changed, not by romanticism but by a new longer-range realism, by an accurate counting up of costs, present and future. Suzuki said he had travelled the world and spoken to scientists and indigenous people all over. He continued, speaking amid the cheers: "And what I have heard is that this planet is sick, and it's in trouble. This planet is sick. This planet is in trouble. This planet is dying."

He spoke about canaries in mines from long ago used to detect toxic gases. "When the canaries died they knew they were breathing the same air so they got their asses out of there. We can't get our asses off this planet, and all around us the canaries are dying. Our canaries nowadays are beluga whales and Quebec's deciduous forests. Our canaries are the plant and animal species that are continually becoming extinct at an alarming rate. We cannot go on if we care about what's going to happen to our children. We are driven by something called economics. By jobs and profits... Hang in there; we've got to keep this fight up."

112

That afternoon, music legend Gordon Lightfoot arrived, opened his suitcase, and took out a toothbrush. He looked around then took out a can of Sprite, opened it, and prepared to brush his teeth with the pop. Cheryl, as security for the area, saw this. Almost involuntarily, she blurted out, "You can't do that."

"Oh yes, I can, Ma'am," he said.

Near the end of the afternoon, Lightfoot appeared onstage. He looked "weathered, but relaxed." He "gave his all," according to Sherri Horvat, of the *Lethbridge Herald*. Immediately after his performance, he left the concert site in a white Cadillac.

The organizers asked people to clean up after themselves. Take-down was easy, and the land was spotless after the concert. The only thing Cliff and the others found later were quarters and nickels left on ground, coins that had fallen out of the hats when they were passed around.

By the end of the day the organization had bags and bags of money. Cliff had a little Suzuki 4x4, and it was stuffed with green garbage bags full of quarters, ones, fives, twenties. He was not sure how much money he had at first, but he remembers thinking he should have had a Loomis armoured car there.

Cliff drove through the night, arriving home at 6:00 a.m. He woke his wife and together they dumped the garbage bags of money out onto the kitchen floor. He later explained to me, "There were piles of cash. Talk about surreal. We spent the morning counting: $23,000. We really were not trying to make money out of this." Cliff had no idea the Friends had such support.

I later asked Martha why she thought Maycroft was so important. She replied, "There was little public interest until that time, little public awareness. There was a lot of media attention to the rally itself. Public opinion really started to change at that point. And not just with the Oldman, but with environmental issues more broadly. It was a really important turning point."

Because of Maycroft, the national media had at last become interested in the dam story. Stephen Duncan, a writer for the *Financial Post*, wrote: "Many Albertans consider the southwestern foothills, with the snow-capped Rockies as a backdrop, the most beautiful part of the province. Here, flooding a valley is like clear-cutting British Columbia's mountain ranges." He suggested that when you are "burying a historic river valley under 45 feet of water," aesthetics is part of the discussion. He also queried the economics of the dam: "Nor does there seem a strong economic case for the Oldman Dam; or, if one exists, the Alberta government has yet to make it. It is estimated that about 300 farmers would benefit from the additional irrigation that the project would bring. With the project's price tag of $350 million, cost recovery would seem a long way into the future." Duncan noted that the provincial budget released just before the concert projected a $1.49 billion deficit.

Like it or not, Maycroft had changed things.

Alberta:
Defying the Law

In July 1989, Martha Kostuch was back in federal court. Martha's lawyers argued that Canada had to do an environmental assessment of the Oldman Dam because various government departments—including Fisheries and Oceans—had responsibilities under the Constitution in relation to the dam. Martha's lawyers claimed that the Department of Fisheries and Oceans was responsible because the dam would destroy fish habitat. In a meeting with the Friends, Alberta Minister of the Environment Ralph Klein explained, "If there were any deficiencies in the way the environmental concerns were addressed, I have faith in the courts."

During the court hearing, lawyers for the Canadian government explained that Canada did not have to do an environmental assessment because Alberta had not asked the Minister of Fisheries and Oceans to issue an authorization for the destruction of fish habitat. The Alberta government intervened in the case and agreed with Canada that no assessment was triggered. Alberta explained that "the fish habitat issue could be dealt with by the criminal courts."

Both Canada and Alberta knew that if Alberta had applied for an authorization for the destruction of fish habitat, it might have forced Canada to do an environmental assessment, something both governments were desperately seeking to avoid. It took Jack

Glenn many chapters to set out the ways in which the Government of Canada defaulted on its obligations to Native people and the environment in order to allow Alberta to gets its dam. Jack sagely remarked that governments study public opinion polls, which show that we as citizens hold protecting the environment at a much lower priority than we say we do.

Why did Martha's prosecution file languish for years in Canada's bureaucracy? Why was it languishing as the environmental case was being argued? And why did Alberta do what it could to stop the prosecutions? Was this some grand plan to ensure that the Oldman Dam was not stopped? Or, were the representatives of the Canadian and Alberta governments merely inept?

Martha and Friends of Oldman River lost their case, so they appealed to the Federal Court of Appeal. In the spring of 1990, Martha and the Friends won a great victory: the Federal Court of Appeal cancelled Alberta's license to build the Oldman Dam until the Canadian government did a full environmental assessment of the project.

Newspapers called on the government to halt construction of the dam. "Stop Dam Work Now" was the headline of the *Calgary Herald's* lead editorial on March 14. The March 27 edition of the *Lethbridge Herald* carried an editorial written by Joanne Helmer under the headline, "Respect the Law." The article noted that by continuing construction of the dam without a permit, the Alberta government was "ignoring Federal law." The article's conclusion suggests that "water management projects should be and they must be built within the law. Surely that is not too much to ask."

The court ruling provoked a crisis. There was an emergency session of the Alberta Legislature on March 14, 1990. After the day's prayer to God, the Leader of the Opposition, Ray Martin, rose to ask Jim Horseman—an MLA from southern Alberta, the deputy premier of Alberta, and a lawyer—about the court decision of the day before. "We see from comments yesterday that they're arrogantly going to defy the law, and yesterday the Minister of Public Works tried to convince us that he didn't have to stop construction of the Oldman River Dam despite the Federal Court of Appeal's decision to quash the approval allowing construction in the first place. Doesn't this government realize that this government no longer has a permit for the construction of the Oldman River Dam?"

Horseman explained that the Government of Alberta intended to appeal the decision and that it was "committed to ensuring that the water needs of southern Alberta are met." He repeated that the government was "intensely interested" in ensuring that there was "an adequate water supply" for southern Alberta. "That's what we're doing, that's what we are all about." Horseman did not directly answer the assertion that he and the province of Alberta were defying the law.

Martin stood up, turned to Horseman, and asked a second question: "My question, then, is to the Deputy Premier, who is a lawyer. It says clearly in there that there is not a permit for construction. How does he continue to justify construction when to do so shows contempt for the Federal Court of Canada's ruling?"

Horseman spoke for some time about the importance of water to southern Alberta, and that it was the Government of Alberta's view that the court had been "in error." Again, Horseman did not answer the assertion that his government was defying the law.

"The Deputy Premier knows more than the Federal Court of Appeal, he said it so today. When the same thing happened in Saskatchewan, the Conservative government in that province halted the dam. They understood the law. The Deputy Premier at that time said in the Legislature, and I quote: 'This government believes in this project... but this government also believes in obeying the law.'

Why doesn't this government believe in obeying the law?"

Horseman stood and spoke about the importance of water in southern Alberta. He did not answer the question. Nor did he mention the importance of the rule of law.

In an editorial titled "Dam Not Vital to Survival" on March 16, 1990, in the *Lethbridge Herald*, Joanne Helmer responds to Horseman's remarks, which had been widely reported in the media. Joanne suggested that Horseman's comments about the Oldman Dam's being "vital to the economic survival of the whole of southern Alberta" were "nothing more than the attempt to create hysteria among southern Albertans so they will support the provincial government's decision to continue construction of the dam in the face of a federal appeal court decision to quash the earlier federal approval of the project."

———————

A week after Alberta's license to build the dam was cancelled by the courts, construction at the dam site was proceeding normally. Journalist Mike Lamb flew over the dam site. From behind the Plexiglas windows of the plane, he saw "frantic" construction continuing. Gravel trucks traversed the site throwing "thick dust into an unusually calm southern Alberta sky. Bulldozers dig into mounds of stockpiled earth resembling mini-pyramids." He continued, "One of the province's own studies calls this area 'an oasis on the prairie,' a unique landform that the region's wildlife depend on." He noted a "timbered sheltered haven that will soon become a reservoir." He concluded: "Great horned owls, falcons, hawks and Canada geese are returning, looking for their traditional nesting areas. But their homes are gone, turned into carved hillsides and stumps."

On March 20, 1990, the *Lethbridge Herald* headline was

"Dam Shutdown Inevitable." The article quoted an MLA from the area who said "the dam was likely to be mothballed by the end of the month." He was worried about "leaving the half-built structure exposed to the wind, rain and spring snowmelt that threatens to be bigger than usual."

Alberta said it wasn't safe to stop building a half-finished dam. Jack Glenn later suggested that since the Alberta government created the danger, it was their responsibility to fix it and conform to the law.

Martha tried to get a court to order the Alberta government to stop building the illegal dam, but the judge refused. He said that the Canadian government had to decide if it would order the dam stopped. The Government of Canada decided on May 22, 1990, not to order the cessation of building due to the perceived risk of stopping when the dam was half-finished. At the court hearing brought by Martha, and in the media, Alberta government representatives suggested that the spring runoff might endanger the dam, given that it was not at its full height. As a matter of scientific proof, it was never clear how much risk leaving the dam uncompleted would pose, but these arguments allowed the Canadian government to resist stopping the dam construction. It looked again as if nothing could stop the Alberta government's Oldman Dam.

The Warrior: Milton Born With A Tooth

In April of 1990, Elijah Harper of the Cree people, and an MLA in Manitoba, "eagle feather in hand," refused to agree with the attempt to change Canada's Constitution known as the Meech Lake Accord. Shortly after, Harper explained to CBC's *As it Happens* why he was opposed: "We as Aboriginal people have not been dealt with fairly. We have always been dealt with as second-class citizens. We would like to see recognition as a part of this country, as a founder of this country. We are not even recognized as founders of this country. Only the French and English are recognized. And yet, when we welcomed people, on the St. Lawrence River, and the West, through Hudson Bay, we have welcomed all people. But we have yet to be recognized for the positive developments that we have made in this country. And yet, we have made the greatest sacrifices all across this country—such as giving land and resources…"

In the spring of that same year, in a little town northwest of Montreal called Oka, town officials approved a piece of land called Pines to be developed into a golf course. Mohawks, however, claimed Pines as tribal land. In the spring of 1990, in response to the golf course development, a group of Mohawk people occupied the land and barred everyone from entry except for other Native people. The Mohawks ignored a court injunction to leave. In July the

120

occupation evolved into an armed standoff between the Mohawks and Quebec police. When police tried to remove roadblocks on July 11, the resulting skirmish ended with the death of a police officer. The Mohawks remained at their barricades. Quebec Premier Robert Bourassa appealed for help from the Canadian Armed Forces on August 8, leading to the end of what was called the Oka Crisis in late September.

First Nations people protested across Canada during the summer of 1990, spurred on by frustration with the Meech Lake Accord and support for the Mohawk cause. These protests, however, did not directly cause Milton Born With A Tooth to enact his own protest in southern Alberta— Milton was, for better or worse, an original.

By the summer of 1990, archaeologists hired by the Alberta government were getting ready to finish the job of scouring the Oldman River valley upstream from the dam site for Native artefacts. During the process of their commission to catalogue the history of the Piikani people and their ancestors in the part of the Oldman valley to be flooded by the dam, no one consulted the Piikani First Nation.

The *Lethbridge Herald* documented what was happening with the items being found and catalogued when they caught up with senior archaeologist Barry Dau, who worked with Ethos Consultants. Archaeologists had already found 175,000 pieces of Native past and taken them away. The archaeologists found some "rare and significant pieces," they said. Archaeologist Barry Dau said, "This is the most interesting site I have worked on in 20 years." He found the bison bones used for straightening arrows "intriguing." They found pieces of Native pottery covered in silt in the river valley. They were able to put a pot together, which archaeologists had never before been able to do in southern Alberta. They also found "pieces of bone in incredibly good shape" that "yielded clues to a period about 250 years ago." When asked if he didn't feel emotional about knowing the site may soon be underwater, Dau said with a laugh, "Archaeologists don't get that way. We do the best we can... We probably have enough to discover what went on there." Hundreds of boxes of artefacts were taken from the area to Medicine Hat, where they were stored for a time before they were moved to Edmonton.

Later, another archaeologist, Brian Reeves, wrote, "The cultural and ecological genocide of both the past and present of Napi's river will be complete. The world will be poorer for it." The flooding and the dam project in general were branded an "outrage against the law" by Nelbert Little Mustache. He said the flooding was like obliterating the bread and wine of the Christian Eucharist.

——— • ———

As the archaeologists were preparing to finish the job in the spring of 1990, Cliff Wallis received an unexpected offer. He called Dianne Pachal at the Friends of Oldman River headquarters in Calgary and told her, "There is this Piikani guy who wants to work on stopping the dam and wants some office space. Can you find some space for him?"

"Sure, I will make some space for him, we've got a big building," Dianne said.

The person who arrived was Milton Born With A Tooth, recently returned from the United States. Dianne later talked about the day she first met Milton: "You just knew from the day he walked in that he was on a mission. That he was very passionate, that he wanted to stop the dam." Dianne explained, "He had that presence, he saw himself as having a job to do, and that he was going to do it. I wanted to give him space and get out of the way."

Dianne and Milton spoke about the dam all the time. They came from very different cultures and perspectives, yet they had the same goal. They also shared an interest in ecology, an area of study in which traditional Native knowledge and modern science meet. Dianne explained, "The closest non-Native science gets to Black-foot science is how the world and earth works—ecology—and their belief that everything is animate and is a being and it all has a place and function and role. [Milton] had been out of country, and had returned, and was going to stop the dam. He was in the Lonefighter Society, and they were going to take the lead to stop the dam."

Cliff met Milton many times to discuss their opposition to the dam. Occasionally, Milton would call Cliff in the evening and ask to meet him at a coffee shop or pizza joint. Milton would sometimes arrive for these meetings in a stretch limousine. His driver was a South Asian man named PK. Cliff would ask Milton if he needed money for the limo, and Milton always said, "No." Cliff later said, "When Milton needed money, I would know about it."

———— •• ————

For many years, Milton's family lived just metres from the Oldman River. His sister Lorna said the sound of the river was the first thing she heard in the morning and the last thing she heard at night. They grew up beside the river and played on its banks. Even small children would go alone to the river. They got firewood and game from the river valley. They would go fishing, berry picking. They would get willow sticks for ceremonies and sweat rocks from the river. Even as small kids they had many duties. The river provided an escape from the poverty of life.

Years later, when Milton spoke about his relationship with the Oldman River, he always talked about his first day of school with white children. It ended at recess, when "the white children laughed at his name." So, Milton left for home. First he followed a creek, then the Oldman River, for eighteen kilometres, until he got home. "We were shoved into each other's worlds. We were never taught about them and they knew nothing about us." The Royal Canadian Mounted Police forced Milton back to school, but he didn't stay. Milton "preferred the river to books," so he quit school in Grade 8.

Milton's "teenage years were lost in booze... travelling the wino routes." Then an elderly man—fresh from the Sioux battle with police at Wounded Knee, Pine Ridge Reservation in South Dakota 1975—mentored Milton. "I started to see that my lifestyle had been really great before alcohol. I found this understanding, who I really was. It only took one second to quit." He returned home with "vengeance" on his mind. "I wanted to make trouble. I wanted to create chaos among my enemies. I figured they had made my life miserable."

Milton Born With A Tooth grew up on the Piikani Reserve, along with fifteen brothers and sisters. In the late 1960s, laws changed and alcohol was again allowed on the reserve. According to police reports, in the late 1960s a number of Piikani died of starvation, including a child. The police were sufficiently concerned to mount a house-to-house check. During this check, they found that "most households had virtually no food—no game or other meat and often only flour or tea." One of Milton's fellow Lonefighters later told me that she remembered her family bringing food over to Milton's house, as they had none.

Milton's childhood friend, Leonard Hungry Wolf told me in flinty sentences what he remembered of their childhood. Years after I first spoke to Leonard, he and Milton had a falling out; he no longer wanted his name in this book, so I call him Leonard. He explained that the main village, Brocket, became a slum after the ban on alcohol on the reserve was lifted. I have tried to find out exactly when the ban was put in place, and when it was lifted, and I have received different answers. What is clear is that the ban was lifted when Milton was a child. This event shattered Milton's home, and the homes of everyone he knew. A generation of children had to learn to survive the destructive power of alcohol. When these children were very young, people got along; they helped out; they shared. When alcohol was allowed back on the reserve, life as the children knew it collapsed. At a young age they experienced many things. The old traditions, such as ceremonies, were dwarfed by destructive actions that were not spoken about—alcohol abuse, glue and gas sniffing.

As small children, the young Piikani stood in long winding lineups with their mothers to pick up their treaty cheques. Based on their treaty with Canada, in 1877 each person got five dollars a year. They would be there for hours, all these children with their mothers.

"Where are all the dads?" many wondered. Leonard told me that the kids knew the answer: "They are six feet under."

At ages nine or ten the kids began drinking booze. Later, many died of cirrhosis of the liver; they were killed while drunk in cars, or while walking on the railroad lines or roads. Others hanged or shot themselves, or cut their wrists—they all died cruel deaths. Milton Born With A Tooth's dad died in a car wreck—while drunk, people said. Over the next few years, four of Milton's brothers and one sister died—deaths one way or another linked to alcohol. One brother was murdered. Everyone expected to be dead by thirty. Of one hundred men of their generation, all good friends, ten managed to reach the age of forty.

At fifteen or sixteen, the young Piikani made houses from willow branches and cardboard and placed them on the valley floor near the Oldman River, or in nearby towns. They would live in them and buy wine and food in Lethbridge or Fort Macleod. The cops would see them and chase them home because they were underage, but they continued to act out. They also lived off the hostels, hitting up different churches for whatever they needed. Many of them went to school with white children in Pincher Creek. They were called "dumb," "sausage," "prairie nigger." They would fight back. Leonard said that "they knew how to steal the best lunches." After the fighting, they would be punished: strapped or whipped. They were wild. They would go around town, stealing and fighting. They skipped classes. Some of them broke into houses. They thought, "If this is your world, we don't want it."

As they grew up, they learned about their history from their parents and from the stories that were passed down through the Elders. The past was interpreted to keep alive the knowledge of who they were, of what was done, as well as to serve the present. Leonard told me that they learned the Blackfoot words for many things: priest, smallpox, tuberculosis, and sour meat. They learned about their people freezing in their tents and how Great Britain took over the world with the help of the police. They learned about the death of the seemingly endless supply of buffalo—of their defeat, not at the hands of the men from the East, but because of the emptiness of the plains.

———— • ————

"'Destroy the Indian to save the man' was the rallying cry of humanitarians" in the era after the treaties. Many non-Native people at the time felt that "conversion to Christianity, especially the Protestant version… was the indispensable element to being civilized." Not everyone, even then, saw it this way. According to historian Hana Samek, in one magazine, an anonymous writer, calling himself "fair-play," posed this question: "Would it not be pleasanter, even safer, for us to have living in our midst a contented, well-to-do, self-respecting community of Indians, rather than a set of dependent, dissatisfied, half-educated, and half-Anglicized paupers?"

The Canadian government also wanted the Indians (as they were called at the time) self-sufficient as soon as possible to save money. Otherwise, as one highly-placed Canadian civil servant said in another context, "we should be compelled to feed them and get nothing in return." In the years after Treaty 7, alongside assimilation, the other main goal of the Department of Indian Affairs was "encouraging austerity in the Indian service." This brought "great suffering to the plains tribes left unprovided for after the disappearance of the buffalo."

The Canadian government gave control over Indian education, religious "training," and health care to Christian churches, paying the churches for each Indian in their care. Missionaries worked hard to destroy Native customs and ways of life, including "marriage and divorce, clothing and personal adornment, activities of the medicine men, the authority of the Chiefs, the various Indian Dances, and Leisure pastimes such as gambling and horse racing."

Much of this information comes from historian Hana Samek's book, *The Blackfoot Confederacy: A Comparative Study of Canadian and U.S. Indian Policy.* It is required reading for those who want to see a detailed study of these issues. Samek describes the way the churches approached Indian education:

> Each denomination clamoured for the establishment of more industrial schools, clung tenaciously to every existing school and pupil, and lived in fear that a competing institution would enter their "field" if these schools closed. Canadian denominations also transported Indian children long distances to

fill the rosters of their institutions and to receive government grants. With every child representing an investment, there were virtually no critics of this system among denominations… In their haste to claim more schools than their rivals, churches often paid little attention to the conditions of these facilities, which were dismal as a rule.

On the Piikani Reserve, Rev. H.T. Bourne's school was described as "completely unsuitable for its purpose." In 1899 Catholic Bishop Emil Legal tried to get as many pupils and as much money as possible for the Sacred Heart School on the Piikani Reserve. He argued that the school "could accommodate forty or fifty pupils" even though government appropriations only allowed twenty. The government denied this request. It denied a further request in 1909, because, as Samek writes: "As D.C. Scott pointed out, twenty-two of the thirty-nine Catholic pupils at Sacred Heart School had contracted tuberculosis, and seven had died in school. Instead of remedying the situation, Catholic authorities called the medical findings a 'specious pretense' to prevent the admission of more children to Catholic schools."

Many children ran away from the schools. In 1920 the Mounties "chased nine runaways, one of whom had already been returned to school eight times." When one nurse went to the Crowfoot School on the Blackfoot Reserve, "the children told her that they were chained to benches for punishment, and some were whipped by the sisters." The government inquired about this. The principal said "the department merely invited trouble by encouraging the Indians to voice 'pretended grievances.'" The government knew about the poor conditions the students faced and did nothing.

In addition, Canada did not take responsibility for Native health care. This was "not unusual, since churches provided health care" for much of the non-Native society until after the First World

War. Yet, the situation for Natives was much worse than it was for others. In 1904 the government finally tried to deal with the problem of Native health. It created the position of medical inspector. "Dr. Peter H. Bryce occupied this position until 1914, when his irritating and depressing reports of health conditions among Indians led the Government to relieve him of his post."

In 1907 Dr. Bryce inspected Indian schools in the West. He "presented a damning report," detailing the terrible state of health among Natives. He noted that of 1,537 pupils from fifteen schools, one quarter of the pupils had died during or soon after their school period. Sixty-nine percent of pupils at one school died soon after leaving school. He wrote a further report saying that the Native people were not living in "Arcadian simplicity;" rather, they were "dying of Tuberculosis." Later, he revealed the "disinterested attitudes of government officials who pigeonholed his reports and postponed decisions during a time of dire need in Indian health care" in a pamphlet entitled "The Story of a National Crime."

Statistics from that era show "just how perilously close the Blackfoot came to extinction." The Piikani came "the closest to extinction ....round the turn of the century smallpox and 'grippe' claimed a number of young children, and in 1909 the population hovered at 471." In 1909 Indian Agent Yeomans "wrote that the Peigan's health was satisfactory, except that they suffered from Tuberculosis."

In May of 2005, I went to visit, among others, Lorna Born With A Tooth, Milton's sister, in downtown Calgary. When I had been trying to find Milton, without much success, I learned about Lorna. Months before, I had begun my search for Milton, naively calling directory assistance. I learned through experience that Native people often use cell phones, and the phone numbers change frequently. I found a Born With A Tooth with a different first name in Calgary, so I called there. After several rings, a fellow answered the phone. I told him I was searching for Milton. He said, "We don't know those people," and hung up. Next, I called the Piikani First Nation band office on the reserve and asked if anybody knew Milton's phone number. The first woman who answered the phone sounded suspicious; the second spoke very slowly. I tried to imagine what her life was like out there on the plains, the slow rhythm of the days. I tried to imagine how it must be like for her, to hear this guy calling from Toronto, this guy who rushed through his sentences and finished hers.

Finally, another woman said I should call a man who grew up with Milton, someone I refer to as Leonard Hungry Wolf. A week after I called him, he called me back. Early in our first conversation, he asked, "Are you an informant for the government?"

"No," I said. I added that I was writing a book to inform about what had happened with the Lonefighters and the river. After several conversations, he gave me the cell phone number of Lorna Born With a Tooth.

I called Lorna a few times to see if she wanted to speak to me on the record. She later explained that if I was "all right" I might be able to speak to Milton. Just before we were to meet, I called her house. A relative said she had stayed up late speaking with Milton, who, as was his habit, had showed up unexpectedly. They had chatted late into the evening, so she was still sleeping.

"Is Milton there right now?" I asked.

"Yep. He is sleeping."

With some effort I resisted the urge to ask this fellow to wake him up.

I met Lorna at a downtown Starbucks inside a busy shopping mall. Lorna was late, as one of her brothers was ill in hospital, so I sat in the mall, clanging noise and canned music accosting me for two hours. Finally, Lorna arrived. She looked to be in her mid-forties, had big brown eyes and long black hair down to her waist. She wore a long white leather coat. Her voice was gravelly as a result of a bout with throat cancer some time ago. Carefully dressed business people turned to look at her as they walked by. She gave me a firm handshake, a shy smile, and sat with her legs crossed. The skin on her face was more ruby than yellow and had seen a lot of sun, a lot of tough living, and a lot of death. Six of her brothers and sisters had died from alcohol.

We quickly agreed to get out of the shopping mall.

"I know a place," she said.

We left the office towers and walked along a path, over a bridge, into Prince's Island Park. We were surrounded by the green grass and trees. We walked to a secluded section of the park. Through the trees in front of us, we caught glimpses of the fast-flowing Bow River, silver and flashing brightly as it flowed. The smell of the trees was fresh, sweet, and calming. It was quiet. We were alone at last, sitting on a park bench, facing one river to talk about another. We spoke for almost four hours, from the heat of mid-afternoon to the cool of early evening.

I did not record our conversation. I thought it would be the first of many to come. We spoke of many things, about her life and Milton. After three hours of talking, she said to me, "I wanted to make sure you were okay before Milton spoke to you. I was a leader, too, in the Lonefighters. Milton listens to me. I am prepared to do all I can to help you. They took the honour away from my brother. I want to put it back, through a book I want to write, and through your book. Nobody told it who saw it like us, except Joanne Helmer, the journalist. Nobody. I am prepared to let you write about us."

"Thank you," I said.

We agreed that I would call her after I returned to the city from a visit to the Piikani Reserve, a week or so later. When I returned to Calgary, Lorna's cell number was out of service. After several more unsuccessful attempts to contact her, including sending her a stamped self-addressed envelope, I finally had to give up. I never spoke to Lorna again, or to Milton, for that matter.

I heard later that both Lorna and Milton were sick, but whether these rumours were fact or fiction or something in between, I cannot say. We all have the sense—accurate or not—that a face-to-face meeting allows us to get a feel for the essence of a person. I have not met Milton, and so, like everyone else, must try to piece together the man from all the words, the testimony, and his actions. I knew Milton had spoken to the media a lot. More importantly, I knew he had had two trials. I hoped that he had testified on his own behalf. If he did, and I could get the transcripts, I would have his exact words.

Years later, during his second trial, Milton would tell a court why he formed the Lonefighters in the summer of 1990. In a prosecution, the prosecutor puts forward the charges on a piece of paper called an Indictment. In defending himself, Milton Born With A Tooth laid out his own Indictment. He said, "They were disrespecting and desecrating not only the river, but there was also a burial site there." Milton was frustrated, disheartened. "The dam would take the river and choke its life slowly." He did not know much about the "environment"—but he could use that word to describe what was happening, to make people understand. There was going to be an "environmental catastrophe." The crisis brought something to life inside Milton. He knew he had to do something.

He decided he had to act, so he visited an Elder he had always known, Tiny Man Heavy Runner. Milton explained that some of the old people are more than just Elders, "they are people you can go to, and you know that they are going to tell you the right thing about what you feel." The Alberta government didn't want to talk to the Piikani or listen to their true feelings about the river.

Somehow, Heavy Runner knew Milton was coming. Milton offered him tobacco so he would know his was a serious conversation and told Heavy Runner that the Oldman River was in danger.

"What should I do?" Milton asked.

"If you are serious about wanting to do something for the river, you should go and see the caretaker of the river," Heavy Runner told him.

Milton didn't have "the foggiest clue" what he meant, so he asked, "Who is the caretaker?"

"The Beaver," he told Milton.

Milton did not know what to do, but he knew the answer would come. "That was the way these things worked. Sometimes, what medicine people tell you, it means something right there, but sometimes it may take generations before you understand it." He knew the answer would come because of his deep need for an answer.

After seeing Heavy Runner, Milton let things sit. Before the Time of the First Thunder, the answer came. Devalon Small Legs told me, "The Time of First Thunder in the Piikani way is when the medicine pipes come out for the year, and that is in the spring." As he was making an offering to the river and the beaver spirit, Milton realized that the beaver is the only one that has the right to make dams, and that it does it in a way that "does not hurt nothing." As well, it came to him that the beaver's concern is for the future. At that moment, Milton knew that if he was really serious about protecting the river, he would have to become as serious as the beaver was about being a protector of the river.

He went home and let his "thoughts grow." It took a while for his mind to settle on a plan. After that, he "was able to go to the end of a tip of a pen." He wrote five letters: to the Canadian government, the Department of Indian Affairs, the Canadian Minister of the Environment, the Alberta Minister of the Environment, and chief and council of the Piikani First Nation. He charged everyone—even the government of his own reserve—with genocide, under the Geneva Convention, for their direct action or complicity in the damming of the river. He quoted some passages from the convention. Then, he waited. And waited. No answer ever came, from anybody.

So he went back to see Heavy Runner. He spoke to other Elders, as well, including Joe Crowshoe in the spring or early summer of 1990. He spoke to Joe because "Joe is further along on the journey we all share as a people. He knows a lot. He knows about the ceremonies, maybe he might be our library, our Indian library. Joe has served the things that are important. Joe's mother was one of the last medicine women who ran a Sundance. So he got all the right information passed to him."

It was hard for Milton to see Joe Crowshoe. At one point, Milton remembered that Joe looked at him and said, "I'm tired of people coming to me and telling me we are going to do this, we are going to do that. What I want to see is—I want to see you do it. Go do it. Don't tell anybody, just go do it."

After his meeting with Joe, Milton went to see another Elder to get the commitment of the pipe. Milton explained why the pipe was important: "There comes a point in time when you have to make a commitment that is not yourself. It is not a personal thing anymore. For us, if it's going to be done right, if it's going to be a success, or anything else, we remember the pipe. With the pipe, we know our intentions will be respected, wherever we go with it. Without the pipe, it means nothing."

Around this time, the federal court ruling came down. Milton knew that the Alberta government had refused again to follow the law and stop building the dam until the court-ordered environmental assessment of the dam's effect on the river and the Piikani people began. As a result of Alberta's actions, Milton "realized that we had to go to the next level."

He was still hoping that his letters would get answered. "That maybe the laws would come true—that they would follow the law. That maybe we wouldn't have to do our protest. But when that [the federal ruling followed by Alberta's continued work on the dam] happened, we knew that nothing is going to happen no more."

He wanted to make sure the chief and council knew what he was doing, so he talked to Leander Strikes With A Gun, who was on the band council at the time. Milton explained, "I went to see Leander ....et's see—I always base my timing on the moon. It was the in-between from the first thunder to the last moon, and then in between that time. It might have been around May." He asked, "What happened to my letter to council?"

"It went in the garbage," Strikes With A Gun said.

They talked about doing a demonstration. Strikes With A Gun told Milton about an idea that had been around for years; the Piikani called it their "ace-in-the-hole idea." He explained to Milton how they could divert the Oldman River down an old channel and away from the farmers. He showed Milton the place where the old riverbed was. Milton was struck by the power of the idea, and he began to feel more confident about protesting the dam. "It is always kind of like going in the dark a little bit all the time, but the faith is that you know the answer will come to you."

As he walked through the bush with Leander Strikes With A Gun, he thought about the beaver. When Milton was there, by the river, everything made sense. "Not that the beaver told me in his voice, but just by the way I always learned things, what made sense then was that the beaver is only about, you know, one foot high, yet he can divert rivers, with no tools or no nothing." Milton realized: "Wow, it can be done." It was then that Milton decided to go out and get some "capable beavers" to work with him. He needed people with the courage to stand up for what they believed in. He looked first to Devalon Small Legs and Evelyn Kelman. They not only joined Milton's cause but remained loyal to him all the way through the endeavour, even testifying at his final trial, many years later.

The Pipe Carrier: Devalon Small Legs

Devalon Small Legs comes from a family of political leaders and activists. His father, Nelson Small Legs, Sr., had been a respected chief of the Piikani and had defended the rights of the people. Devalon's brother, Nelson Small Legs, Jr., died tragically trying to defend the rights of First Nations people. I knew Devalon had good reason to be wary of white people bearing gifts. The day I spoke to Devalon, he told me he wanted to see my credentials back to 1976. The date seemed arbitrary to me, but I knew it wasn't the time to quibble with dates. "I don't have a lot of trust," he said. He agreed to meet me the next day at his family's house, on the edge of the Oldman River valley, near the Lonefighters' camp of so long ago.

I drove out to Devalon's house late in the afternoon. The steady rain had stopped. The weather was raw and cold and wet, with the temperature in the low teens. It was the kind of day in which you are never quite warm; to be warm would have required a winter coat, and it was June. Another thunderstorm was coming, this time from the east, with heavy dark clouds and signs of rain falling in black sheets.

West of Fort Macleod stood a sign with peeling paint: The Piikani First Nation.

It is easy to miss the Piikani Reserve. It does not appear on most maps of Alberta, even as a blank space or a series of boundary lines. I turned north after passing an electrical transformer station and made my way along a wet rocky road toward the river valley. The land was empty, flat, and fenced, with short yellow grass. It was too dry for trees. Here and there, each far apart from the next, brown houses with peeling paint stood on the lonely prairie. One moment the vast prairie seemed desolate and the next beautiful—the beauty of absence, of wide space.

At the house with the tattered American flag flapping in the wind, I turned east and drove along the edge of the Oldman River valley. Down in the valley, the fences were replaced by cottonwood trees, wild grass, and various kinds of bushes. Behind, beyond the dark trees, silvery and alive—reflecting even the dull light—flowed the river. It began to rain hard; the storm was arriving. I found the brown house on the prairie as Devalon had described it, but I couldn't see the red truck he'd said would be in the driveway.

As I drove up to the house a mean-looking German shepherd lifted his head and wagged his tail. A middle-aged woman answered the door and invited me inside. The house was small and simply furnished. Sitting at the wooden kitchen table was a thin, very old woman, who had big high cheekbones. I later discovered that this was Devalon's mother, Florence. Beside Florence was a walker. (Later she told me she had broken her back many years before and lived in great pain.) I told her that I had a meeting with Devalon at 3:00 p.m.; it was now after that time.

"He isn't here," she said.

"Right," I said then added, "Did he perhaps mention that I was coming?"

"No."

The middle-aged woman, who I found out was Florence's nurse, invited me to stay for juice. I said yes and drank a lot of juice over the next two hours waiting for Devalon to get back from the store. Florence told me that her husband, Nelson Small Legs, Sr., had been chief and that she had two children—Devalon and his brother, Murray—who worked in Germany teaching Native culture. She had a daughter in the States. She told me she had lots of grandkids, but she didn't see them much. I asked if this was hard for her.

"Yes," she said, nodding her head up and down slowly. "I used to work in town as a nurse, now I am here alone all the time."

A few weeks after I met her, Florence died of a heart attack alone in her bedroom. It happened so quickly she did not have the time to press a button she had been given to activate in an emergency

Devalon arrived at 5:00 p.m. He is a big man, close to six feet and big in girth. His face is broad, almost square, or so it seemed to me that day when he arrived with his dark-rimmed glasses on. He wore a big black cowboy hat and a long, heavy, flowing rain jacket. His skin was bronzed by the sun.

He put away his coat and hat with slow measured movements. He told me that he had remembered our meeting, but he just had to get that sledgehammer to fix a fence to keep in his few cows. His mother shuffled off with her walker into another room, and the nurse left, so we were alone. He made tea and put down a plate of biscuits on the kitchen table. He sat down across from me, sipped his tea, then spoke, "Tell me about yourself." So, I did, telling him about my background, going into more detail than normal, so he could know me. Then I told him I thought what the Lonefighters tried to do was important, and a little about the book I hoped to write.

He watched me intently as I spoke. His face was closed, inscrutable, as impassive as a judge's might be during a trial. I told him why I wanted to write the book, hoping and feeling that what I said was the truth; again, I wasn't yet sure what the truth would turn out to be. I hoped it would be what I was saying.

For a long time, Devalon Small Legs had felt immune to death. When he was five years old, he began his life in a residential school called Sacred Heart, run by the Catholic Church. He explained to me that he found it terribly lonesome to be forced away from his parents. He was supposed to get rid of his own language—Blackfoot—and speak English, but he didn't know the English way, and the difference, in English, between "mistake" and "on purpose." If the kids were found speaking Blackfoot, they would be punished. Devalon later explained, "If people around you are hurting you, you crawl around inside and you don't come out. I did a lot of crying at night." He heard a lot of others crying, too. Then, he got "lucky." He fell out of the back of a pickup truck when his dad was driving and was injured. The resulting cut took forty-three stitches to close. His parents were told he was going to die. The lucky part was that he didn't have to go to school for a long time.

When he was a boy, the Oldman River was Devalon's best friend. He swam it, fished it, and played in it. He and his friends and family fished up and down the river—on and off the reserve—and picked berries on its banks. He learned the names of plants in Blackfoot. He explained to me that his great aunt was an herbalist who took care of many people through the medicinal power of plants. She came to Devalon and his friends and she showed them what to pick, paying them in candy. His favourite plant had an orange root and looked like a big leafy sage. His great aunt—or "aunty," as he called her—told him often, "You eat this all the time, you will live a long, long life." Every chance he got he chewed the plant.

Almost half a century later, he remembered chewing the root and told me, "Maybe that is why I am still here." Devalon gave a warm laugh, then added with soft slow words, barely above a whisper, "Everybody else is gone." By 2012 Devalon had one sibling left: his brother, Murray.

Of all the deaths Devalon has faced, one of the hardest to bear was that of his beloved brother, Nelson Small Legs, Jr., who died when he was twenty-three and Devalon was twenty-one. They were very close. As he remembered their brotherhood years later, Devalon held his two hands out in front him, parallel to each other, nearly touching, and said, "Like this, eh?" They grew up together. They were in the same situation and had the same schooling.

In her book, *Wall of Words*, anthropologist Joan Ryan tells the story of the fate of Devalon's brother, Nelson. In 1972 an innovative program, funded on a temporary basis by Indian Affairs, began in Calgary. Many First Nations people were migrating to the cities from the reserves. Through the new program, urban Aboriginals were empowered with the responsibility of helping others in need in the city. Despite promises of steady funding to the program, however no money materialized. In a final desperate attempt to get funding, local urban Aboriginal families, and members of the American Indian Movement (AIM), occupied an Indian Affairs office on payday. They chose that day to give civil servants a sense of what it feels like not to have assured money. One of the young persons involved in this protest was Nelson Small Legs, Jr. The occupation ended quickly, without violence. The program never received funding, and it disbanded.

One high-level civil servant explained to Joan Ryan how the Department of Indian Affairs worked: "It is indicative of the way the bureaucracy works to serve personal ends. You must remember, to finance officers and others at headquarters who have never served at the field level, the Indian people are invisible and not very real, so it is easy for selfish personal reasons to take precedence."

In 1976, after he was expelled from university for what appears to be no good reason, Nelson Small Legs, Jr., went home, put on his traditional ceremonial dress, and shot himself through the heart. He wrote two suicide notes. In his public note, he wrote: "I give up my life in protest to the present conditions concerning Indian people of southern Alberta... for 100 years Indians have suffered. Must they suffer another 100 years? My suicide should open the eyes of non-Indians into how much we've suffered."

In her book about this incident, Ryan wrote: "The very nature of a powerful bureaucracy which is perceived as abusing that power raises serious questions about institutional arrangements in our society... We begin to realize that race relations are not the issue, but that the nature of power, its maintenance, and its abuse, is the most fundamental problem in society."

Ryan also wrote about Nelson Small Legs, Jr.'s funeral: the wailing women, the angry young men with fists raised high, the restraint of Nelson Small Legs, Sr., who stood beside those raised fists, yet resisted the urge to raise his own. And, the young man named Devalon, riding a white horse.

———————

"How do you put everything into a story?" Devalon asked me in 2005. "How do you do that? All these things that have happened— it goes right back to Treaty 7. The swindle started there. All these things that have happened to my people... how do you put all that into a story?"

I said nothing for a few moments. I could think of no answer that equalled his question about stories. Then I spoke, "Perhaps I can

WHO SPEAKS FOR THE RIVER?

speak to the people and tell a story ` in a story."

He paused before sav... angle? Why
are you interested in N...

I told him ... f Native
people, b... ought
wha... ly, I
... g

... ...nter camp."
"... ...eater and raincoat.
It w... , and it was still raining.
The sky was ... ...uck. I wondered out loud why
the Alberta gov... determined to build the dam.

"You've g... ...and your mind. Follow the money. Follow
the money. Think of what this water is worth. Think about water
diversion to the States," he answered.

We drove down into the river valley onto land expropriated
from the reserve land of the Piikani and sold to irrigation farmers
back in 1922. In front of us was the LNID Weir. The weir is a small
dam that funnels up to half the water of the Oldman River out of the
main channel, away from the Piikani, and sends it down a canal,
over many kilometres, to local farmers, to irrigate their lands. There
are dikes built alongside the river near the weir to stop the water
from simply meandering around the canal entrance.

In 1910 a man known as Pop Pearson filed an application
asking the federal government to pump water out of the Oldman
River to irrigate his land. The federal government's Department of
the Interior studied this idea and found it impractical. Their surveyors

studied several locations, including a place in the Rockies known as the Gap. They found the Gap impractical, as well. It turned out that the best spot to take water out of the Oldman River happened to be on the Piikani Reserve. All of the other spots were either not practical from an engineering point of view, or there was not enough water. The economics did not make sense. The spot chosen on the Piikani Reserve was excellent, though. It was practical from an engineering perspective with enough water. Due to the elevation of the land at that location, the water would be moved in part by gravity, making the cost feasible. As a result, that spot on the Piikani Reserve was valuable, indeed, for irrigation.

When the Canadian government discovered that the only feasible place to take water out of the Oldman River was on the Piikani Reserve, it could have asked the Piikani to sell the land, but this would have required a referendum of all the Piikani. Instead, the government expropriated the land from the Piikani and sold it to the LNID. For many years, the LNID took water out of the Oldman River without anyone questioning the legality of their ownership of the land or their right to the water. In 1978 Devalon's father, Chief Nelson Small Legs, led a water blockade to protest against this injustice. To the Piikani, the taking of this land, and the use of the water without their permission, was an open wound. More than ten years after the 1978 blockade, when the Lonefighters were protesting the construction of the Oldman Dam, the protesters created a camp near the disputed land, symbolic of their treatment at the hands of the local settlers, farmers, as well as federal and provincial governments.

In the summer of 1990, Milton Born With A Tooth went to a trailer park in Pincher Creek to see Devalon Small Legs. When he visited

Devalon, Milton knew he was not simply appealing to a man but to man whose family had been at the centre of power and protest within the Piikani people for a long time.

Devalon was in his mid-thirties when Milton came to see him. Milton needed a pipe carrier for a protest he was planning. He had already seen an Elder and had permission to use his pipe for the protest. The pipe would give them power—in English, one would say "sacred or religious" power. Now that Milton had a pipe, he needed a pipe carrier, someone who had the right relationship to Creator and knew how to go about things in the right way. Milton later explained, "How you get a pipe carrier is not complicated in our world," he said, "but now that I have to explain it, half of it I can almost say, and the other half I really can't say, because there is a certain process that goes along with it." He knew that the pipe would help him find the carrier. It would work like a magnet. "It kind of makes you go to the right place, to the right person ....ho has that ability."

Devalon Small Legs had become a pipe carrier for his people. Milton came to see Devalon and told him his plan. Devalon did not immediately decide whether or not he would join with Milton. Instead, he told Milton, "You have to get more organized. You have to do a number of things, then come back to me." Milton later explained, "We had to slow down. I had to go back and do things right and then go back to him, because he needed some things to be understood better." Milton came back to him a second time. Devalon didn't give his answer this time, either.

Devalon later said, "I was interested, because something needed to be done. The completion of the Oldman Dam was almost in place. Everything was going ahead, but nobody was doing anything. Friends of Oldman River were doing something, but nobody was getting anywhere." The third time Milton came to him, Devalon said, "I will be your pipe carrier." Looking back on it, Devalon remembered: "The summer of 1990 was a very heated, very intense time. The Alberta government were pushing their way—hard. We had to do something." They decided to go and camp on land surrounding the LNID Weir—land the Piikani say was stolen from them in 1922.

Devalon and I walked over the weir and along the top of a rocky road about eight metres above the bottom of the valley. Devalon pointed to where the Lonefighters had dug their channel to divert the river. "Some water had started to go down there," he said. Now it was just an indentation of land covered with tall grass. No one would know what they had tried to do here in the hot summer of 1990, what dreams were born and what dreams died here. It was silent now, except for the birds calling and the splatting of raindrops on our jackets.

"The morning they came we were not prepared. We didn't know what we were going to do. There were five leaders. Milton, Lorna, Evelyn, and I forget the others. And there was the spiritual leader—me. If they did not know what to do, they came to me. Each had a role."

It rained hard as we walked the straight road built into the bush and trees.

"The part about the land and the river being sacred—was that real or was it a tactic?" I asked.

"It was real; it was real." He pointed out the area where the confrontation with police had occurred.

"What do you think about Milton?" I asked.

He was silent for a long time. "I respect him for what he did. I respect him. He paid the price." He paused a long moment, then added, "It would have been better if it had been non-violent. That was the plan. We lost everybody over that."

"The camp was over there," he said, pointing with his walking stick. We walked off the road, over to a barbed-wire fence. He parted two strands of wire for me, then I did the same for him and we squeezed through. We trudged through the tall grass and the shrubs, between the cottonwood trees. I began to shiver. The rain stung my face. No longer was the Oldman River valley an abstraction for me or a mere romantic vision. I wasn't looking down on the valley, now; I was in it, surrounded by it. I could only see a few feet around me, to the next tree or bush. I knew very little of the names of all this nature around me—what must it feel like to know this land intimately, like one's own body? The smell was terrifically pungent.

"It is the leaves of the cottonwoods," he said, touching one of the leaves without breaking it. Then he added, "The land spoke to us that day. The land called upon us. We acted. In acting, we became ourselves." He picked up a dark grey rock with a striking white circle on it, handed it to me, and said, "This is for you."

We walked through heavy brush to a small clearing with tall grass weighed down by the rain. "Our camp was here," he said. Devalon told me the group had built an arbour out of tree branches. It was a meeting place, a storytelling place. We stopped. I tried to imagine what it must have been like when the camp was here. Nothing came. It was cold and wet, and I was tired. Perhaps I did not yet know enough about the story. All I saw was field and bush and grey sky. We left the pasture and walked back to the truck.

Devalon said, "When it got hard, we buried the medicine."

"Does that mean you gave up?" I asked.

"No, no, no," he said, quickening his step.

As we walked back there were no signs of so-called civilization, nothing to suggest we weren't walking thousands of years ago, before the ancient Greeks discovered that numbers did not have to be attached to things. Here the land looked young and new and fresh and wild. Behind me came a high-pitched scream, like the cry of a baby. I heard it a second time. "What is that? I asked.

"Coyote."

I knew that Devalon spent many months each year working with his brother in Germany, teaching Native culture and traditions. As we crossed the weir I asked him if he ever considered staying on the reserve and helping his people.

"I have one fight left in me. I have tried before. Nobody will hire me. I am too radical. I am part of the American Indian Movement."

I told him that I had spoken to somebody who had known Milton since he was young, and he had told me that out of a hundred young friends he once had on the reserve, only about ten were left alive. I asked if Devalon had the same experience.

"Only seven of the twenty-four kids I began with in kindergarten are still left. The rest are all gone. It is apartheid, eh? This reserve is a prison. You look all the way back—it is genocide. It goes all the way back to Treaty 7. The injustice, the unfairness starts there. They blocked us every way they could. The Government of Alberta, of Canada." I nodded but said nothing. My head was throbbing now, as if I'd been hit in the head with a shovel.

We reached the truck and got in. As we drove, I said it must be hard for him to go to Germany so many months each year. "Do you miss Alberta when you go over there?" I asked.

"I don't miss Alberta, but I do miss this land. It is part of me. I miss this land, my children, this water."

As we drove up to the house it was near 7:30 p.m. "This rain won't let up," I said, as we walked outside into it.

"The rain is good," he said.

At the doorway his three-year-old boy, from his second

marriage to a German woman, came rushing to the door to see his father and ran into his arms. He had his father's dark hair and brown skin. I knew I could do no more work that day. I had to get off the reserve, back to the house on the leafy white-picket-fenced street while I was saying in Lethbridge.

We stood at the doorway. My head was a waterlogged sponge. He seemed perplexed when I told him that I had to go, but that I would come back to the West again in late summer, as many more times as it took. When we were at his kitchen table, he said, "Next time write out a thousand questions. Next time bring a camera. You need to look 360 degrees. When you are leaning one way, I will push you back up straight."

I drove back to Lethbridge hardly seeing the road. I went to bed without much hope.

The next morning, strengthened by a good night's sleep, I resolved to keep trying to understand the Piikani history, without forgetting my own. I needed to somehow hold them both, contradictory though they were, in my mind. Back in Toronto, I read book after book about Piikani history. Then I read them again. I knew I also had to understand the oral history.

I did come back to see Devalon again, in August 2005. It was a sunny day, and his mood was sunny, too. I will always remember Devalon's compelling voice. It is not deep in tone but deep at the source. His words feel heavy, particularly when he speaks about his past, and the past and present of his people. He speaks haltingly, yet his words have the feel of song, a song of lamentation. The first day I met him, his mood was dark as the day itself. He didn't laugh or smile. As I got to know him better, I heard his great laugh. It begins in tragedy and ends in roaring mirth. He particularly enjoys laughing about the stupidities of the Albertan and Canadian governments. When he speaks about the government of his own reserve, he does not laugh or smile. Many months after our first meeting, he gave me a book, *The Sun Came Down: The History of the World as My Blackfeet Elders Told It*, by Percy Bullchild, inscribing it with the following words: "For all the hardships, this world is still a beautiful place." When I read those words I remember that this man has buried eight of his ten brothers and sisters, and he is only in his fifties.

The Piikani
and the LNID

As more and more people settled the West in the beginning of the 1900s, there was more pressure on the federal government to break their treaties with First Nations' peoples, take their land away from them, and give it to the settlers. In the era immediately after Treaty 7, no reserve land could be taken away from First Nations without their consent, other than for a narrow range of items listed in their treaties, such as public roads. As pressure mounted, however, the law changed. The government began taking land from First Nations and leasing it out to others, without the consent of the Natives.

The government did all it could to encourage land "surrenders," where a First Nation would be pressured to sell its land. According to historian Hana Samek, in 1904, Indian Agent J.A. Markle approached the Piikani, then known as the Peigan, with the idea of surrender. Nothing happened for several years, "marked by a mounting interest in the reserve lands." The Peigans "grew uneasy," and in 1908 "they complained to Markle about rumours that part of their reserve was going to be taken away." In response, Markle "dangled before them the potential benefits of selling their land." He told his superiors that he had "rejected the Peigan's request for a thresher and farming implements, explaining to them that if they wanted these articles they must surrender the land."

As the months passed, the band was "severely divided" on this issue. Markle "worked on the vacillators." Most of the Peigans "adamantly opposed any sale... Markle persisted, tantalizing the Peigans with visions of new wagons, cattle, implements, seeds, houses, and rations." In the summer of 1909, the Peigans voted against the land sale. A democratic vote "invigorated" Markle. He was "exasperated by the opposition of the Old Warriors, but noting that several of them were in poor health, he believed that once they passed away their place would be taken by more 'progressive men,' meaning those who favoured surrender." Later the same summer Markle held a second vote. This time he had swayed enough Peigans to vote yes, so 23,000 acres (9308 hectares) of reserve land was sold. The Peigans realized their folly and hired a lawyer to help them, but despite their protests, the land sale stood.

There were so many questionable reserve land sales in southern Alberta at the time that the government adopted new guidelines. Still, that did not end the problems. Later, in relation to another nation's land sale, there was talk of a judicial investigation. In June 1920, D.C. Scott spoke to Minister Arthur Meighan (soon to be prime minister), and said: "While no doubt the holding of a judicial investigation would clear the air, I am not sure the Department would come out of it very well. [While] I have no objections personally to this ordeal, I think it would be better policy to avoid it."

The only other way to get Indian land for local settlement was simply to ignore their treaties and take it away from them through expropriation. The problem for the Native people was that unlike white settlers who could take the money and move somewhere else, land taken away from the reserve was lost forever. It was like Canada expropriating land from Alberta and telling the residents to move somewhere else. In 1911 the *Indian Act* was changed again to make it even easier to expropriate reserve land. In parliamentary debate about this new law, Minister for Indian Affairs Frank Oliver, whose job it was to protect Native people, said, "The *Indian Act* is to protect the rights and interests of the Indians, and while the… Indian Department is for this special purpose, it is not right that the requirements of the expansion of white settlement should be ignored, that is, that the right of the Indian should be allowed to become a wrong to the white man…" In response to a question, he added, "[I]t may be, we are infringing on the treaty rights of the Indians; I am inclined to think that probably we are." This act became law. Canada used this expanded power to take land from the Piikani when it expropriated land from their reserve and sold it to the LNID for their weir on the Oldman River.

For decades, no one on the Piikani Reserve formally challenged the LNID's right to the weir land or its right to take water out of the Oldman River within the reserve. On May 10, 1978, however, the Piikani—led by Chief Nelson Small Legs Sr., Joe Crowshoe, and other Elders—blockaded the weir to stop the LNID from taking water from the river, as well as to try to settle the issue of the ownership of the weir land and the water. With this protest, something new came into the world; the Piikani fought back against an overwhelming legacy of broken promises, mistreatment, and unfairness.

Although support on the reserve for the protest was overwhelming, negotiations made no progress. Both Alberta and the Piikani claimed ownership of the Oldman River. Both sides put forward their points of view to the media. As I noted earlier, Rick Ross appeared on TV with a document purporting to prove that the LNID owned the land and the water. The Piikani said they owned the riverbed as it passes though the reserve and had a right to the water. According to the *Lethbridge Herald*, "Jack Tully, director of operations for Indian Affairs Alberta region, said the government believes with the information now available the Peigan can likely claim the river and the provincial government irrigation facilities that span it."

On May 23, LNID lawyer, Laurie MacLean, got an injunction from the Court of Queen's Bench, to stop the Piikani from continuing their protest. When we met in the summer of 2006, Roy Jenson told me that normally the LNID used a different lawyer, "a wonderful man. But he was too straight, too forward, too honest, something like that. We did not feel that he was hard enough to deal with those Indians. So we used Laurie MacLean. It was an insult to our other lawyer—but I told him it was because we think you are such a wonderful person— and we did. He was just such a good guy."

On May 30, a disaster looked imminent when between seventy-five and a hundred RCMP officers, "riot-equipped" with rifles, hard hats, and tear gas, "converged on the site, surrounding the six unarmed Peigan guarding" the area, and an LNID helicopter landed near the Piikani protestors. Nelson Small Legs, Sr., approached the helicopter. He was respected at the LNID because of his great physical strength. The first man who emerged from the helicopter was Clarence Jenson. He and Chief Small Legs knew one another from when the chief worked at the LNID. For a moment, Chief Small Legs blocked Clarence Jenson; Jenson could not pass him and proceed to the weir.

Chief Small Legs hesitated before letting his "old acquaintance" pass. But he did not give up. Chief Small Legs walked with him, spoke to him, and tried to reason with him. He told him of their plight, and why the Piikani had blockaded the weir, and why the water was theirs. The immediate crisis had passed.

After the crisis was over, MacLean, on behalf of the LNID,

launched a court action to have the Piikani cited for contempt of court because they had continued the blockade despite a court order to stop (though they did stop their blockade on June 1). A few days later, on behalf of the LNID, MacLean launched two lawsuits: one was filed in Alberta against the entire Piikani tribe and claimed ownership of the land on which the LNID Weir sits; the second was filed in federal court and claimed ownership of the same land.

After the blockade, the Piikani faced a contempt of court hearing. Chief Justice Milvain warned that "a deliberate and public challenge to the judicial system would not be tolerated and ordered six Piikani to appear before him in Lethbridge to show cause why they should not be held in contempt of court." The justice did not order "Chief Nelson Small Legs, Sr. to appear, though he was named in the LNID notice. Instead, he merely asked Small Legs to come to talk to him in Lethbridge. Chief Justice Milvain explained, 'I too am a Chief. Chiefs like to speak to one another at the same level. Therefore, I request my brother the chief to be here.'"

Chief Justice Milvain made a speech during the contempt of court hearing. He said: "I have been in law for 50 years and the snows of many winters are on my top—and I know the laws of the land are not perfect. But—as John Locke said—'Where there is no law, there is no freedom.' George Bernard Shaw said that anarchy is the system under which each person does what he pleases. Laws, including imperfect laws, must be obeyed until they are properly changed. This is a *prima facie* case of a deliberate, open, public, and evident challenge to the judicial system."

On June 7, Chief Justice Milvain withdrew all contempt charges against the Piikani. He said that the "Court [was] more than fully satisfied with [the] explanation" by Small Legs about why he had disobeyed the injunction. Justice Milvain repeated that "[c]hiefs like to speak on the same level." During the hearing, at Milvain's invitation, Small Legs stood and said, "Our people have got a lot of respect for the law. If we have broken the law, we are very sorry."

In 1981, with the help of Justice Milvain, a final agreement was worked out between the Piikani and the Alberta government over use of the weir. It was agreed that Alberta would receive not ownership but a "permit" under the *Indian Act* to operate the irrigation system on the reserve. When Alberta no longer needed the irrigation system, it was to clear off the land. The agreement implied that all natural resources of the land were confirmed to belong to the Peigan people, yet the Alberta government still had formal title to the land.

When Justice Milvain retired in 1979, he said, "I can remember members of the Indian Communities coming around to the ranch. They used to come and I used to like them, to know them. They're essentially a very proud people. They shouldn't be kicked around." When I asked Devalon about Chief Justice Milvain, he said, "We respect him."

The LNID's lawyer, Laurie MacLean, would return to the story, in 1990, as the Court of Queen's Bench justice presiding over Milton's trial for alleged criminal offences occurring on the same piece of land.

The Sister & Brother: Evelyn Kelman & Reg Crowshoe

The more I read about the Lonefighters the more I wanted to meet Evelyn Kelman. During the crisis, when police arrived with their guns and the helicopters whirling overhead, she went to the river to pray. I also learned that she is the daughter of Joe Crowshoe, one of the most revered Piikani ceremonialists in recent times, respected both by whites who care about such things and by the Piikani. The term "spiritual leader" is hackneyed in English; the best word for what Joe was is "ceremonialist," but it must be explained. A ceremonialist is someone who is a leader of the spirit of the community; he (for a Piikani ceremonialist is usually a man) was a combination of religious and moral leader, and preserver of the laws. A crucial part of his role was to conduct the ceremonies through which the people express their religious and moral vision. At the height of the Oldman Dam crisis with police in 1990, a photo of Joe Crowshoe coming to the Lonefighters' camp made the front page of the local newspaper.

Evelyn Kelman comes from a family of some of the greatest ceremonialists of the Piikani people. In an oral culture, these leaders had the vital task of not only keeping the cultural and legal practices alive but also of renewing them. They were, at their best, men of vision, men of justice—the wise men of the people. These men were the repositories of the knowledge that had been passed down. They were the keepers of the famed—at least within the people—Thunder Pipe Bundle. One of Evelyn's ancestors was a well-known ceremonialist named Brings Down The Sun, whose exemplary life is known today by many Piikani.

Evelyn told me that the Thunder Pipe Bundle that came from Brings Down The Sun later came to be held by her father, Joe Crowshoe. She explained that the bundle is not something you keep but something you are honoured to look after. Joe Crowshoe was in his thirties when he got the bundle. As kids, Evelyn and her siblings grew up with the bundle and know how powerful it is. Joe once told Evelyn that the bundle has not always been used for good things but that he had tried to use it for good things. He said, "If I tried to use it for a negative thing, it would come back to me ten times worse than I sent it out. Because that is the way the circle is. You do something; that is what comes back to you. You have to treat people good. You have to be kind, give respect—even though some people don't give respect back—because it will come back to you."

———— • ————

Evelyn had told me how to get to her place a few days before on the telephone. As part of the directions, she said, "Where you see two big trees on the right side, go left." I was going to a place where the streets have no names. She said you will know the house because of the big, yellow, two-storey school bus in the backyard, and the three old cars in the front: a Mercedes, a Toyota, and a Nova. I asked her if it would be appropriate to bring a pouch of tobacco to her. She said it would. She used it for ceremonies.

I went into a tobacco shop in Lethbridge and bought some tobacco. I didn't know if cigarette tobacco was good enough for the ceremonies, or if I should buy the more expensive pipe tobacco, so I bought lots of packages of each.

Evelyn's house was painted white and yellow. A big blue tarp covered the opening where a front door would normally be. Above the tarp a red and black sign read, "End the Apartheid." When I arrived, two tough-looking dogs ran off the porch to my car, tails wagging. The house was surrounded by yellow and green wild grasses, and there were lots of old cars in the back.

Evelyn lived on the northwest part of the reserve, at a place where the emptiness tips toward startling beauty. Her house is in the valley, not far from the river. To the west and northwest, the land rolls up and down then up into the Porcupine Hills, which rise dramatically on the horizon. The land is bare with no trees or bushes, with the hills rising darker in the distance. It is from these hills that her paternal ancestors drove buffalo off cliffs. This area is now named Head-Smashed-In Buffalo Jump and is a Canadian National Historic Site and a UNESCO World Heritage Site. It is as close as most tourists get to the Piikani Reserve.

Evelyn came outside to meet me. She has long black hair, a round face, big brown eyes, and looks ten years younger than her sixty-nine years. We sat across from each other in her well-lit kitchen, at an old wooden table. I told her I thought what they had tried to do was important. I hoped that the truth as I later saw it would honour the things I felt then to be true; but I couldn't know for sure. I could only hope. The potential gulf between what I was saying and what I might think later made me uneasy as I stared at Evelyn's trusting face—trusting, despite many reasons not to trust. I need not have worried.

She listened quietly then said, "Are you from CSIS?" I said

no. She nodded. Her big brown eyes did not blink. "I will speak to you," she said. Before I asked any questions, she said, "People never understood. It wasn't about Milton. It was about supporting the river. The river is one of the four elements: fire, land, water, air. The river is part of us. Part of my being. It was the same with my dad. One time one of Milton's sisters came here and said, 'Thanks for supporting Milton.' It wasn't about Milton. It was about the river."

Early in that first conversation, she said, "They call me a radical. I just tell the truth." After that first meeting, I knew I had found what I was looking for. I came back to speak to Evelyn again in August 2005. We spoke for six hours while drinking many cups of good strong coffee. She made us lunch, using fresh bread she had baked that day for her six kids. She had a quietness about her that was both calming and perplexing to a guy like me, used to people who talk all the time, even when there is nothing to say. Evelyn did not speak unless I asked her a question. Her stories held me in rapt attention. She remembered tiny details and emotional moments from up to fifty years ago.

After our meeting, I was exhausted from asking so many questions; I couldn't imagine how tired she must have felt, so I asked.

"It was painful, but it was good. Like a healing. I don't talk about that stuff very often."

When Evelyn was a child, her family lived in Brocket, right across the highway from an old church, near the river. Her grandfather had built a log house there. As a child, she often went down to the river to the thriving community there, which was called Highbush. People had gardens. As kids, Evelyn and her family did everything there: pick berries, ride horses, swim—boys and girls together. She lamented, "People don't grow gardens anymore on the reserve. It is too bad."

As a child, the river was a lifeline for Evelyn, her family, and her people. Years later, she said of the Oldman River, "It has always been part of our culture and our people. That river is very important. It has always been important to my people. You are part of water, your body has water. Without water you would not exist."

They all went down to the river in those days—the water was good to drink then. Her dad would load two big wooden barrels with canvas covers and a two-inch band of wire on the wagon then drive it into the middle of the river. On hot days, the kids jumped in the river and walked around the wagon and the horses. They were grateful for the water. Once her father had filled the barrels, they would return home. They used the water in the barrels for cooking and drinking; they watered their garden with it. At the time, they did not have running water or electricity, but they got along just fine.

Evelyn left home when she was six and went to live at St. Cyprian Residential School, run by the Anglican Church, remaining there until she was sixteen. Every child had a number. Everything that belonged to that child bore that number. Evelyn's number was 66. All her clothing was labelled with "66," never her name. When she got to the school, the teachers cut her hair short. Evelyn remembers how they ran that place like an army camp. She had loving parents and a loving grandmother. To leave them was traumatizing. Hardly any academic subjects were offered to the students because the government gave Native people a limited education. The kids were told, "You go and get married and start raising kids and we will baptize them into the Church." Some students at the school suffered from sexual abuse, many more were physically and verbally abused. The kids were deathly afraid of certain staff members.

Evelyn remembers that she and her classmates learned to lie in order to get out of trouble. The authorities at the school would ask the children, "Did you speak Blackfoot?"

"No," they would say.

Evelyn described for me the daily schedule at school: "First thing in the morning we prayed by our beds. Then we went downstairs. Before we ate, we prayed again. After we ate breakfast, we prayed, and then we went to the chapel and had a service. Then we would do cleaning and get ready for school. Then we would pray some more. After that, we had school for the morning, and work for the afternoon.

"At first, I started to believe in their god. It seemed okay. I told my grandmother, and she would say, 'That is not who you are. Try to be who you are, not what they want you to be.' Later, my ideas changed. I thought that this god was a real terrible god who sat on a golden chair. A rich god who was evil and not good to people. I thought this because of the way the teachers were at my school, all these women who were supposed to be good Christian people."

When Evelyn was seventeen or eighteen, she returned to her residential school to work. She was able to earn her own money, and she could be close to her brothers and sisters, who were still in school. She eventually met her husband, Bruce, a man of Scottish ancestry. They transferred to Alert Bay, on Vancouver Island. She and Bruce had been together for forty-six years when I first interviewed Evelyn in 2005. They had six children. After living on Vancouver Island, Evelyn and Bruce moved to Manitoba. She said she came back to the reserve to help her parents, as they were getting older. She did not want to come back to the reserve and is not happy there. She said in British Columbia, and in other places, she found that she had friends and a real sense of community. On the reserve, she feels there is no community; people don't associate with one another unless they are doing something related to traditional Piikani culture. She feels that there is a lot of mistrust, which is a legacy of the residential school system. When I met Evelyn, she was working as a Native counsellor for a Native counselling service. She had worked as a counsellor for many years, and as a social worker for the Department of Indian Affairs.

In late July 1990, Milton went to see Evelyn to ask if she would take part in the protest. She was to be in charge of the women at camp or, as Milton put it—"camp mom." Evelyn was in her early fifties when Milton came to her door. She agreed to Milton's proposal, but she became much more than "camp mom." When she came down to the Lonefighters' camp, she brought with her the great and honoured pedigree of her family: the Crowshoes.

Evelyn was living in Lethbridge when Milton approached her. He told her his plan to save the river. He asked if she would support his cause. She knew immediately what she would do. "Yeah, I will support this cause—to stop the dam, to cut off the irrigation. We are not getting anything from Alberta, from the Lethbridge irrigation guys, and all those people." She knew that the river was part of her people: they couldn't lose it or have it destroyed. Evelyn had seen with her own eyes the damage that dams can do. She explained, "Look at the Peace River. The mighty Peace River is now a trickle. And to me, I thought these things, I thought them out. I wanted this river to stay the way it is."

She had heard a few years before the Lonefighters' protest that there was going to be a dam built, apparently on the reserve. "A lot of Elders really put up a stink about it. They said, 'No.' The young people said, 'Yeah, we're going to be getting jobs. We are going to be doing this and all that.' The Elders said, 'No—that is not the way the white man thinks. That is how they say; that is not how they do.' Then they moved the dam off the reserve."

The Piikani chief in 1990 was Leonard Bastien. Evelyn

remembers the time he came to her folks' house. She was there helping her parents. Evelyn brought coffee. She heard her dad tell Chief Bastien, "Don't ever sell this river. It does not belong to you, it does not belong to me; it belongs to future generations. Don't ever sell this river."

When Milton told Evelyn of his plan to divert the river, Evelyn immediately agreed to take part. She told Milton, "We have to do something for the river, even if it means to divert it away from the farmers... we have rights to this river." Her decision caused a division in her family. Everybody except her parents thought she was crazy. Her brothers and sisters wanted nothing to do with the Lonefighters' protest. When I met with Evelyn, I had not yet had the chance to speak with her brother Reg, who had opposed the Lonefighters. I wondered about his position, about the position of those on the reserve (and off) who didn't agree with the Lonefighters, and by extension those who actually favoured the dam.

———— •—

The first day I met Reg Crowshoe saw a strange mixture of rain and cold, sun and heat. A big red-and-white sign at the Calgary Stampede entrance promised: "Richer, Rougher, Rodeo." As I walked into the grounds, "Appalachian Spring" by Aaron Copeland blasted from loudspeakers. I walked between narrow rows of kiosks selling popcorn and pizza, past a midway, a rollercoaster, across the Elbow River, to Indian Village, where I was to meet Reg.

At the entrance to the village a six-metre-wide, three-floor-high, TV screen advertised the rodeo and various products for sale. To the left of the huge screen, a sign: "Welcome to Indian Village." A buffalo was in the middle of the sign. Nearby, another sign: "Proudly presented by Husky Energy and Wells Fargo Financial."

And another: "Authentic Traditional Dances."

Before speaking to Reg, I had watched the Piikani Show on the main stage. Reg, a Native woman in a Calgary police uniform, and three RCMP were dancing side by side in time to the music. A person with a microphone spoke, as Reg and the officers danced: "Reg Crowshoe has been coming here for forty years. I want to acknowledge that history ... The pride of the Piikani are represented here." Reg had on white formal dress, as well as a headdress. He approached the microphone, spoke Blackfoot, then he translated to English: "I acknowledge Creator in my own language." As he spoke, the RCMP officers and the Calgary police officer bowed their heads in prayer.

When I found Reg in his trailer, his wife Rose was making breakfast. She served Reg a heaping plate of scrambled eggs, cheese, and well-buttered toast. Rose offered me some, and I could not resist.

We put the tape recorder on the table between us. I began to ask questions, and he answered. At the beginning of our interview, Reg was obviously tired. His words and ideas were very clear and came from a place of deep cultural understanding, but each word seemed to be a struggle to pull out of fatigue and the maelstrom around us. But as time passed, Reg seemed to become involved in our discussion, and his words gained emphasis, force, and even passion. Yet, the passion seemed to be weighed down with the knowledge that he was confronting an almost superhuman task in trying to renew the culture of his people.

Over those two mornings in July, I asked Reg the toughest questions I could think of, regarding the dam, the law, and the current plight of First Nations people. We spoke about Milton Born With A Tooth, with his flowing hair and gun pointed at the sky. At one point, Reg said, "The black people were persecuted for being black down in the south. They were enslaved, and they had to fight for their rights in a rough way. Here we think we have it easier, but romanticism is just as hard as persecution. And you have to fight through that, especially as a traditional people. Opportunists will take the romanticism and make an opportunity out of it."

During the Lonefighters crisis, Leonard Bastien was chief. Later, Reg Crowshoe would have a term as chief of the Piikani First Nation, but when I spoke with him in 2006 he was the steward of the Thunder Pipe Bundle. As a young man, Reg was "hit" by dreams and concepts of his traditional knowledge. People encouraged him to get his own bundle. So he met with an old Blackfoot couple from Browning, Montana. They agreed to transfer him their Thunder Pipe Bundle through a ceremony. He kept it for many years and ran ceremonies with it until the early 1990s, when his son died tragically in a house fire on the reserve. Identifying his son's body was the hardest moment of Reg's life. After the death of his son, Reg transferred the Thunder Pipe Bundle away, and he became a former Thunder Pipe Bundle carrier.

After the time of the Lonefighters, when Reg's dad Joe Crowshoe got sick, Joe told Reg to come and see him. Joe told him, "Nobody can handle these Thunder Pipe Bundles unless he is a Thunder Pipe owner, or a former Thunder Pipe owner. Take it, and I will transfer it to you." So the Short Thunder Pipe Bundle was transferred to Reg Crowshoe. A day before he died, Joe told Reg to come and take the bundle. Reg later explained, "It wasn't just handed to me because of lineage. I had to earn it, first of all, by being a Thunder Pipe Bundle owner myself, and by looking after the old man. It would not have been proper if I had just taken it.

166

That's not the right way to do it."

When I read the transcripts of the two trials of Milton Born With A Tooth, the Crown attorney in Milton's second trial characterized Reg as a "world renowned ceremonialist." I felt that it was important to speak to him about this, to try to understand the point of view on the reserve of those who opposed the Lonefighters, and to understand Reg's specific vision of how the Piikani saw the land.

In July 2006, when I interviewed Evelyn, I learned that Reg had been a police officer with the Royal Canadian Mounted Police. I also learned that Reg had written a book about Blackfoot law and ran an orientation camp for Crown attorneys, judges, and defence lawyers, to help them understand Blackfoot culture, law, and that culture's vision of justice. At the time I met him at the Calgary Stampede, Reg was a cultural leader on the reserve.

Before he answered my questions, he told me, "I am a traditionalist." He tried to explain what gave him the right to speak about Piikani history, law, and culture. He explained that in First Nations culture, lineage is very important. He added that all his teachers, whether they were formally part of his family or not, could become part of his extended family. When I spoke with Reg, he was still the keeper of the Short Thunder Pipe Bundle. In the book Reg co-authored, *Akak'stiman,* bundles are described as objects that contain sacred articles. The Thunder Pipe Bundle includes a medicine pipe, the hides of animals, and other objects. The power of the Thunder Pipe Bundle comes from Thunder itself and brings "supernatural power and strength" and the power to "settle conflicts and disputes between people and groups." As a result, a keeper of the Thunder Pipe Bundle is accorded the highest respect within the Piikani and other Blackfoot communities.

Reg told me that his bundle had "never seen the inside of the museum through all the years that we were… ah… in the colonization process."

———— • ————

When I asked Reg Crowshoe about the Lonefighters' protest, he compared it to the protest in 1978. He explained that in 1978 the Elders and traditional people had initiated the protest. The Elders refused to let the young people take control of the process, telling them:"You guys don't know what negotiating is right now… we know what it is from a traditional perspective. Those guys—politicians, RCMP, powers on the hill—they know how to negotiate from a Western perspective. We got to get together and negotiate. You guys don't know either side, so don't come in yet." Reg said that it was very different in 1990, with Milton's protest, which was initiated by young people.

Reg said he believed in the cause the Lonefighters were fighting for; everybody in the community believed in the cause. "I believe that the old people still believe they have the authority to this land, and they have to be part of that decision to deal with the LNID and province. But the old people should be the ones to negotiate, and that's what I felt." He recalled that it was the Elders who had acted during the water blockade in 1978; that protest had been resolved peacefully.

I asked Reg if he felt the protest was legitimate, given the treatment of the Piikani by Alberta, and the treatment of the law by Alberta. He replied, "I think a group of people can be pushed so far. After you have pushed them so far action starts happening. I think the Piikani were being pushed that far. I give tremendous recognition and credit to the patience and trying of the old people through the oral culture, but they were totally pushed aside and not heard.

I give credit to the politicians who tried through council, and they were pushed aside. And .... recognize the group of young people who tried to get their point heard, because we were getting pushed to that. You've got all the ingredients for something to happen when you are being pushed to that level."

Despite the strong opinion of Reg and others in her family, some of Evelyn's nephews were silent supporters of the protest. Later, when the group was at the Lonefighters' camp, she would see deer hanging from the trees. Her nephews, Wesley and Chris Crowshoe, would hunt for the deer, prepare them, and leave them hanging in the trees for the protesters to eat. Then, they would drive away to their jobs.

———— •– ————

Near the end of our discussions on the second morning, I asked Reg if he liked coming to Indian Village at the Calgary Stampede. He paused before answering my question. Then, he spoke:

"After we signed the treaties, we were put on the reserves and couldn't leave without a permit. I witnessed some of this. On the permit you had to say where you were going, how many days you were going for, and who you were seeing. That began after the treaty and lasted until 1968. You were not usually refused, but some people were. We were told, 'If you don't come back, we're going to start putting your relatives in jail until you come back.' That's why you had to put your relatives on there.

"They also started taking away the kids and bringing them to the residential school. If my family wanted to visit their kids at the residential school, they had to give up whatever they held sacred—like bundles—to the Indian Agent. A lot of bundles were lost that way. Ninety per cent of the time, when the bundle was brought to the Indian agent there was a collector sitting in the other room. He would buy the bundle, and sell it to a museum. Without those bundles, we couldn't do our ceremonies.

"With all the controls we had, the Elders were worried about losing their culture or their language, but they didn't want to say it. The Indian Agent wanted everybody to farm and ranch. One day a fellow called and wanted the Indians to come to the Stampede. The Indian Agent refused. He wrote that he didn't want the Indians to regress back to savages, wearing their clothing, living in tipis; that they did so much work to get them to farming, being civilized, he refused to let them go to Stampede. The issue went all the way to Ottawa. The Canadian government agreed to send Indians to the Stampede because the white community goes to the Stampede, and they out-numbered the Indian Agent.

"Now, at that time, all the Indians were separated in different tribes. They couldn't get together as a big nation any more. The last time they all came together in a big camp of Treaty 7 tribes was at Blackfoot Crossing at the signing of Treaty 7. So when they got invited [to the Stampede], they took the opportunity to come in a big camp, all together again. This was 1912.

"Since then, we have been camping here, protecting and preserving our culture, and just recently we have started renewing our culture. So I think this link is the only link to 1912, past then to the 1800s, for our tribes. To come to the Stampede for me, is like maintaining the duty of that link, of what we had in the old days. I have heard lots of comments: we are being exploited; white people are using us; the Calgary Stampede's Indian petting zoo. You hear all these things. But I don't think they know the history."

—— · ——

When Milton decided to do his protest, he was entering a complicated political situation on and off the reserve. At the time, an ongoing, though unresolved, lawsuit was in place regarding the water rights to the Oldman River and riverbed launched by lawyers Thomas Berger and Louise Mandell. This use of the legal process and the courts was supported by some on the reserve. Then there were the traditionalists like Reg Crowshoe, who did not oppose the lawsuits but preferred the traditional way of proceeding, meaning that they preferred to use the ties to the land in oral history from Treaty 7 to argue points rather than a formal court process based on the Queen's law. Finally, there were the young people, people like Milton, who wanted action.

PART THREE

The Showdown

The Lonefighters:
Back to the Land

In July 1990 the Lonefighters were ready to discuss their plan with the reserve leaders, so they went to see Chief Leonard Bastien and the council at the band office in Brocket. Devalon told me that Milton was supposed to go, but for some reason he left before the meeting took place. Devalon and Milton's brother, Sam Born With A Tooth, went to speak to the chief. They told him about their plan and offered him their pipe to smoke. Devalon explained to me that, in the "Indian way," to offer the pipe is to ask for help, in this case for the blockade. To smoke the pipe is to agree to help. Over twenty years later, Devalon remembered Chief Bastien's exact words, "Okay, I will help. If I don't help, I shouldn't be chief."

Later, Chief Bastien would make many contradictory statements about whether or not he supported the Lonefighters. I asked Devalon why he thought Chief Bastien did this. He explained, "You've got to remember, Chief Bastien had a position to hold as chief of the whole reserve. A blockade would be a deep political move far to the left. But at the same time he was committed to the rights of the Piikani. He believed in the pipe, he believed in the Indian way. He was in a hard spot. He is a man worthy of respect."

Later in the month, Milton, Sam Born With A Tooth, and Devalon met Chief Bastien, some council members, and

Joe Crowshoe beside the Oldman River. They sat in a circle and discussed the issues facing them: the dam, historic injustices, conditions on the reserve, and the way in which the Alberta government was treating them. They also discussed the proposed diversion of the river to stop the dam, and to bring the legal position of the Piikani people forward.

The meeting progressed though the passing of the pipe. Each person took the pipe and stated his case in English. The chief translated from English to Blackfoot for Joe Crowshoe. The chief drew on a little Styrofoam cup to show Joe the plan. Joe nodded and said, in Blackfoot, "Good, it was done right." Finally, the pipe ended up back with the pipe carrier. Milton said, "We had to get everybody understanding from their own selves and their own commitment about the issue."

Devalon said Joe knew his daughter Evelyn would be part of the protest. He told the Lonefighters, "Watch how you do everything. Be careful what you do. Remember: if anything should happen, you should not fight back. This is just a protest. We should do the protest. Go ahead." A copy of a band resolution made by chief and council was entered as evidence at Milton's first trial. The Judge at Milton's trial said that the band resolution spoke about the "advisability of getting arrested" [the Judge's wording] at the protest, which suggests that the protest was meant to be non-violent.

Everyone smoked the pipe, giving the group the approval to go down and divert the Oldman River. Milton was excited "because then it was a go-to-the-store kind of feeling," he said, "got to get things." Each person who was to be part of the diversion had a different area of responsibility. Everyone was preparing. Some of the Elders had already called a meeting, "to alert the Elders on the reserve it was a go." By then Milton was already off "trying to muster supplies." The protest was set to begin on August 3, 1990, the night of the full moon. Milton and the others had to find a place to set up camp and an arbour.

Since the ill-fated highway blockade in 1988, there had been a few discussions between the Piikani and Friends of Oldman River, but there had been no joint agreement to work together. When Milton and his group arrived on the scene, however, the Friends' relationship with the Piikani broadened. Cliff said, "People thought he [Milton] was a loose cannon, but he was very open and always honest to me. He told me about his rage and drinking in the past, and how he had gotten through that, and what he wanted to do with his people."

The Friends worked closely with the Lonefighters on their protest. On July 29, 1990, Martha's journal entry states, "Things are set to go this weekend. The Peigans have got a legal opinion from [the law firm] Bennett Jones that says nothing they are planning is illegal. Cliff is planning to be down there. Cliff is wondering if we can give them some money. They have some from the US. They are looking for about $15,000. I said I think we can commit $5000. We won't give them money until something happens."

In Martha's journal entry on July 30, she mentions Milton Born With A Tooth for the first time: "Milton Born With Tooth called. He first said how much I have done. He said they appreciate it. He said it is now a time of unity and they need 2000 right away. I found out who the cheque should be made out to—I said I will try to arrange it and call him back."

Then, on August 2, Martha writes, "Cliff called. Everything is ready to go for tomorrow. He is making last minute calls to the media. I wish I could be there. I do wish I could be down there now and be part of the action, even though it is better that I'm not. It's time for the Indians to be in the limelight not me. But I do like being in the limelight, and it is so hard to miss the action. I have waited for so long; it is so hard not knowing what is happening."

———

The Lonefighters made camp in early August. Devalon knew the area well—from the mountains in the west to the grasslands in the east. The whole area had been his playground when he was young. He chose the campsite because it was out of the wind and close to the water. The landowner, Ralph Greir, told Devalon that they could use the land if they brought him a few groceries now and then. Devalon left his trailer park. Evelyn left her home. Others came down from Calgary. Glen North Peigan and Lorna Born With A Tooth also came to camp, along with Elder Romeo Yellowhorn and his wife, Margaret. Lorna brought her kids to camp. Milton's brother, Sam Born With A Tooth, Frank English, Evelyn's son, Raymond Crowshoe, Jessie Scott, Charles English, and others came down to camp. Devalon remembers there being thirty Lonefighters in all. Press reports would later suggest that the number fluctuated, depending on the day.

Some had never camped before. They left behind the fences surrounding their reserve, as well as the heavily cultivated farmland, and went into the broad valley of the Oldman. They made camp on the northwest corner of their reserve, near the river, in a little pasture surrounded by cottonwood forest. They set up tipis, tents, a kitchen, and a great brown tent. They made an arbour of the trees they found nearby. The arbour was a meeting place, a storytelling place. Milton Born With A Tooth later said, "We did not want to just build a house." Their arbour was a gesture demonstrating they were doing things "right within our own way." Glen North Peigan explained to the press that this was "a family camp. Some parents wanted their children here and it is a good idea. They play, and enjoy the area; they swim, pick berries, and play all around."

Many times in interviews Milton explained why he called the group the Lonefighters. Devalon explained that they chose the name during a ceremony conducted by him around the time that they met by the river with chief and council, but not during that meeting. According to Milton, the group needed a "shield." So they chose the Lonefighters, because it was a historic "authority within the Blackfoot Confederacy." "We wanted something in our way of life that was real strong, that had not been used in a real long time," Milton said. He said the Lonefighters had been "outlawed"; he chose a name that hadn't been "tainted by ABCs and stuff like that." Milton was a direct descendant of that society, through his father and his father's father. What sent chills down his back was that the land where they made their camp was Lonefighters' land. Lonefighters' graves were also part of that landscape. Being there made them feel that their struggle was connected with the past. "It made sense."

When they set up camp, they laid down some ground rules: no drinking, no fighting. The camp had to be safe because they had women and children there. Also, everybody had to be part of the decisions, or at least understand them. When an important decision was to be made, they went into their arbour to "talk it out, and then it would go through the pipe."

Every morning Devalon made prayer and they raised the

Piikani flag. According to Devalon, when they got to camp, they needed to purify themselves, to create a medicine that would help them in their struggle. Early in the process, they made a sweat lodge with willows, which looked like an upside-down basket on the ground. They put rocks in a pit in the centre of the lodge. Later, they started a fire and heated the rocks until they glowed red. At the front of the sweat lodge they made an altar. That night they purified everybody who was going to be part of the struggle. They wanted to use these "sweats" as much as possible to help people stay focussed, to purify them, to take stress away from the whole situation, and to try to get some spiritual assistance.

Six boys—street kids—from Brocket moved into camp. They helped to build the sweat lodge. Some people from the reserve said, "You've got alcoholics." Evelyn and the other Lonefighters did not think this. Evelyn thought, "Oh, good, they're here." These boys set up tents and tipis in a clearing near the river. For three months the boys did not drink, and they stayed in the camp. They believed in their culture, and it really helped them.

Evelyn was the oldest member of the camp. She later said, "I was really treated with respect." When they first got there, she took a walk up a hill, sat down, and watched the boys cutting down little branches to finish the arbour. One of the boys told her, "You know we put tobacco in the ground before we took the trees." Whenever they took something, they put something back. The camp provided the boys from Brocket with a crash course in their own culture. Evelyn respected those boys, whose "real selves began to shine through" as they became more and more immersed in camp life. Years later, when she would go to Brocket, she would say, "Hey, hello, Lonefighter," and they gave her hugs. They would say, "It always makes me feel good to see you." She would reply, "Me, too."

During the early days of the camp, there was a lot of sun.

One Elder came down and said, "This is the closest I have ever been to my culture." Others came down and held ceremonies. Evelyn said, "We were honest and trusting as a family." By August 3 everything was ready, or nearly ready, for the action that had pulled them all together.

By the morning of August 3, 1990, events were unfolding as planned by the Government of Alberta. Construction companies raced to finish the dam, using the latest engineering principles, as well as bulldozers and other heavy equipment. Archaeologists busily removed Native artefacts from the area that was to be flooded. Businesses, farmers, engineering companies, and the Alberta government were all getting ready to receive the benefits—in money and popular support—of the new supply of water, the liquid gold diverted from the Oldman River valley, and from the Piikani.

———— -- ————

Cliff Wallis phoned newspapers throughout Alberta and told them, "A hole is being punched today in the weir on the Oldman River on the Peigan Indian Reserve, in protest against the Oldman Dam project." The newspapers tried to get comment from the LNID officials, but they were touring the Oldman Dam construction site and could not be reached. Cliff told the media that there would be a "groundbreaking ceremony," not far upstream from the LNID Weir.

The outside world knew nothing about this protest, nothing about its leaders, and little about the Piikani; they had been fed a great deal of misinformation about the Piikani from some media. The press arrived at the camp by the Oldman River on the afternoon of August 3, ready for a controversy for the evening edition, but nothing happened. They waited and waited. Some left without getting the story they needed. Everyone waited for one thing—the bulldozer.

For Milton Born With A Tooth, there was no turning back. August 3 had been hectic. He had found out that morning that the huge Caterpillar (CAT) they had been expecting was not going to be there. The Lonefighters had rented the CAT for "irrigation work" from a construction company building the Oldman Dam. When they learned the CAT might not arrive as planned, the protesters didn't know what to do, but they were committed. They were determined that the groundbreaking ceremony would go ahead that day. The Lonefighters had invited everyone they could think of to the ceremony: chief and council, Andy Russell, and lots of media. Everyone was there, everything was ready, but there was no CAT. According to Milton, it was a "kind of at-the-wire feeling." The media "were getting kind of antsy." They had deadlines.

"We told them we weren't trying to design this thing to meet the designs of whatever—there was a serious intent. Still, some of the media left," Milton later said.

At long last, Milton got the word that the CAT was on its way. He was jubilant. Everybody was excited. Finally, in the far distance, coming out of the trees, they saw and heard the great CAT rumbling down the dirt road. For Milton, it was "the most beautiful sight of the day."

Luckily, they found a band councillor who could drive the CAT, so it was fired up and began to clear brush from the currently water-free channel into which the Lonefighters wanted to send the river. They explained to the press how they planned to divert the water around the weir and send it down the old waterway.

After the CAT demonstration, a press conference was held near Head-Smashed-In Buffalo Jump. Milton told the press, "This dam is an outright genocidal act against nature and the Peigan people's way of life. We can no longer sit idly by and watch one of the last free-flowing rivers in North America be destroyed."

At this point, Chief Leonard Bastien told the press that neither he "nor band council endorsed the actions of the Lonefighters." He hoped negotiations would settle the dispute. Bastien added that he would be calling a public meeting to allow reserve residents "to express their concerns about the Lonefighters' decision to divert the river flow."

The Lonefighters explained their plan to move the river to protest the dam, conditions on their reserve, and the wrongful expropriation of land away from them for the irrigation weir. They said that they intended to dig through the LNID dike with their D-9 CAT. They hoped water would leak through this hole and go down the channel, rendering the farmers' canal high, dry, and useless. Even though it was late in the growing season, farmers and some towns still desperately needed the water from that canal to provide them with a reserve for winter, since the irrigation system would shut down in the fall.

At the press conference, Cliff said Friends of the Oldman River "endorsed the action of the Lonefighters as a lawful, non-violent action."

Late that day, after the media left, the CAT got stuck in the marsh of the old channel. The water table there was so high it was hard to keep any piece of heavy equipment from getting stuck. Milton later told the story: "It was stuck enough to make us all at that moment in time think that maybe we should go home. Oh, jeez, it was not stuck; it was sunk in the mud. It just about disappeared." The D-9 CAT had tracks as high as a man, and that day, "the tracks weren't even showing." It was a make-or-break moment for them. At first, they tried to blame each other. By evening, they just sat around. The next day they went into the sweat lodge to try to get guidance. Everyone they approached for help asked them how deep the CAT was stuck. When Milton told them, they answered, "It is going to stay there a long time."

"I need something that has to be immediate . . ."

"Well, if you can carry it out…"

Milton said it was "those kinds of times" that one has the "strongest conversations." At some point the group was joking about how a car would often be stuck somewhere on the reserve and they would have to dig it out. While they were talking, "a few people got it in their head," and eventually somebody came back and said, "We are digging it out." They only had two shovels and some railroad ties for leverage. It took them sixteen hours to dig the CAT out. Unfortunately, it got stuck another half-dozen times, but after the first time, digging it out became easier and less time-consuming.

———————

Martha Kostuch arrived at camp on August 4. When she arrived, not too much was happening. At about 3:00 p.m., she went down to look at the CAT, which was still stuck. Martha wrote in her journal: "What they need is a moral[e] boost. The day was very, very hot, and we were all tired and dry." Martha got a phone call from someone from Pincher Creek on August 6: "'Do you realize what you have turned loose down there. It will get ugly. You have unleashed a bunch of criminals and hatred.'"

The day before, on August 3, Doug Clark, an engineer with Alberta's Department of the Environment, watched the groundbreaking ceremony on television. It was his job to make sure that the weir was working properly and delivering its precious water to the irrigation district and local towns. He was worried, so he decided to go over to the weir to see if any damage had been done by the CAT. Under the circumstances, he thought it prudent to bring RCMP Sergeant Gary Mills with him. Early on August 4, they drove to the weir, parked, then walked toward the main dike. They passed a plywood sign, with the following words painted on it: "No trespassing by Order of the Peigan Nation. Violators will be prosecuted immediately. Sanctioned by Lonefighters."

Clark walked past the sign onto the main dike. He did not see any damage. He heard a vehicle start up on top of the river valley. Moments later, a van pulled up beside him and Sergeant Mills. Four or five Native people got out, including Milton. Milton came over to them and said, "Who are you and what are you doing? Can't you read? You are violating the Peigan law."

Milton was determined to take Clark's camera, and Clark was equally determined to keep it. Milton stopped when he realized Clark was not going to give up the camera without a fight. Sergeant Mills offered to give Milton the film if Clark could keep the camera, and the crisis passed. Sergeant Mills later said that Milton "asked for our names, and said he would report us." After that, Milton and the others escorted the sergeant and Clark off the reserve.

That afternoon, Mills and Clark flew over the site in a helicopter. The CAT was working, but there was no "damage" yet. Mills told his bosses in a written report that it was a media event and that with only the one machine they could not divert the river. He recommended that no police action be taken at that time. He later said, "At that time it was my own personal opinion that this was a political matter between the Peigan Nation and the Alberta government, and I didn't think it would be appropriate if the RCMP were to take action at that time, to come to the reserve and start arresting people. I felt that maybe things could be discussed between the Peigan Nation and the Alberta government." Behind the scenes, the Alberta government, up to the highest levels of power, was carefully monitoring events and planning to meet with the Lonefighters to talk.

And so, in the early days of August, through days of heat and sunshine, the Lonefighters' camp established its rituals and sense of community, as the CAT continued its fitful digging. Early on, the camp more closely resembled a family and community course in culture than a protest. Lonefighters would pick berries near camp, and afterward, they had berry soup. Years later, Evelyn remembered Lorna's five-year-old daughter, MJ, on one side of a bush, and Evelyn on the other. MJ prayed in Blackfoot. She did not know the language, but she had heard people praying in Blackfoot at camp. Evelyn listened to her. When she finished, MJ turned to Evelyn and said, "Grandma, what do you think of my prayer?"

"Right on," Evelyn said.

Usually the Lonefighters would be up by 7:00 a.m. Night security would have the coffee ready. After coffee, the Lonefighters would go into the arbour and "smudge." Evelyn explained that to smudge, participants would take coal and put it on the ground. Then they would take rolled-up dried-out sage, put it on the coals, and light it with a match. Then, Evelyn would put sweetgrass on top. She would purify herself with the smoke. Smudging, she told me, is a way of taking away "negative stuff, to cleanse yourself of negative thoughts. When you smudge, you are balanced, and nothing can upset that balance. My dad, before he passed on, he said, 'Never let my smudge die.'"

Every morning before breakfast they sat in a circle and spoke about their dreams, the problems on the reserve, the dam, and how they had been treated. Every night they returned to their circle to discuss the day and to make sure that everyone understood what had happened. People would ask questions, even small children asked questions. They were not told "go away and play," they were invited in. Everyone there felt good being together, in a circle. Everyone, including the children, was treated with respect. The young men were the security. They would stay up all night, looking after the fire and standing guard; then they would sleep during the day.

This "idyllic" view of the camp early on was shared by the RCMP—at least publicly. Sergeant Mills reported that the RCMP did not plan to stop the digging. The police were flying over the Lonefighters' site daily and had seen no ammunition, no guns, no firearms, no explosives. Mills reported to the *Edmonton Journal* that the Lonefighters' camp was "nothing to get excited about ...basically, it's approximately ten male adults with their families camped in a little area fooling around with a bulldozer. The protesters are playing to the media and when reporters aren't around they relax—sometimes swimming in the river."

The same article from the *Edmonton Journal* contained the following quote: "Furious southern Alberta farmers Saturday called for police or the army to be brought in to stop the natives. From his farm near Lethbridge, Bill Arsene said, 'They should bring in the army and I don't have to tell you the rest of it. We support the construction of the Oldman River dam and have no sympathy for the natives. When they start getting militant, then it's time to put your foot down. There are 48 little towns that need the water.'"

As time passed, the RCMP would come under heavier and heavier pressure to intervene with force, which was something they were desperately seeking to avoid.

———————

The Lonefighters' CAT kept working and getting stuck. By August 7 it had broken through the main dike, but Doug Clark wasn't worried.

He wrote in a memo to his bosses, "My personal observation is that this work does not have much chance of success as only one dozer was working, and no surveys had been done." Farmers, on the other hand, were worried, and their feelings started to show in their comments to the media. Roy Jenson told the press, "I doubt the Lonefighter action will ever be complete. It's a way bigger operation than they thought. The farmers are upset about the Lonefighters' tactic. It's really maddening, terrible, ridiculous, and somebody should do something about it."

Though in its public comments the Alberta government downplayed the Lonefighter situation, Alberta was concerned enough to meet secretly with the Lonefighters and Piikani Chief Bastien at the Lonefighters' camp. Often, those in power will refuse to meet with protesters until they halt their protest. For all its bad press, the Alberta government broke this rule to meet with the Lonefighters, to try to find a solution to the crisis. The government's only condition was that the meeting be held in secret. The only condition the Lonefighters put forward was that the RCMP could not attend the meeting. It is not clear who ultimately agreed to this condition, but the end result was that the leaders for the Alberta negotiating team went into the Lonefighters' camp without protection. Sergeant Mills of the RCMP drove government negotiators down toward the demonstration site until he reached a roadblock.

The meeting took place in the Lonefighters' arbour. Discussions lasted hours. Many Piikani came to the meeting. Milton later explained, "We had our own security to make sure nobody harassed them. Nobody took potshots at them, whatever. It was tempting, because rarely do we get the government in that kind of situation, but we made sure that never happened."

Though the chief had said publicly that he was against the Lonefighters, he made sure he was at the camp for the negotiations,

188

should arise. The Lonefighters had a clear and simple position, as Devalon later said: "Shut the dam down. Close the dam down. Obey your own laws. Shut the dam down until there can be a federal environmental assessment."

Peter Melnychuk and the other Alberta negotiators would not agree to this condition.

The meeting did not produce an agreement, though the Alberta government did make an offer to try to settle the dispute. The Lonefighters held to their position that the dam must be stopped. There is no evidence that the chief put forward any position at the meeting. In the end, according to the Lonefighters, the government negotiators promised that if the RCMP were to come onto the reserve, the protesters would receive twenty-four hours' notice.

After the meeting, Milton phoned Martha Kostuch. She recorded their conversation in her journal: "Milton called. He wants me to call the media for a press conference. He said they had a good meeting with Alberta Environment and Native Affairs—and government officials were ordered to meet with the Peigan. They are continuing work and the work is going well. Needs a backhoe. He said he is acknowledging us always; he doesn't want them to come between us. He sounds so happy!"

Later the same day, Milton called Martha a second time. She noted that conversation, too: "Milton called again. He said he is under a lot of stress. The camp is getting bigger. Work is continuing. The government made an offer. They said no. They want dam construction stopped. The chief and council are going to have to start taking a position. They need a backhoe. Cliff said he could arrange for it."

Peter Melnychuk had a different view of the meeting than Milton. He reported to his superiors that "Milton Born With A Tooth was in charge of the whole operation in spite of the fact that the chief was present. Milton gave us a lengthy history of the Peigan band and the importance of water. I found that the meeting was threatening and confrontational." After the meeting, Department of the Environment officials told police that they did not want to attend any more meetings without police protection.

The next day, Milton spoke to the media about Alberta's environment minister, Ralph Klein, who would later become the province's premier:

> Klein and the project itself are in the same category as Hitler himself, who overrode every law and just went ahead and destroyed a culture. The Oldman Dam project is an illegal act. They've overrode the federal government, every environmental law, but most of all they overrode the law of the Native people. My enemy is not the Peigan people, it is the project. In anything, there has to be a sacrifice, someone has to be out there. I chose to be that. If the Oldman River Dam project and the court systems aren't going to listen to their own kind, then what makes us think they're going to listen to the Peigan people?

Milton told *Kanai News* that he had no concern for farmers, "Not one. Because they are not concerned about us or considering our lives. They don't live here, but we're their means of support. It comes from us. It is just a syringe from our lifestyle, yet they don't even consider that." In a separate news story, Don Lebarron, a prominent politician in southern Alberta who had told the press the dam construction should continue despite court rulings that rendered the dam illegal, was quoted as saying, "We have to have law and order in this province."

In the early weeks of the protest, *Alberta Report* magazine had two articles about the Lonefighters. The first was titled "Playing with Water—and Fire: The Oldman River Ecofreaks Take Up with Some Dangerous Indian Friends." The article characterized the protesters as "A dozen rough vigilantes," "outlaws," and "saboteurs." The article also referred to, and headlined in thick black ink, a very serious criminal conviction of Milton's. In the article, the source for the criminal conviction for the other Lonefighter is given as "sources for the government." In the same issue, *Alberta Report* also ran a "Letter from the Publisher," by Link Byfield. In the article, Byfield explains that treaties between the Indians and Canada are "a lie"—that "treaties are signed between sovereign nations. They are meaningless between a victorious nation and a vanquished one."

———————

Almost daily during the crisis, Roy Jenson would wake up to the sound of helicopters landing on his property, kicking up dust. Journalists would fly out to speak to Milton at the Lonefighters' camp, and then they would fly to Roy's farm. They told Roy what Milton had told them, and then returned to the camp to tell Milton what Roy had said. Roy's deepest conviction was that the law had to apply equally to all. Years later he explained, "I don't think they had a special right to the water in the river—but they have a legal right to water. We're all born out of the womb of woman under the same sun. We should all be equal, with the same rights and responsibilities. It shouldn't matter whether or not your father was born here or your grandfather was born here or [an] ancestor was born here 2,000 years ago."

A Community
Divided

When I asked him about the 1990 Lonefighters camp, Reg said he had been concerned about the integrity of the law itself; not only Blackfoot law, but also Canadian law. The Elders felt that they should be the ones to negotiate these issues, not the younger generation. But according to Reg, nobody was listening to him and the elders, only to Milton. Then he knew: "What is the use of being in camp? The old people are right." The old people said, "We're helpless. What do these young people know about our traditional authorities through songs? What are they going to do if we go down there? In the old days, if they still had traditional understanding, we could send the Brave Dogs, we could send our Thunder Pipe people, and they would put a stop to this, no problem. But these people don't know at all where our language and our culture are." Inherent to the Elders' concerns was another worry—that the "Lonefighters," in their youthful abandon, would end up getting hurt.

Reg told me he did not agree with what he called "new-age" methods:

Canada has a history in developing practices in justice. I have a history in developing justice practices. They are long histories, and we can get along together that way. But what happens if somebody comes along and says—well, for example: "The beaver diverts, so I am going to proceed to do this." I don't agree with that. They have to work with [traditional and Canadian law] to be able to do anything… "Follow the beaver" might be a true message. But if you don't know anything about your culture on how to follow the beaver, then you are going to have your own personal creation of new culture, new-age culture that says, "Okay, don't know what he means, but I am going to divert the river, I guess that's what beavers do. But I am going to make it my personal understanding of what that means." What about the thousands of years of Blackfoot culture with Beaver Bundles that show us the technical [right] way to do things, compared to someone's personal understanding of the beaver?

In this case, Milton's directive, to "Follow the Beaver," according to Reg, was outside both white and "Indian" culture.

When I spoke to Reg at the Calgary Stampede, he also explained that he was in favour of a dam on the Oldman River, provided it was on the reserve and the Piikani were paid a fair share of the revenue that might come from a dam.

———————

The Lonefighters' protest had sharply and passionately divided the Piikani; approximately half of the people believed in the protest, while the other half were against their actions. By mid-August the press had broken a story under the headline "Lonefighters Claim Name Being Misused." It quoted members, purportedly from the "real" Lonefighters Society, who did not want their names used:

A lot of us are very frustrated with these people. They're using the name for what it is not intended. These people are just using this name as a tool just to give them some recognition. The majority of Piikani don't support the protest tactic, have not endorsed the group and are even in favour of the dam. So why say the dam is not going to benefit the tribe as a whole? Sure, some of the burial sites may be wiped out. Don't you have to sacrifice a little bit for long-term gain? Attempts to divert the river are not working. The bulldozer bogged down in the muck. They're going to need a lot more machinery. They're pushing dirt up against the weir. There's not water diversion.

Years later, Native critics of the camp were still afraid to have their names published. As were some former Lonefighters. When I visited the reserve, the division over the issue was still fresh in people's minds.

The division prompted some people to speak against the Lonefighters when they went to Brocket for supplies, or spent time away from camp. Evelyn said to them, "You don't like what we're doing? Let's put up microphones in town hall. Let's talk about it." She went to the town hall and waited. Nobody showed up. Every day was like that. Evelyn knew that they were opposed by many—even among her own people.

Evelyn and Reg are close. Yet, to this day, they still disagree about the Lonefighters' protest. Evelyn responds to Reg's view like this: "Some people think we should just lie down and let them run over us. It is good to live off the reserve, it broadens the mind. Reg does a lot of good for culture. Some people, when we protest, they say, 'You are acting bad—talking back.' I say, 'Yeah, that is what we are doing. We want to make them see what they are doing. You can't hide all your life. You can't just submit. The power is bigger than us, but you still got to make a statement.'"

Devalon agrees with Evelyn. "There was another part of our people who were working so hard against us. Many came down to see what we were doing. Reg Crowshoe, he came down. He didn't say anything against us to our face. He isn't like that."

Devalon explained that the Alberta government was funding culture on the reserve. "Alberta was paying for Sundances and paying for Pipe Dances. I mean, all these Native people involved, who are they praying for to have success in our court case, us or Alberta? Our cultural people, getting together and having a hernia about what we were doing. They were afraid the provincial government would close the tap on their funding." He laughed. "I mean, you should have seen the bullshit happening in those years."

On August 20, Doug Clark flew over the site and saw, for the first time, a backhoe working in the river and a hole in the middle of the main dike, with water advancing through the hole down the proposed diversion route. The camp was growing. There were more tents and vehicles. Still, he did not think the planned diversion would work. Little new work had been done with the backhoe; the flow of the river had not been affected. A few nights later, shortly after all the bars had closed in Fort Macleod, young men came to the camp in pickup trucks, yelling and screaming at the Lonefighters. The Lonefighters managed to turn them back. This was the only direct attempt to attack the Lonefighters' camp, until the RCMP arrived in September.

At the same time, the sense of community broadened as many Piikani on the reserve pitched in and brought hot meals and cakes to the people at the camp. Cliff Wallis, Martha Kostuch, Andy Russell, and others from the Friends came down to camp. Environmentalists and Native activists from all across Canada also arrived at the camp to show their support.

Evelyn later explained, "We all worked together—we were one. I had a vegetarian woman cutting dried meat for me. Colour didn't matter. It should be like that all the time; that is how it should be. People sent in, or brought, food." They had vegetables and fruit trucked in from a reserve in Kelowna. Others brought clothes to the protesters.

On August 14 the Piikani held a five-hour community meeting in a sweltering gymnasium in Brocket. Anyone who wanted to was given the chance to speak. The press expected Chief Leonard Bastien to announce his position after the meeting, but he refused to do so. After the meeting, people told the press that the reserve membership was "virtually split on whether to support the group or denounce its actions."

The next day, Bastien spoke to the press: "The actions of band members claiming to be part of the Lonefighters Society had brought issues forward which need to be addressed at the bargaining table—issues that likely wouldn't have come forward had it not been for the protest. But, the actions of the Lonefighters have to be considered from the legal aspect." He added that he was against the involvement of Friends of Oldman River, because the issues should be decided by the Piikani people. He also said that he was against the Oldman Dam "because of the cultural genocide it is having on our people. But I would be willing to negotiate and talk with dam officials concerning river flow which would guarantee to nurture river vegetation and thereby ensure life of the flora and fauna in the river valley." Chief Bastien acknowledged that "some band members want Chief and council to step in and stop the protest. Some want to bring in the RCMP and whatever force necessary. But we want to look at this realistically from all band members' viewpoints. The core group [Lonefighters] at the weir receives support from a fair number of our membership, from fellowship in support of their endeavours to the supplying of food."

Two days later, on August 16, the *Lethbridge Herald* headline read: "RCMP Have No Proof Yet of Any Native Illegalities." RCMP Superintendent Owen Maguire told the press, "[T]he police role is to get people communicating. Unless there's a criminal offence, we're not going to get involved. The RCMP will explore all other avenues before moving in to quell the protest. The last thing we want is a confrontation. The longer the protest drags on, the likelihood of a confrontation increases."

Milton said, "To me, whether chief and council says yes or no to our action, the Lonefighters Society is going to continue. You don't see any violence here, no guns. You just see a whole lot of people who are concerned. I want you to look at who diverted the river first ....e are in a process of healing the river."

———————

As the end of August approached, it was beginning to look like the protest had failed. Water had not been diverted; the public still didn't understand why the Lonefighters were holding the protest; and the story had hardly made it out of Alberta. The crisis in Oka, Quebec, continued to receive the national media's attention. Attorney General for Alberta Ken Rostad commented, "[T]he attempt to divert the Oldman River has all but fizzled out... Anybody who has flown over the area can see the project is not going anywhere." He added that the Piikani "aren't serious" and compared them to "children playing with Tonka toys."

Yet things were not quite as they seemed. In an article on August 26, journalist Mike Lamb reported about his visit to the Lonefighters' camp. He saw a renewed effort to divert the river. Lamb wrote, "The feel of winter was in the air and new snow dotted the mountains, as a huge slow-moving bulldozer operated behind ground workers who worked late into the night Friday clearing the way... Heavy equipment reinforcements including a backhoe and dump trucks had arrived." The Lonefighters "laboured through the rain and mud Saturday to divert the Oldman River." Milton had quit predicting completion dates the week before. He "would only say: 'The job will be finished.'" Lamb continued, "But a ground inspection Saturday showed considerable headway during the past few days. A more orderly work pattern may also reflect donations of engineering advice and money the Peigans say have trickled in recently. One man who drove the heavy equipment said, 'People ridicule us; they say we are not serious. We'll see who looks stupid next week.'"

Cliff Wallis told me that the Alberta government could have stopped the protest, and he had no idea why they let it go on as long as they did. Later, when the water started to flow, Alberta started getting nervous. "And that is when the RCMP and others were called in."

To this day, Cliff has vivid memories of the Lonefighters' camp. "I remember the seasons changing. We had a concert during that period right down at the Lonefighters' camp... I would spend the night there occasionally. It was a very friendly thing... The Elders came in, children, and women. There was no feeling of anger or rage. It was very peaceful. That was the thing that always kept me there; I still am opposed to violent action."

On August 27 Doug Clark flew over the site again and took photos. He told his bosses that "one of the dikes had been dozed up for a considerable length." However, the backhoe driver did not seem to know how to drive. The protesters were having "no effect on the river," and "considerable work remains." From his engineering perspective, he concluded they either had to "deepen the channel or build a dike across the river." He felt the new trench was having "zero" effect on the river.

Some journalists reported that the Lonefighters had altered their plan. They were now trying to move large boulders into the river to force the water down their diversion channel. Whether because of this plan, or the added equipment, one Alberta government engineer would, for the first time, conclude that the Lonefighters might actually have a chance at moving the river. Alberta stopped laughing and the dangerous endgame began.

The Breakthrough: At Last!

Many times over the course of August 1990, the Lonefighters told the press that the river was now "diverted." Sometimes, Milton would say that the river was diverted, and the other Lonefighters would say that it wasn't.

On August 28 Doug Clark flew over again. He watched the Lonefighters' bulldozer drive back and forth in the river, trying to push gravel out far enough to block the flow of water. He could tell they were becoming more and more knowledgeable about their task. They had dug sixty-one metres of a deepening, lengthening canal from the river. They still had to dig 610 metres before that canal could rejoin the river and bypass the farmers' weir. He still felt that they "probably . . . would not finish before the end of the season." But something special happened the night of August 28, 1990, long after Clark had gone home.

By this time, the Lonefighters had two CATS and one backhoe on the job. Earlier that day, they had told the press that the river would be diverted early in the morning. Then the deadline was noon. Then it was 3:00 p.m. "The camp was busier than usual throughout the day and there was a feeling of tension and suspicion as sentries posted at the camp entrance kept the press well back from the brink of the hill overlooking the area where the diversion work is being carried out." At 4:00 p.m., Devalon spoke to the press "atop a windy hill overlooking the Lonefighter encampment." He said, "We are only a couple of hours' work away from cutting through. There have been a lot of difficulties, but the river is going to flow this evening." At 7:00 p.m., the members of the media, more than a dozen strong at one time during the late afternoon, were told to go home.

The press later learned that the backhoe had broken down the day before. The Lonefighters tried to fix it themselves but could not. The broken part would have to be taken to a supplier for repairs. Devalon guessed that at first 30 per cent of the river would be diverted. "Eventually, huge boulders will be used to block the entire flow and bypass the irrigation headworks." *The Calgary Herald* headline read: "No Diversion Yet: Backhoe Breaks Down; Peigans Will Persevere." Attorney General Ken Rostad "dismissed the activity and said there's no reason for the government to interfere." He added, "If they want to muck around with dirt on their reserve that's their privilege."

Even though most of the press had left by 7:00 p.m., an initiated few remained—including Bert Crowfoot, staff writer for *Windspeaker* magazine and great-great-grandson of Chief Crowfoot, one of the key negotiators for the Blackfoot people during the negotiation of Treaty 7. Bert Crowfoot was there at around 8:00 p.m. when, somehow, the Lonefighters got the backhoe running again. The Lonefighters were tense and tired. They felt victory was close. Would it happen that night? They had waited so long for a victory— some would say more than a century. Perhaps by then the hope of changing public opinion had faded; the means had become an end. It was now an existential situation: to roll the rock all the way up the mountain, and damn the fact that it would roll back down again.

They gathered by the river in the evening to make "a pipe ceremony and offering to the river." They "only had a few feet to go before they would break through and 'correct' the diversion done in the 1920s." The ceremony began. "A loud smack in the river startled everyone .… beaver was gathering twigs and small branches to help dam the river just below the 'correction' canal." The beaver was using the branches and twigs from a tree the CAT had earlier pushed into the river. Each person spoke about how they felt now that their task seemed nearly complete. "It was an outpouring of grief, joy and determination. Then the pipe ceremony was held, and an offering made to the river."

Devalon later told me: "We needed something to pull the group back together… This was what we needed to get the momentum back again."

Evelyn said, "We really felt great. We were whooping and hollering. We needed this. It gave us the energy to keep going. This energy was coming back to us from the river."

After the ceremony, they fired up the backhoe again and "began to work on the final few feet between the river and the canal." At 8:54 p.m. water began to "trickle" into the Lonefighter canal. "As the shovel dug out the final bit of earth, the water began to pour into the canal." They had done it—or so it seemed—on what was to them a glorious night. "All that was left now," according to Bert Crowfoot, "was for the CAT to build a dam across the Oldman River, and the river would change its course to the original riverbed it ran for thousands of years before." In a newspaper article the next day, Glen North Peigan said, "This is the first time anybody has diverted a river like this: anybody. It was a joyous occasion last night. You had to be there to feel it."

The next day, under a two-inch heading in the newspaper— "Through At Last"—Bert Crowfoot proclaimed the victory, consciously or perhaps unconsciously echoing the words "free at last" from Martin Luther King, Jr.'s great speech in praise of freedom

202

made in Washington in 1963.

The *Calgary Herald* reported that "aerial inspections of the site Monday showed only a portion of the Oldman, perhaps 25 percent, would flow into the new three-meter-deep channel... The rest of the river will continue to bypass the ditch unless the Peigans block its course with huge boulders, which have been stockpiled. Work on that part of the project is expected to take several days."

Milton told the press that the river "should be fully closed off within twenty-four hours." He added, "We are willing to die for our actions. But that doesn't mean we will promote the violence." Milton added that the Lonefighters had been told that about twenty army vehicles had been spotted in Fort Macleod. He concluded, "We'll sit back and wait, for the army or whatever process they use to come to us."

Many engineering experts doubted that the river would ever be diverted, even though some water was heading down the Lonefighters' trench. But the perception of impending success put pressure on everybody. The next morning, Alberta Environment engineer Dennis McGowan flew over the site. He watched the CAT working in the water beside a small dike, pushing gravel into the river. He estimated that the Lonefighters had closed off half the river and was worried. He told Doug Clark and others that he felt the Lonefighters "could possibly achieve the objective of blocking the river off." For the first time, an Alberta government engineer thought that the protesters might actually succeed.

The afternoon of August 29, Doug Clark flew over the site again and took photos. He knew that the only way the Lonefighters could divert the river would be to build an earth dike across it. So far, the "stuff they were putting in was just washing away as close to the channel the water moves with more force." He later said, "I concluded that the present method was unlikely to be successful."

After flying over the camp, Clark flew up to Edmonton, on orders from his bosses. He had been asked to provide the information necessary to his superiors and their lawyers so they could go to court to get an injunction to order the Lonefighters to stop working.

—————•—

Government lawyers and employees, including Peter Melnychuk, met to prepare an affidavit, which would be part of their application for an injunction, and to explain the situation to the judge. Alberta was concerned that if the breach was not repaired by spring, runoff and high water might force the river to flow down the Lonefighters' channel around the weir. The affidavit mentions McGowan's observations and worries. But Clark's opinion—the Lonefighters likely could not divert the river—is not in the affidavit. Doug Clark would not have been the one to decide what would go in his affidavit.

The government lawyers would be alone with the judge to get the injunction. The Lonefighters would not know about this court order until later. This procedure is legal, but there is an added onus on the lawyers and government to fully disclose the situation to the judge, since the other side does not have a chance to put forward their point of view until later. Alberta succeeded in getting its injunction, which would allow government engineers to fix the damage the Lonefighters had done. Police also served a statement of claim—the beginning of a lawsuit advanced by the Alberta government—saying that the government owned the Oldman River.

Attorney General Ken Rostad told the press: "Until [the Lonefighters began digging in the riverbed] they were on Peigan land. The riverbed is Crown-owned and digging in it breaches the Water Resources Act." He warned the protesters that they could "face contempt charges if they ignore the order." Rostad defended the government's decision to wait this long before intervening: "I think clearly that patience and reason usually end up resolving something peacefully and without violence." Don Lebarron told the press, "The laws of this country are going to be upheld, there shouldn't be two sets of law."

The day after Alberta received its court order, fifty Mounties drove out to the end of the LNID Weir, near the camp. A few police walked down to the camp. One of them was Raymond Gaultier, an RCMP corporal. Later, he would be appointed sergeant. He was one of the RCMP officers assigned to police the Piikani Reserve, and had done so for many years. Many of the Lonefighters knew and did not like Officer Gaultier because of past experiences they allege they had with him. Glen North Peigan would later tell *Windspeaker*, "We despise him." Reg Crowshoe, however, who was once an RCMP officer and did not like or respect some of his former colleagues, told me that he "could work with Sergeant Gaultier." That he was "okay."

Despite the animosity some Lonefighters felt for Gaultier, Devalon Small Legs made sure that everyone gathered to listen to the police and cooperate with them when they arrived. Officer Gaultier read the injunction out loud; then he tacked it up on one of the posts in the arbour.

Devalon turned to Gaultier and said, "This is a provincial court injunction. It has no power on the reserve. Only the federal government has jurisdiction here."

Devalon told the press, "They haven't stopped us. We're going to continue on with our actions. Construction will begin again as soon as possible." He added, "There was a court injunction against the people at the Oldman River Dam, and you don't see any of them in jail."

Milton was away from camp that day at an emergency meeting to discuss First Nations' issues, but the next day, after he returned, he said, "We started this without guns, but if it means we have to die to protect the situation, that's what we're going to do."

Chief Bastien urged the Lonefighters to avoid a violent confrontation. He said, "It is my hope that there is no bloodshed. I instructed them not to give up their lives. Hopefully, they will listen to me." He told the press that he would find out if band council would "support the Lonefighters in light of the injunction. The majority of the band elders had urged the group not to divert the river. But they decided they were going to do it regardless of the objections they might run into."

Through the press, Milton told the RCMP that they shouldn't try to enforce the injunction. He said, "If they come anywhere near this place, we're going to move them out. We're going to divert the river regardless of who says what we can do. When it comes to the last second, you are going to see how we are going to defend ourselves. Provincial threats of legal action are empty, because it has been twenty-six days since the diversion work started and the province hasn't acted. They say we're militant, more or less stupid Indians. There's a smear campaign. But they will have to come to us and negotiate."

Roy Jenson told the press that although "communities have been storing water," some would need to refill reservoirs up until October in order to get them through the winter. "We're hoping the government steps in. We're being held ransom here."

Environment Minister Ralph Klein told the press, "Had this occurred under any other circumstances, the environmentalists who are supporting this cause would have been screaming bloody murder."

For the first time, the story received national coverage in the *Globe and Mail*, whose reporter noted, "Initially officials and reporters took the threat seriously, but it soon became apparent that the inexperienced Indians were undertaking an engineering project that would test the mettle of the U.S. Army Corps of Engineers ...but the natives doggedly dug on, creating a deep channel and embankment almost ten meters high."

——— — ———

As September approached, a tense quiet came to camp, despite the growing numbers of people arriving almost daily. A dozen activists, representing Greenpeace and other environmental groups, had also moved into camp. The Lonefighters were preparing for an "invasion" of RCMP, as Devalon explained to me.

On September 10, *Alberta Report* painted a picture of the Lonefighters' camp, where one evening, while sitting by a roaring fire, Glen North Peigan laid out a strategy for when the police arrived. First, the environmentalists and human rights activists would be used. "We would put them first in line, like a human barrier," he said. "That would force the RCMP to pull them away and arrest them. That's what [the activists] like to do." After that, the police would come up against a second human chain consisting of women and children. "They too would insist on being forcibly removed." The final barrier would be about a dozen men, North Peigan continued. The final line of resistance, a dozen men, would be armed with "rifles and shotguns." He refused to tell anyone where the rifles were, nor would he "prove their existence." North Peigan said, "We don't have a lot. But we might be getting more from the United States. I think if we fired two or three shots, that would make them back off, like at the Native conflict in Oka, Quebec."

I wondered about the accuracy of this *Alberta Report* article and about the character of Glen North Peigan, who apparently said these things. Since Glen North Peigan did not speak to me,

I asked Devalon about it. Devalon did not deny that comments of that nature were made to the press. He told me that one had to understand their situation. They knew that they were surrounded. They knew—they had inside information—that the army or police would be moving in on the camp soon. Devalon told me they had one old hunting rifle at the camp. That was it. They had no other guns and were not getting any. Why, then, did Glen North Peigan say what he said? Devalon explained, "We were living with our situation every night. By saying what he did, Glen was hoping to set the night on fire."

August 30 was "bright and windy." Everyone "gathered around a big drum, singing and beating it with branches while the Peigan women raised the Peigan flag." The Lonefighters told the press they were ready for a confrontation. That morning, two men got into the backhoe and began working with it in the river valley. "The backhoe clawed at the earth in part of the ditch away from the riverbank for several minutes, then stopped." Milton told the press that they would resume working in the river, but he did not say when.

As the day progressed, Glen North Peigan became more and more "melancholy." He was expecting a raid from police. He continued "giving tours of the diversion for the press. He said, 'It's a beautiful morning, isn't it? And we're getting ready for doomsday. It might be the end of it for me, I guess. I just got a feeling there's a little bullet out there with my name on it.'" As the clock approached noon, "a rumour swept the camp that the RCMP would be arriving before 1:00 pm."

The tension that had been ebbing since morning began to build. The activists picked up placards and banners and went to the camp entrance to wait for police. As the wind blew hard over the land, over two dozen journalists waited with them. They were afraid to leave and miss the promised raid. More rumours of the Canadian military getting ready to move in swept the camp. Another rumour suggested that the RCMP was waiting for dark to attack.

By late in the evening, most of the journalists and many of the activists had left the front line, "abandoning the blockade to the wind and dust and grasshoppers... Except for the dogs, the distant coyotes and the comings and goings of sentries—camp was quiet." Lonefighter Raymond Crowshoe, Evelyn's son, told the press that the "security was not so much to protect against police but to protect against the rest of the Peigan band."

Unknown to the police, and much to the surprise of most of his fellow Lonefighters, Milton Born With A Tooth had left camp. Devalon told me that Milton was heading to New York, hoping to get an audience with the United Nations, and also, on the way back, to see the leaders of the Mohawk protest. Devalon explained to me that he did not know for sure where Milton went, but that's what Milton had told him he was doing. According to Martha's journal entry for the day, Milton had called her and asked her to fax the court injunction to someone, so she did. Martha didn't identify the person she faxed the injunction to.

On September 1, the *Calgary Herald* headline read: "Peigans Defy Injunction: Lonefighters Warn RCMP Not to Stop Diversion." Supporters poured into the Lonefighter camp. RCMP Superintendent Maguire told the press, "It is my belief we had another media event." Superintendent Maguire had flown over the site the day before. He was reported in the press on September 1 as saying that the Lonefighters were not trying to divert the river. They were only digging a few holes. "I have to see actual intent to divert the river before I can act."

Chief Bastien told the press that "the protesters should stop their diversion until they are certain their actions are legal" and that such work would increase "growing hostilities between the reserve and white businessmen." He continued: "The band council doesn't support the protest, at least at this time. A clear majority of residents don't support their actions, and if they're to continue we'd have nothing but a fiasco on our hands." He said he avoided voicing a personal opinion before because "everyone should have the right to protest… Time and time again they have said they have everything, legally or otherwise, under control. I am not so sure that's the case." Bastien told the protesters to park their equipment until they and the band got further legal advice. "I don't have any magic formula to end this dispute, but I certainly think the province would be well advised to respect Peigan wishes and halt dam construction until we can sort out all these problems."

On September 5, Doug Clark flew over the site. He saw evidence that the Lonefighters were working in the river. The same day, Martha Kostuch wrote in her journal that Milton had visited the Mohawks in eastern Canada, after a futile visit to the UN: "He is back in Calgary and planning to head back down to the reserve tonight. He was talking about the need to have good conflict resolution." On September 5, Milton told the press: "If the band council asks the army to intervene, the band council will become part of the enemy."

The next day, Doug Clark once again flew over the site and noticed that since the day before more work had been done. The Lonefighters were building up gravel in the riverbed. He concluded that the CAT had been in the river working since the injunction. He could see that water was continuing to go through the breach in the dike and had moved up the old channel, even though the level of the Oldman River had gone down. Since the injunction, Clark could see certain improvements and a deepening of the ditch. Water was now slowly flowing through the Lonefighters' ditch. He was concerned that while the majority of the river was still flowing down the existing river channel, over time there would be progressively more and more erosion in the Lonefighters' ditch, eventually to the point that a significant portion of the river would, in fact, go around the farmers' canal. He and others in his department told the RCMP that they thought the Lonefighters' breach should be fixed.

Superintendent Maguire was on vacation in British Columbia when he received the call from a representative of the Alberta Cabinet; he was told the Department of the Environment was going to fix the Lonefighters' breach, and the RCMP would be protecting them. As midnight approached, Raymond Gaultier and the RCMP Tactical Squad drove toward the Lonefighters' camp. Another group of sixty or so RCMP from all over southern Alberta was getting ready to move in.

The RCMP: Invasion?

Years later, during the two trials of Milton Born With A Tooth, RCMP Police Officer Raymond Gaultier and the other RCMP officers testified about what happened that day.

Just after midnight, on Saturday, September 7, 1990, while the men, women, and children in the camp slept, Gaultier led the RCMP version of a SWAT team onto the Piikani Reserve and set up a command post on a hill near the Lonefighters' camp. At a meeting earlier on September 6, at the Fort Macleod hockey arena, the RCMP Emergency Response Team (ERT) had explained its plan to go down to the area of the Lonefighters' camp and the breach to see if the Lonefighters were breaking the court injunction. The team was from Calgary and didn't know the area. Gaultier had policed the reserve for over eight years and knew the area well. He quickly realized that the proposed ERT route to the camp would be fairly difficult; he knew a better way. So, he became part of the team that went in that morning. The Lonefighters would not know until much later that Gaultier may have saved Milton's life that day.

Gaultier led the team of between seven and nine men on foot from the command post, down an old wagon trail, and into the river valley. They carried night-vision cameras and night scopes. They wore battle gear—green khaki uniforms, with camouflage pants—and had smeared dark grease on their faces. They walked as silently as possible through the cottonwood groves, carrying their semi-automatic rifles, approaching as close as possible to the

Lonefighters' camp and the site of the diversion attempt. The team stopped just south of the camp. For over an hour they listened for the sound of machinery working in the river but heard only the sound of their own breathing, and perhaps the wind in the trees. When they were satisfied that the Lonefighters were sleeping, they walked quietly back through the river valley, and then followed the old wagon road to their command post. They arrived back at the Fort Macleod hockey arena at around 7:15 a.m. It was packed with police vehicles.

Gaultier had not slept that night and had to have been very tired. As far as he was concerned, his shift was over. He was done. As he was getting ready to leave, however, Staff Sergeant Campbell told him that he was going on another mission that morning, back to the weir. Again, the RCMP had gathered officers from around southern Alberta. Nobody else knew the area as well as Gaultier did, so he had to go back. He got in his car and drove back toward the camp. Years later, at Milton's first trial, Gaultier testified, "I had very little knowledge of what was going on. I had knowledge that heavy equipment was coming to assess the damage. Then I saw heavy equipment arriving. I could only assume what was going to happen."

Gaultier entered the reserve, drove along a small dirt road for three miles, then down a small steep hill to the weir. He arrived at 8:20 a.m. Immediately, he saw Murray Small Legs and Celina Littlehorn run across the top of the weir across the footbridge, then west, onto the dike, toward the Lonefighters' camp. The rest of the police cars began to arrive. It was a big operation. The RCMP plan called for between thirty and thirty-five police officers—in six teams of five men each—to go out onto the dike to protect the people from the Department of the Environment, who were there to assess the damage and make repairs. Dozens of police officers arrived in squad cars. Some parked at the top of the hill overlooking the valley, but most came down to the weir. The police had also rented Jeeps for the operation that morning. They brought prisoner vans, which were guarded by six more police officers. Back in Fort Macleod, the Calgary Tactical Troop was on standby. Their standard equipment included batons, shields, visors, and helmets. The RCMP had also included female police officers in the operation; they were expecting passive resistance.

The police expected the Lonefighters to block them and the Department of the Environment workers using non-violent tactics. This behaviour would likely have led to dozens of arrests. When a person is arrested, police usually search him or her to find evidence of a crime or simply to ensure that the police are not at risk if someone has a weapon. The RCMP needed to have women officers at the site, ready to search any women who might be arrested during the operation.

When he testified at Milton's first trial, Superintendent Maguire said he was not expecting violence. On the other hand, other officers said they were expecting "trouble." The officers did not know precisely what to expect, but at least some of them would have been given an overview of the situation, and it was reasonable to expect that there was a real danger of violence in the unpredictable circumstances.

As the police arrived, heavy vehicles from the Department of the Environment began to show up, including a flatbed truck carrying one of Alberta's own D-7 CAT tractors and several other trucks from the Department of the Environment. Later that morning, the ERT, which had been heading back to Calgary, were recalled to the weir site. They came to the hill overlooking the weir and remained there, fully armed.

With everything now in place, the RCMP tried to seal off the area by closing all the roads nearby. Anyone who wanted to get down to the weir or the camp had to go through RCMP checkpoints placed at strategic locations on the reserve. An RCMP helicopter was also sent to the scene to provide air support to the operation.

There were more than seventy police officers outside camp that day. The cumulative roar of all those engines—the cars, vans, Jeeps, and big trucks—combined with the sporadic whine of the helicopter, must have sounded like an armoured division moving in, shattering the silence of the morning.

Nobody had told the Lonefighters that the police were coming that day.

———— • ————

Gaultier led the first team. He still wore the casual shirt and jeans he'd put on after his nighttime foray, when he thought he would be going home. The other RCMP officers wore standard dress, what they call their "long blues," khaki-coloured shirts, their Sam Brown gun belts and .38 Smith & Wesson revolvers. Gaultier had a gun, according to him, holstered by his side. He walked in front. Behind him were four RCMP officers and men from the Department of the Environment. He told the court at Milton's first trial, "We walked in a slow pace, there was no hurry." He explained that they were "marching" down the dike toward the breach and the camp. It took ten minutes.

He could not see the breach until he was fairly close because the dike meanders through the bush. As they walked, a helicopter roared overhead and made the first of several passes over the area. Once they reached the dike, Gaultier and the others walked on top of it toward the Lonefighters' camp. Halfway to the breach, in the dike made by the Piikani, they heard a bulldozer engine start, somewhere in front of them, on the Piikani side. Moments later, they heard the uneven roar of a bulldozer that had water in its fuel lines (from all this time in the river valley), as it broke its way through the bush toward the breach that they were approaching. Gaultier and the others kept marching. Several Native people gathered across the breach from them, on the other side of the dike. Some beat on drums and others gathered behind them. Gaultier recognized Milton Born With A Tooth, Devalon Small Legs, and others.

The breach in the dike was forty feet wide, twenty feet deep, and was edged by high banks of sand, dirt, and rocks that had been dug out of the river valley and pushed up by the bulldozer. Water ran along the bottom of the dike, four feet deep. Trees lay this way and that nearby, having been pushed over or run over by the bulldozer.

Gaultier's group included Doug Clark from Alberta's Department of the Environment. They walked up to the edge of the dike then waited for the other groups to catch up. Gaultier saw Devalon Small Legs, and other Lonefighters. They began to yell at Gaultier.

"You're on Indian land."

"You're trespassing."

"Get off our land."

Chris Buffalo beat on a tom-tom. The Lonefighters kept yelling. The moment was ripe with possibility. Gaultier turned back toward Clark and said, "This is going to get a little dicey; do you want to go any further?"

Clark nodded, "Yes."

Gaultier began walking along the side of the dike, on a pile of gravel and dirt pushed up by the bulldozer. After he had gone fifteen feet, one of the Lonefighters said, "We're armed."

Gaultier didn't pay attention. He kept walking. When he had moved another twenty or thirty feet, rocks started to land around him, so he ducked behind part of the dike. "They were baseball-sized rocks, rocks that could cave a man's head in," he told the court at Milton's first trial. As he tried to decide what to do, he heard the muffled sound of a gunshot, as if it had been fired into sand or water or dirt. He didn't know who fired the shot. Then he heard another officer yell, "He's got a gun!"

———————

Milton's version of events, as he told them at his second trial, begins with: "The inevitable woke me up." Milton was groggy, half-awake. He didn't know what was going on. Then he understood that the army was coming—an army of police. A cold feeling came over him; the worst thing that could happen was happening. He felt betrayed. They had been told that the police would give them notice before coming to the camp, and here they were, coming out of the early morning. Milton later said in those first moments, "We were like chickens running with heads chopped off—running around, trying to get ourselves together."

Milton remembered that Devalon said, "Stop!" firmly to everyone. "Every morning we do the pipe ceremony—and we haven't done that yet today." So everybody stopped running, calmed down, and Devalon performed the ceremony in the arbour, quickly because he didn't know how much time they had. The helicopter kept making passes overhead.

The ceremony calmed everyone. That calm would not last long. Devalon turned to Jeff, an environmental activist and helper to the Piikani. Devalon said, "Go look, find out where they are." Jeff sped away on his bike.

Next, Devalon turned to Gord Kelman: "Go get the CAT moving."

Almost immediately Jeff returned on his bike, pedalling furiously. He screamed, "They're all marching up the road. There's bunches of them. You know, coming up. They are real close. They're almost here!"

———•—•———

Evelyn told me that she woke up that morning to the frantic screams of Devalon's brother, Murray Small Legs, who ran into camp yelling, "I saw sixteen cop cars. The police are coming—they have guns, they have guns. There are sixteen cop cars, and about a hundred policemen, up there at the substation. There are trailers, and all kinds of armor, they got the army."

Another group of people ran in from the north. They said, "There's a bunch of cops with battle gear, and ambulances." Panicked, everyone got out of their tents or tipis. From inside their tents they had heard the loud whine of a helicopter circling over camp. Evelyn was sleeping in a tent with Lorna Born With A Tooth and her two young girls. They jumped up and clambered out.

———•—•———

Devalon told me that he saw his brother waving and yelling and screaming and running. He looked at him and thought, "What in the world is going on? We were scrambly. We thought, 'What do we do?' Somebody said, 'How about we go and see them?'" Devalon thought, "The invasion has come." He told everyone to go and meet the RCMP at the breach.

———•—•———

For a moment, Milton and Devalon were alone. Milton told the court at his second trial that he felt that if the government was going to come and get them this way they should have done it before. He felt it was his responsibility to take the "initial brunt of whatever was going to happen." The helicopter was roaring overhead again. He looked quickly at Devalon and said, "We're not going to let them disrespect us in that manner. I'm not going to let them do this—plus it's our territory here; you know, they're the ones trespassing. I am going to defend this land."

Milton remembered that Devalon said, "Well, I'm going to go ahead. The decision is with you." Devalon turned and followed the others, who moved in single-file down a narrow path toward the breach and the police. Milton stood alone. The helicopter roared overhead again. He tried to think about what to do. He had only a few seconds, but the time seemed endless. The hunting rifle was there beside him. So he picked it up. It was a matter of making the stand. Milton felt that the police had to realize that the Lonefighters meant what they had talked about. It had to be understood. Over and over in Milton's head circled the words: "It wasn't right. The way it was happening that morning, it wasn't right. That shouldn't be the way it should end."

Milton waited until the helicopter flew away. At that moment, Gord Kelman drove by with the CAT, heading toward the breach. When Gord drove by, Milton went in behind the bulldozer, so the helicopter couldn't see him.

———— •— ————

Evelyn told me that her first thought that morning—having being brought up in her culture and knowing the way her grandmother used to do things—was to go to the river. She heard her grandmother saying to her: "The river is alive. You have to respect it." Evelyn always kept tobacco and sweetgrass with her when she slept, so she rushed back into her tent, got it, and walked toward the river along a little trail that followed the diversion. Evelyn went to the top of a bank overlooking the Oldman River. She stopped and threw her tobacco in the river. The helicopter came over and flew just above her head, with the choppy whine of its engines in her ears. Her long hair flew skyward. Calmly, Evelyn looked at the whirling machine above her. She could not see men, just the machine. Evelyn looked back to the river and began to pray.

"Help me, I am in need. I need strength and courage, your help, your energy, I need you to give me that strength, that help—this is what I want from you. And here, I am giving you this tobacco," she said as she threw more tobacco into the river. Afterward, she felt better, calmer. She felt something come to her. As she later said, "If you put good energy out, it comes back in a good way."

Just as she started back to the path, her son, Gord, was driving past with the CAT toward where they had diverted the river. Milton was right behind him. Evelyn crossed paths with Milton. He was carrying a hunting rifle. She turned to him and said, "I hope you are not going to use that."

"I won't. I will just shoot up in the air," he said.

Evelyn went back inside the arbour. Other Piikani—friends and former foes—came from across the weir to their side in support. The kids, who were in the arbour with Evelyn and the others, began to cry. Evelyn and the others told the children, "They are not going to hurt us." She was scared but felt that she had to be strong for the others. She did not want to let her emotions take over, even as she wondered about what might happen. A lot of people were scared. They came to Evelyn, and she helped them. Evelyn and the other women and children decided to pray. Louise English prayed in the Roman Catholic way—and that was accepted. She prayed using a rosary, the others prayed by smudging.

When Evelyn went to get coffee, she heard a shot. From where she was in the arbour, she could not see what was happening. She and her group did not go outside at that time—they were scared, really scared.

———— • ————

Years later, Devalon told me he did not know that Milton had a gun in his hands until he heard the first shot go off. Before that, he and the others had gone down the path, until they reached the breach in the dike. Many people crowded on the other side. Devalon warned them that they were trespassing, that they should get off the reserve. Then he saw a Department of the Environment person nod to Ray Gaultier, and they started moving again toward the Lonefighters. They had their guns drawn. To try to stop them, Devalon told everyone to pick up rocks and throw them, and they did. Then, Devalon heard and felt a gunshot come from behind him, to the right; it was nearly right in his ear, or so it seemed to him. He thought, "Oh, shit, Jesus Christ, what the hell?" He later said, "But, you know, you can't have a split decision inside a group. You have to follow the leader. Even if that takes you in a totally different direction. You have to keep pointing in the right direction. And everybody considered Milton to be the leader."

After Milton fired his shot, the helicopter ducked away. According to Devalon, the noise from the CAT was horrendous. The bulldozer was making "peculiar noises." It was backfiring because, after all, it wasn't in the best running condition. One could hear the CAT from miles away. "Close by, you couldn't even hear yourself."

Milton fired a second shot.

Then Devalon thought he heard a third shot, but to this day he is not sure about that. He thought one of the police fired, but he couldn't be sure. The police were in the water already, with their guns drawn. Devalon saw Officer Gaultier in the front.

———— • ————

At his second trial, Milton told the court why he fired two shots that day. When he arrived at the breach, his heart was just about jumping out of his body. He saw the RCMP moving to the left and thought, "Oh, no, they're going to get us, right now." He thought he could fire a warning shot. After all, it was Piikani property.

So he fired. The RCMP froze. Seconds later, Milton shot again. He had been kneeling. After the second shot, he stood up and saw that they were all running. He thought, "Wow, they're running." When he saw them running, he felt good.

He waited. That's when he remembered the rock-throwing starting. He went over to the bulldozer and climbed on top of it. He knew what he had done. He was afraid they would shoot back at somebody else. He thought, "If this is the day to die, better me than somebody else." So he climbed on top to give them a chance to do it. He stood on top of the bulldozer and waited. After a while he began to feel really good, because they didn't shoot. He wanted to let the RCMP know who had fired the shots over their heads.

Milton stayed on the bulldozer long enough to know that the RCMP weren't going to shoot him. Then he climbed down and put the gun behind the bulldozer. A few moments later, the Lonefighters decided to use the bulldozer to build a fort. Milton jumped off the bulldozer as it started backing up. He noticed, too late, that the bulldozer had flattened the gun, embedded in the ground. The Lonefighters were surrounded by police and helicopters and what seemed to be the army, and the only gun they had was run over.

Leander Strikes With A Gun arrived at this point. Milton

remembered asking him, "Where is the chief?"

"Don't worry, we'll see who's responsible for this," Strikes With A Gun said.

Milton told him, "You guys told us there was a [notice] thing that was supposed to happen. It didn't." Then Milton ran over to a truck and used its cellular phone to call CBC Radio. They had given him a number and said if anything happened to call them. So he did.

Milton and some others looked at the gun and decided they couldn't do much about it. Milton explained, "It was embedded pretty good." He waited until nobody was looking before putting it beside a tree. Later, it disappeared.

Officer Gaultier testified at court that he (like Devalon) had heard three shots fired that day. When he heard that somebody had [fired] a gun, he knew he would be a target—though he did not say why. Exposing himself would be foolish, so he stayed low, out of sight. He could not see what was happening in front of him. He watched the other RCMP and the Environment people run away, back along the dike. Constable McKenna was higher than he was. He was looking over the top, with his handgun drawn. Everything was happening so fast.

McKenna yelled to him, "Stay down, here comes another one."

A second shot rang out. The RCMP screamed to each other to take cover. Directly behind them was a large pool of water. Gaultier knew they were in a good position not to be shot where they were, "but rocks were still coming in." They had to make a move to get around the pool of water and back to the cottonwood trees. He later said he did not have his handgun drawn, despite the two shots.

Gaultier looked over at Constable McKenna, who was looking

over the top of the dike. His gun was drawn and pointed toward the Lonefighters.

"I can take him."

"No, don't shoot," Gaultier said.

Gaultier decided to run. He started to his right, hunched down, crouching as low as he could, trying to make it around the pool of water. As he climbed up the dike, he realized that he might be exposing himself to the Lonefighters, because he was gaining altitude. Then he heard Constable Whittington yell from somewhere behind him, "Look out, Ray!"

At Milton's first trial, Gaultier explained what happened next. "As a result of Constable Whittington yelling at me, I looked over my right shoulder as I'm running in a crouched position, and I remember Milton Born With A Tooth with a .303 British Lee-Enfield rifle with the rifle shouldered, and he was aiming down the barrel, and that barrel was pointed directly at my back. His hands were in the proper position to fire. I know those rifles; I hunted with them when I was a kid on the farm. It crossed my mind that I'd had it. The distance was not all that great. He had a good bead on me. I felt I was a goner. However, I rolled into the bush. Within seconds, within milliseconds of that time of myself rolling into the bush, I heard the rifle go off. And I didn't hear the bullet whiz past me. I didn't hear it hit anything behind me. I don't know where the bullet went. (This would have been the third shot, according to Gaultier.) I had passed the pond by this point, so I crawled into a lower spot, into the bush, and got cover behind a cottonwood tree. At that time I drew my service revolver."

After running to take a position farther back, while behind a cottonwood tree, Gaultier radioed his superiors. He asked that some rifles and shotguns "be brought up the line as our firepower isn't adequate if we were to face this much further." He also requested that the helicopter take a look at what was going on. Later, two rifles with power scopes and three shotguns arrived, and Gaultier passed them out. He stayed behind the cottonwood tree for half an hour, then he climbed on top of the dike and found cover behind another tree. During this time, as he later explained in court, Gaultier exposed himself to a clear shot by the Lonefighters on purpose—three times. "I would walk from behind the trees and stand on the middle of the dike with my arms crossed... On three occasions Milton lifted the rifle over the top of the gravel pile and aimed it in our direction or in my direction." At 12:30 p.m. that day, Gaultier was relieved and sent off duty. Finally, he could sleep.

After Milton fired his two shots and the RCMP retreated, each side tried to strengthen its position. The Lonefighters used their CAT to build bunkers to protect themselves. Despite the roadblocks that police had set up, people came to the camp walking, any way they could—supporters from nearby Lethbridge, the press, and the Piikani themselves. While many Piikani did not support the Lonefighters, when their own people were in trouble, with police and what seemed to be the army on the reserve—they showed their support for the camp.

The Lonefighters were thrilled when the RCMP decided that the Department of the Environment workers had to move their heavy equipment away. The dike would not be repaired that day.

According to newspaper reports, the Lonefighters told the police that if the helicopter did not leave the area, they would shoot it down. At the same time, the media reported that "no weapons were visible" during the day on the Lonefighters' side. There was no evidence of Milton pointing a gun at anyone after the press arrived. High up, overlooking the Lonefighters' camp, the police "set up an observation post, where they controlled the weir area." As the morning wore on, dozens of RCMP dug into the ground to protect themselves in the trees near the camp. The Lonefighters dug a bunker for a dozen or so Lonefighters.

Piikani leaders negotiated with police for many hours that Friday, September 7. The RCMP wanted Milton to turn himself in for discharging a firearm. If he was turned in, the RCMP promised to leave. The press reported that a negotiated settlement was nearly reached between Glen North Peigan and the police, but the Lonefighters "remained defiant." Negotiations ended after several hours. According to one source, there was a "twenty-four-hour truce." According to another, both parties were "close" to such a truce. One of the Lonefighters' demands was that Gaultier not be in "full view" of the Lonefighters. Was this why Gaultier was relieved from duty that midday?

A photo of Milton from that morning shows him wearing jeans, cowboy boots, and no shirt, his hair tied back. Late in the day, Milton told the press, "We've given them till sundown—this is our territory and we know it very well—we're moving in on them."

Superintendent Maguire, on the other side of the weir, refused to comment on the ultimatum. He said, "Once again, I am dealing with the chief and council, not Milton Born With A Tooth."

Milton spoke to the press often during the day. "Born With A Tooth called negotiations between RCMP and Chief Leonard Bastien useless because the Lonefighters no longer consider him their chief. He said they have already told Bastien he is not welcome here and they have replaced him with another." As well, Milton proudly showed the media a fax from the Mohawks in Quebec. It read, "You know in your heads and minds that you are right. Don't ever surrender. The Lonefighters Society of the Peigan Nation has given us strength in our struggle." With visible anger, Milton "condemned" the RCMP "invasion" of the Piikani land.

On the other side of the weir, Superintendent Maguire told the press that "there were reports of three gunshots, one fairly close to an officer."

On the contrary, Milton explained, that "no one was in any danger." He continued, "I have been a hunter all my life. I know what a warning shot is. I can guarantee the next will be dead centre." Milton added that "the public should judge the Lonefighters not by Friday's actions, but by our peaceful actions throughout the first thirty-one days of protest. If violence should erupt, we're ready. All I can say is that today is a good day to die. There's no way they're going to come in and do this. I am going to leave here free or dead."

The Lonefighters' lawyer Drew Galbraith came to the scene to consult with his clients. He told the press his opinion: "'The provincial government and the Court of Queen's Bench have no jurisdiction over Indian land.' He also questioned whether an earlier court order forbidding further diversion attempts had been breached." He said that he intended to challenge the provincial jurisdiction in court and was in contact with a judge on "an emergency basis."

Reporters were hard at work all day on September 7, gleaning quotes from everyone involved, from the Lonefighters and RCMP at the standoff, to the politicians in the provincial capital, as well as in Ottawa. The Lonefighters wanted as many media representatives present as possible, so they could report what had happened to the outside world.

One newspaper reporter told Evelyn that he had seen four ambulances. He also said that the army (with machine guns) was over at Head-Smashed-In Buffalo Jump. He asked, "Are you afraid?"

"No, it is one of those things to put scare in us."

"I am glad you feel this way," he said.

At a news conference in Edmonton, Attorney General Ken Rostad told the press, "The Lonefighters are breaking the law, and will have to suffer the consequences."

Tensions remained high at the Lonefighters' camp. Both sides had dug in, literally and metaphorically. More and more people came onto the weir site and joined the Lonefighters. They came on foot or on horseback, skirting the blocked roads. Evelyn and the women cooked food for everyone. Later that day, somebody brought a bunch of pork chops. It was like having a party.

The police wanted one man: Milton. And the Lonefighters refused to give him up. One reporter at the scene, Garry Allison of the *Lethbridge Herald*, suggested that Milton was so dedicated to the cause that "negotiation is lost on him," whereas "[Devalon] Small Legs and [Glen] North Peigan don't seem as pumped with adrenalin or blind to negotiation as their partner." When we spoke about the negotiations, Evelyn said, "In the old days being a warrior was dangerous stuff. They painted their whole body with red ochre paint. Milton did this. Then he put on his ribboned shirt... There was an old log cabin—he said he would sleep there. He said to us, 'If they come in, without any warning, so there will not be any commotion—that is where I will be. Just tell them.' But we never told anybody."

Day turned to dusk, then to night. The stalemate continued. Late Friday evening tensions were high. Medicine Man and Elder Romeo Yellowhorn came to the Lonefighters' camp with his medicine bundle and pipe. He gathered the Lonefighters into a circle. Then they prayed. The "possibility of death . . . lingered in the air." Devalon, Romeo Yellowhorn, and his wife, Margaret, tried to alleviate the tension. One witness there that night later wrote, "They prayed the crisis would end peacefully and they even prayed for the 'men with guns' out in the darkness, who had wives and small children who were worried about their well-being."

That Friday night few people slept. Overnight, peace groups and people bringing food snuck into camp. The RCMP helicopter was in the air, and the sound of whirring blades echoed across the valley.

The Peacemaker: Joe Crowshoe

When the sun rose on Saturday morning, lighting the valley and the Lonefighters' camp, it became clear that hundreds of people had come to camp during the night. Early that morning, Evelyn returned to the river, threw tobacco in, and prayed in the Blackfoot way.

Most journalists could not get all the way to the Lonefighters' camp by road. Joanne Helmer and another reporter, who was doing a freelance piece for the *Globe and Mail*, tried to get to the camp that day. Joanne later told me the story. They were stopped by police at a roadblock on a reserve road not far from the site. The police wanted to see inside the car trunk. As one officer searched the trunk of the car, another officer came to the window and said, "So, you girls coming to see the boys, eh?"

When Joanne and the other reporter got to the camp, it was very tense. They weren't allowed to be in the camp. The media were all directed up onto the bluff overlooking the site in the valley. One could see people moving in camp with dozens and dozens of RCMP surrounding them, and the helicopter making passes overhead. Of the experience, Joanne later told me, "It was an overwhelming feeling."

Saturday afternoon, Joe Crowshoe was at his home with his wife, Josephine. The wind blew hard over the prairie. Inside the house, the atmosphere was "tense, and quiet." Eighty-year-old Joe smoked cigarette after cigarette. In the afternoon, at about 4:00 p.m., the phone rang. It was Evelyn. Joe wanted to know about everything that was going on. They spoke for a while, and then Evelyn put her son, Gord, on the telephone.

"Grandpa, I want you to come down, I am really scared. I want to talk to you. I want to see you."

Joe put the phone down. He and Josephine sat at their wooden kitchen table. Again they debated whether or not Joe should go to the camp. They had learned by radio that Milton had fired shots into the air as police had advanced. Joe was angry. Josephine said, "If we go to camp it might help stop the violence. What about the women and children? Evelyn?"

Joe "rubbed his furrowed forehead." He "hunched over" the table. Finally, he blurted out, whether to himself or Josephine, it was impossible to say, "It's bad. I don't want to be involved with violence. I told them I would come if they would take away all the guns, but they haven't. They didn't listen to the Chief, they won't listen to me."

Josephine refused to give up. She said that Milton might listen to them. They had to try. They spoke back and forth for a time, and then the room went silent. Finally, Joe turned to his wife and spoke quietly in Blackfoot. She nodded. Then she put on her shoes. Joe left to change his clothes for the visit. He came back wearing a white western shirt and cowboy hat. Later, Josephine said, "We decided we might as well try. Then, if something happens, at least we know we tried to help Milton."

They drove down to the camp. When they arrived, everyone ran toward their truck, thrilled to see them. Joe got out and everybody came up to him, kissing him, hugging him. Somebody said, "How did you get through the road block?"

"They stopped me and searched the car. They asked if I had any guns. I said no, I only have my pipe," he said. Everybody shook his hand, and then, slowly, he walked over to the arbour, as nearly one hundred police looked on. Joe sat inside the arbour, and the Lonefighters and others made a deepening circle around him. Milton emerged from hiding and joined the group.

Joe Crowshoe sat before an open fire, under cottonwood branches. The Piikani flag few above him as he led a prayer in the Blackfoot language. Then, he spoke, "We know how the white man has treated us. He has not been fair to us. We all know that. This river we have known for thousands of years. This river has been our lifeline. For what is happening here now we all have to think about what we believe. Go the peaceful way. Work from your treaties, then you can bring about what you want. But do not practice violence. Do it in a good way. They may try to push you to violence, but do not do it the way they want—that is when they have got you. What we are doing now is excellent. The time has come to get back to the responsibility and human rights we lost when the treaties were signed, rights which were guaranteed by those treaties. We have to work together with one voice, support each other in a friendly and powerful way, and educate other people."

According to an article by witness Dianne Meili, "The Lonefighters listened politely to his words, but it is obvious they are not about to heed the restraining advice. One by one, they deliver their own speeches about bravery and a willingness to die for Napi's river, the Old Man's River... Joe maintains his stance against violence and asks the Lonefighters to go slow, attempting to calm their excited bursts of bravado."

Evelyn recalls the moment differently. She explained, "Everybody was really peaceful after that. We gave them some tea. We were cooking a big supper, for everybody. He and my mom stayed for the meal. Everybody felt really good about what was happening." The *Lethbridge Herald* report about the speech concurred with Evelyn's version of events and didn't mention any aggressive response to Joe's speech.

After supper, Joe and Josephine Crowshoe went home. Dianne Meili later wrote about that day. Josephine told her, "Great Spirit gives him the strength to stand up for non-violence and he isn't offended if his pacifist's approach is considered wishy-washy." Meili also wrote that both he and Josephine had "taken a passive stance in their opposition to the dam, believing the situation is in the hands of the Creator and the structure will come crashing down of its own accord if it is not supposed to be there."

———————

Reg Crowshoe told me that when Joe came back from the Lonefighter camp, he was angry. When Reg came by the house, he turned to Reg, and said, "You should be down there in camp. You speak the language. They should be listening to you. What are our bundles all about? What are our traditional ways all about? You should be helping to run that place; then they wouldn't be in trouble."

Joe and Reg did not discuss the matter further. Reg knew that if the Lonefighters wouldn't listen to Joe, why would they listen to him? Reg later said, "When my dad spoke about non-violence that was really him saying, 'Let's use our traditional legal terms in talking about the treaty.' Those old-timers are still thinking a hundred years ahead." According to Reg, some Piikani have lost their traditional wisdom in relation to the treaties, and the Canadian government. In thinking about the treaties, the old-timers are actually thinking ahead of everyone else, in a direction the First Nations people must go. For them, paradoxically, keeping the historic treaties fresh in their minds, as their own sacred documents of foundational rights, the old-timers are not stuck in the past but rather are thinking "ahead" of those who have forgotten about them.

———◆———

On Saturday afternoon, the Lonefighters learned that a judge of the Court of Queen's Bench in Calgary had told everyone to maintain the status quo. The police were not to move in; and the Lonefighters were to do nothing to escalate the crisis. During a special court hearing that Saturday morning, Justice William Egbert made an impassioned plea for "cooler heads to prevail" after he heard Drew Galbraith's request to lift the injunction and allow the Lonefighters to continue working. Justice Egbert said, "I ask all parties to act in a calm and dispassionate manner. The status quo has to be maintained. If there are any breaches on either side of this volatile and dangerous dispute, the Court will deal with them very seriously."

As the afternoon progressed, it became apparent that the police were pulling out. Milton Born With A Tooth repeatedly told the press that he "will defy" the judge's order and continue to "heal" the Oldman River. Milton said, "We are continuing. No court, no policeman, no provincial government is going to stop us." Milton continued, "Today peace showed. The RCMP is gone and the province is left to justify coming in here to our homeland. We want to live in peace and we've got to stand up for truth. The law enforcement people have no right to be here... Those warning shots—anybody

234

in the province has the right to make them—maybe even in Roy Jenson's backyard."

To the Lonefighters, it seemed like a great victory. The RCMP began to pull out. Eventually the RCMP left, taking their weapons, cars, trucks, and helicopter. The valley was left quiet, except for the excited voices of the Lonefighters and their supporters. One witness said, "In the Lonefighters camp there was nothing but joy. The tension was gone and everybody was hugging and sobbing."

Devalon said, "It's a blessing in disguise. I do believe that the tide has turned and the truth has prevailed. The real criminals have left and this will never happen again on Peigan soil." He did not want to comment on whether the RCMP will return. "Who cares? They're gone. For us, it's a victory. Let's celebrate it." That night the Lonefighters "celebrated with a circle dance. The drumbeat reverberated through the Oldman River valley."

When the police left, Elder Romeo Yellowhorn told the press: "It was tense this morning. I prayed slowly and asked spiritual helpers to get everyone in a circle. Now the tension has broken. People were sobbing everywhere. I knew they would succeed, but I never said anything because of the tension. The sobbing became a cry of joy. It's a joyful feeling to see the women and children, everyone, so happy. Maybe now there will be a peaceful solution ...maybe now."

The action by the RCMP swung reserve support toward the Lonefighters. On Monday, September 10, chief and council announced that they supported the Lonefighters' "lawful efforts to stop the Oldman Dam until a further and proper study has been done on the effects the dam will have on the Peigan band, its people, culture, lands and religions." Chief Bastien added that the band did "not support violence or aggression, nor do they support the breaking of any laws of the Peigan band, the Federal Court or the Provincial Court."

On Tuesday, September 11, a few journalists visited the Lonefighters' site. Craig Albrecht of the *Lethbridge Herald* wrote eloquently of the change in the camp. The sound of "the grinding track" and the "groaning diesel engine" was gone. "Where the thunder of the low-flying helicopter and rhythmic pounding of native drums echoed down the river valley during the weekend, only the shrill song of the grasshoppers broke the eerie silence. Gone too are the many conservationists, other supporters and media members who swarmed the site over the weekend." He added that only a half-dozen Lonefighters were in camp, and they "declined all but the shortest questions."

While the camp may have been silent, on September 12 the "pounding of drums and the haunting sound of Native singing" echoed outside the Court of Queen's Bench in Calgary. According to one reporter from the *Edmonton Journal*, the lawyers for Alberta and the Lonefighters "clashed" inside the court. The two sides did clash, but this time with carefully considered words and arguments. They tried to come to a solution based on principles, rather than as a result of violence. At the end of the hearing, Justice Egbert concluded, "If the people receiving water from the Oldman River are deprived of this water, there is no doubt they would suffer irreparable damage and harm." He did not decide that the water belonged to the farmers, rather, that the diversion would cause harm to the farmers that could not be fixed later—by taking away their water, now, before any final decision had been made on their—and the Piikani's—rights to the river.

At midnight on the same date, at the request of its owner, the D-9 CAT the Lonefighters had been using since the beginning of their protest was seized from the reserve. The Lonefighters had rented that particular CAT, legally, from the owner, but the owner was concerned because the Lonefighters owed him $27,000 in rent. They had not returned the CAT when they were supposed to, and the owner had become "concerned about money owed on the rental."

Milton knew the police were looking for him at this point, but he travelled to Calgary anyway for a meeting of the Alberta Wilderness Association. During the meeting, Milton wanted to smoke so badly that he ducked out to get a package of tobacco. While making his purchase, he was arrested.

PART FOUR

Cry for Justice

Southern Trial

On September 13, 1990, Milton Born With A Tooth was arrested by police in Calgary. The next day, he went to the provincial court in Lethbridge for a bail hearing, at which the judge decided whether or not he would be allowed out of jail while waiting for his trial. Judge Martin Hoyt was presiding in bail court on September 14. Years later, at a party, Judge Hoyt told Joanne Helmer what happened that day, and she later wrote an article about these events in the *Lethbridge Herald*.

Martin Hoyt was born in New York City and later moved to southern Alberta. Before he became a lawyer, Judge Hoyt had taught literature in high schools around southern Alberta. He was, and was known as, a liberal, a civil libertarian who listened to Native people, and later, a judge who decided high-profile cases in Native peoples' favour. Joanne explained, "Given his political views, even he was surprised he was appointed by the Conservative government. He had the respect of his colleagues."

Moments before Milton's bail hearing began that morning, Judge Arthur Wood came to see Judge Hoyt and said, "Do you mind if I take the courtroom today?"

"Are you seized with Milton Born With A Tooth's case?" Judge Hoyt asked. (To be "seized" means that a judge had already begun hearing a case and would keep it to finish.) He didn't know if anything had already happened in Milton's case that required Judge Wood to keep it.

"No," Judge Wood said, he wasn't seized with it. He didn't say why he was taking the case. "Judge Wood was assistant chief judge and was in charge of scheduling. Judges are routinely moved last-minute for reasons of expediency."

In Joanne's article, she quoted Judge Hoyt: "He just arbitrarily reassigned me. It was upsetting at the time because of the implication that I might be prejudiced. I felt I could be as impartial as anyone else at a bail hearing. I wondered if he had received instructions. Why else would he do that?"

The article continued: "[H]igh-level sources later said the Chief Judge for Alberta would not have ordered a switch in judges that day." Such sources can only speak freely on the condition of anonymity. One source told Joanne, "I suspect because of the sensitivity of the case there was a feeling a senior judge should take over. Wood was the senior judge in terms of rank but not longevity. Hoyt was one of the finest judges in the province. He was not motivated by the events of the day but by a sense of fairness. Maybe it was thought his view of the case would be different from others."

On April 24, 2007, I spoke to Barbara Hoyt, Martin Hoyt's wife, hoping to discuss these matters with her husband. She told me that her husband would have loved to have spoken to me about these issues, but he had died not long before. Barbara Hoyt told me that Judge Wood and her husband had very different views of the world and were not close.

Judge Wood took over the court that day, and he presided over the bail hearing for Milton Born With A Tooth. The Crown prosecutor alleged that Milton had pointed a rifle at police. Milton's lawyer, Drew Galbraith, claimed that Milton had simply fired a warning shot in the air. The Crown prosecutor stressed that "Born With A Tooth's criminal record indicates he could be a threat." He said that Milton "was found guilty in Colorado of criminal negligence causing death to his infant child in 1989, for which he was sentenced to two years in jail."

Milton had been extradited from Canada to Colorado for that trial, as the crime was alleged to have taken place there. After his sentence, he came back from the United States and met with Friends of Oldman River in Calgary. His guilt was not at all as clear as it seemed at the bail hearing.

The prosecutor also noted that Milton had an assault conviction when he was seventeen. Judge Wood decided that Milton Born With A Tooth must stay in jail until his trial. Because Milton had publicly vowed to halt construction of the dam, his detention was "in the public interest."

Milton appealed the decision to the Court of Queen's Bench. A few days later, Justice Yanosik decided Milton had to remain in jail. Justice Yanosik said, "Suggestions have been made that Born With A Tooth has experienced a change in attitude and that he now realizes he is subject to provincial laws. Facts indicate he does not accept the authority of council or the law."

Drew Galbraith was shocked. "There's no hope now," he said about the possibility of bail. At a town hall meeting at the University of Lethbridge on October 5, 1990, Glen North Peigan told the audience, "Justice and law never walk hand in hand, at least that is the Native experience in southern Alberta." By mid-October, Milton had passed his first month in jail.

The Lonefighters held a press conference naming Evelyn Kelman their new leader. Lonefighter John Holloway told the press: "The fact Milton will be in trial brings out the truth, brings out the injustice we are facing." He called Evelyn "the heart of our movement." He added, "The corporate world hiding behind political leaders has tipped justice in its favour. How else can you explain the use of the civil law against the Peigan when we have never been included in anything that happens off the reserve? Is it not logical to perceive the existence of a hidden agenda behind the Three-River Valley Dam?"

Holloway said, "The apparent division among our people is evidence of the genocidal process of exploitation. The brief violence we were pushed to is evidence of that exploitation. The people who fear, hate and distrust are a burden we must carry in our struggle for self-respect and honour. We are in the process of building a people movement based on non-violence and love your enemy. We are still willing to die for the truth, just as Jesus Christ did, but we are not willing to kill for the truth. The relationship between politics and corporations will kill the spirit of humanity and leave a legacy of loneliness and bitterness..."

Meanwhile, Lorna Born With A Tooth and others protested Milton's detention outside the Lethbridge Correctional Centre (LCC). The small group carried signs saying, "Milton Deserves Justice" and "Free Milton." Lorna told the media, "He's not feeling good. He needs encouragement." Employees near a reception desk inside the LCC closed the curtains so they did not have to watch the protesters.

On November 17, as Milton neared his two-month mark in jail, he was denied bail for a third time. A few days later, Marie Laing, a New Democratic Party MLA and spokesperson for human rights for the NDP, called for Milton's release. She said Milton was "being held as a political prisoner" and had been held in jail "far too long." She continued, "We don't have to go beyond Alberta to find that basic human rights and dignity are denied within our own judicial system... Bail is a constitutional right of all Canadians and only in extreme cases, such as when the accused has a history of failing to appear in court or is considered a serious threat to the public, is it denied." She said courts had been vague in denying bail and that Milton had never failed to attend court.

Just over a month later, on December 19, Milton had another bail hearing at the Court of Queen's Bench before Justice Laurie MacLean. MacLean was the lawyer who had represented the LNID in the conflict with the Piikani during the 1978 blockade. Since then, he had been appointed to the Court of Queen's Bench. By this time, Milton had employed a new lawyer for his case, Karen Gainer. Milton approached Gainer as she had developed a high profile protecting the rights of First Nations peoples in Alberta. That day, Milton was finally released from jail. Despite three decisions in three different bail hearings to keep him in jail, in a "surprise decision," Justice MacLean did not follow the previous decisions and ruled that Milton should be released. Justice MacLean said he had "concerns with Born With A Tooth's attitude toward law and with his intention to obey the law on release," yet he agreed to release him.

Milton was released with several conditions to help control him and protect the public. Just before Christmas, Milton criticized some of his bail conditions, in particular, the condition that he could not go within "one mile" of the LNID Weir, saying that such a condition applied to land on his reserve, and the Alberta courts, in his opinion, did not have jurisdiction on the reserve. Media did not report whether Milton mentioned, during his bail hearing with Justice MacLean, that the Alberta courts had no jurisdiction on the reserve. Had Milton told Justice MacLean this, he likely would not have been free to speak to the press later.

The trial of Milton Born With A Tooth began Monday, February 26, 1991, at the courthouse in Fort Macleod. The courthouse was two blocks from the Royal Canadian Mounted Police Museum.

When I interviewed Karen Gainer, she told me she had been a criminal defence lawyer since 1981. Over the course of her career, she has tried to make the criminal justice system respond better to the needs of First Nations peoples. For example, she tried to change the way juries are selected to ensure that First Nations persons are fairly represented, and she argued for the right of First Nations to have articles necessary for prayers when they are in prison. Gainer twice ran for political office as a Liberal. In 1996 she left private practice to work for non-profit organizations, building fair and transparent legal and democratic systems. At one point, she was the senior country director for the National Democratic Institute in Croatia.

Gainer later told me that Justice MacLean was well known in southern Alberta. When she conducted Milton's bail hearing in front of him, she said that they had a big battle, and she was determined at the trial to remain as polite as possible to avoid another battle. When I asked her what it was like working in southern Alberta as a defence lawyer, she laughed and said, "You don't know southern Alberta very well, do you?"

Before the trial, Gainer had tried to have Milton's trial moved out of southern Alberta because she was afraid that he would not receive a fair hearing. People in the South were so in favour of the dam it would be difficult to find a fair juror for a First Nations person who opposed it. The court ruled against Milton, saying that there was widespread publicity regarding the case, both positive and negative. "Therefore, there wasn't sufficient evidence that there was widespread prejudice against Milton in Fort Macleod."

Devalon told the media, "He is being set up to fall." Milton told the press he was being "crucified." Mike Bruised Head, executive director of the Lethbridge Native Friendship Centre, said, "The Court process is highly questionable." He explained to the media that "southern Alberta is extremely racist towards Natives and he is concerned that Milton Born With A Tooth won't be judged in a neutral environment. A neutral environment would be in the best interest of Natives and non-Natives. The judicial system is leaning towards the establishment. It's in favour of those who support the dam."

Milton had chosen to be tried by a judge and jury. Bruce Fraser, who had twice stopped Martha Kostuch's prosecutions against Alberta, would now prosecute Milton. At 10:00 a.m. Monday morning, the trial began with Justice Laurie MacLean presiding.

——— ——

It is very important that a criminal trial not only be fair but also be perceived as fair by neutral observers. If there is a reasonable perception of bias, the judge, either on his or her own, or after an application by the lawyers, should remove him/herself from the case. When I reviewed the transcripts for this trial, it seemed to me that there was clearly at least an issue of the perception of bias in Justice MacLean's hearing the case. So, I called him in October of 2007.

Former Justice MacLean had retired as a justice and was working as a lawyer. I could hear the intelligence, as well as the quality of plain speaking in his voice. I confirmed with him that he did act as lawyer for the LNID in the 1978 crisis. Then I asked him, "Did you feel that there was any danger that your work for the irrigation district during the crisis in 1978 would put you in a situation where there would be a perceived conflict of interest in you conducting Milton's trial?"

"No," he replied. "The other case was a civil case, and this was a criminal trial. Milton's case had little to do with the title of the land. He was facing a firearms charge, so it did not really matter where it had happened. I had no special information that would impact on my ability to judge the case impartially. Also, Milton chose to have a jury trial, so it was the jury who would decide the facts, not me." Former Justice MacLean also confirmed for me that, to the best of his recollection, there was no formal application or any comments on the record on this issue during the trial. This accords with my reading of the transcript. However, he told me that he did turn his mind to this issue at the time and determined that there was no real or reasonable apprehension of bias.

As I was writing this book, I ruminated on my discussion with MacLean. I struggled with myself to try to formulate a judgement on this issue that was just, and did not criticize someone unfairly, after the fact. It is deceptively easy for a writer to criticize others from the moral simplicity and safety of one's home office, years later. Yet, one must not be afraid to criticize where necessary. Over a few days in 2011, one issue clarified in my mind: If Justice MacLean knew that the issue of his past relationship with the LNID was an issue that he himself had to consider, and that in fact he did consider, why did he not disclose this past relationship in open court, to allow the issue to be raised by the defence and aired publicly? I only wish that my thoughts had crystallized with sufficient clarity to ask him this at the time. By the time I had come to this thought, I learned that MacLean had died, so I could not give him the right to defend himself, a right he deserved.

The judge entered the court. The lawyers faced him. The public gallery behind them had many representatives from Church and Native rights groups. Dianne Pachal sat in on many days of the trial. Joanne Helmer wanted to sit in, but her office was in Lethbridge, which made it difficult for her to attend. That morning the lawyers and the judge discussed various issues before they picked the jury.

The group of men and women who had been summoned to court as potential jurors waited nearby, ready to be called into court. The lawyers dealt with last-moment issues. Justice MacLean explained to the lawyers what he would say to the group of jurors when they came in to the court. He was particularly clear that the lawyers should try not to select jurors who had already made up their minds about the guilt or innocence of the accused, who could not be impartial. He looked at legal cases that had discussed this, as these provided a quality of reasoning and wisdom that no judge could come up with alone during any one trial.

Next, Gainer stood up and asked Justice MacLean if the jury could be asked the following question: "Do you hold any political or other personal views which might interfere with your judgement of this case?"

"Where did you get that one from? Have you ever seen that one in any form in any way?" Justice MacLean asked.

Gainer then mentioned a case in which views were canvassed about abortion and added, "It's a political issue, My Lord, and certainly there are political ramifications to this issue."

"Oh no, no, this is, this is not political, this, this relatively simple incident, that's not political… I appreciate your argument that this is political, has political overtones… I say your submission in that regard is rejected." Justice MacLean then turned to the Crown and told Fraser to focus on the legal issues in the case, "which is what we're here for in society, and if need be, the politicians can take care of the periphery from your point of view."

After these discussions were over, the potential jurors were summoned into the court. There could easily have been a hundred people. This is a moment of real tension, even for experienced counsel. Once those potential jurors have come into the court, informally, the trial has begun.

It is a very public process. The potential jurors—also known as a jury panel—watch, as do spectators in the gallery, including members of the news media. In each trial, the Crown and the defence have the right to say—without giving any reasons—whether or not they want a potential juror to be a juror. This gives both defence and Crown some control over who is chosen. On one hand, the Crown wants to pick witnesses he or she thinks will be favourable to the case. On the other hand, he or she must not step over the bounds of fairness.

After the jury panel was called into the court, a list of potential jurors was called, and citizens lined up along the side of the courtroom. Next, a process began that has gone on for hundreds of years. A potential juror for Milton's trial was chosen. He or she stepped forward.

The court clerk read from a prepared statement: "Potential juror, look upon the accused. Accused, look upon the juror." Milton looked at the potential juror, and the potential juror looked at him. As Milton and the potential juror looked at one another, Karen Gainer and Bruce Fraser had the chance to say either "challenge," meaning they did not want the juror, or "content," meaning they did. If either lawyer said "challenge," the potential juror would not be on the jury. If both said "content," then the potential juror would become a juror.

A number of potential jurors came forward. According to newspaper reports, and author Jack Glenn, two Native people came forward as potential jurors. Everyone watched to see what would happen. A few seconds would pass before the court clerk would speak again. What would the Crown do? Would the Crown let a Native person sit on this jury? Or would the Crown challenge him? Would the Native people, who have been ignored for so long in Canadian and Alberta history, have a role in this process? Some might think a Native person would be biased; others would say he or she would be no more biased than a non-Native. An accused is not entitled to a favourable jury, merely an unbiased one. Probably not many thought of a third possibility: that the Crown might decide, as is his or her legitimate right, to challenge the person, not because she or he was Native, but for some other legitimate reason.

The first Native person and Milton looked at one another. The entire court watched.

"Content," said Gainer.

"Challenge," said Fraser.

Only one other Native person came forward that day. His name was called by the court clerk. Next the court clerk said, "Look upon the accused. Accused, look upon the potential juror."

The potential juror looked at Milton. He looked back.

"Content," said Ms. Gainer.

"Challenge," said Fraser, and the second Native person walked back to the gallery.

And so a jury of twelve people was chosen that day: six men, six women. All were white.

With the jury selected, the court clerk read out the eight criminal charges against Milton. All his charges related to the firing of the gun on the morning of September 7, 1990, when police came onto the Piikani Reserve to break up the Lonefighters' protest. After each charge was read out, Milton spoke: "Not guilty," he said. The judge then told the jury that they could read to the newspapers; they had to "determine the facts and, on the basis of those facts, determine the guilt or innocence of the accused." With this, the trial was ready to begin. At the end of the first day of the trial, Milton explained to the *Lethbridge Herald* that he was upset that the jury did not include any Natives. Of his trial, he said, "It's about to be a massacre."

Fraser stood up, turned to the jury, and delivered his opening address. He said the land where the incident happened "belonged to the Government of Alberta, this was land in the name of the province, and duly registered to the Government of Alberta in the Land Titles Office of Southern Alberta." The Crown prosecutor ended his speech with the following words: "What this trial is really all about, is the accused pointing a loaded rifle at police officers and the Environment people, the accused actually firing that rifle, and the accused holding off the police and the Environment people from making repairs to the damage to the dyke."

The Crown began his case by calling the police officers who were on the dike that day. Police witnesses said Milton pointed a gun at Officer Gaultier, and then fired a shot upward. Some witnesses said Milton pointed his rifle at the RCMP helicopter. One officer said that late in the day, when one of the Lonefighters wanted to leave and RCMP stopped him, Milton said, "Let him through or I will shoot."

After lunch on the first day, the lawyers returned. Gainer said "My Lord" and continued that she thought he had made a mistake when he was speaking to the jury that morning, when he had talked about the jury inquiring into the guilt or innocence of her client, and that "I would respectfully, it's a small point really..."

Justice MacLean cut her off in mid-sentence and said, "It is indeed. It's noted, goodbye, bring the jury in."

When he answered questions from the prosecutor, Officer Gaultier told the court that Milton pointed a gun at him from about "40–50 yards" away. He said he thought he was dead. When Gainer asked him how far away he was from Milton when he saw the gun pointed at him, he said he was "75 yards." Gainer reminded him that in a prior statement he said he was "100, 120 yards" away when he first saw Milton. When she asked him to explain why the answers were different, he said, "I don't know what you're meaning here. But if you want my answer today, when I look back as I'm running back to the bush, I'm 75 yards away."

Gainer continued, "Now, Officer, to be fair to you, at the point in time, when this happened, you were under a great deal of stress; is that correct?"

"I'm concerned. I'm not really stressed."

"You agree you have a certain amount of adrenalin going through you?"

"Definitely."

"Okay. And when you are asked in court to try to dissect this incident in minute detail, it's difficult to do so?"

"Not at all. I rather enjoy it."

"Was this a coordinated operation?" Gainer asked.

"Not well enough."

"You thought he had it aimed at you?"

"I didn't think, I knew he had it aimed at me."

The case for the prosecution seemed simple. It was alleged that Milton had pointed his gun at two police officers—Raymond Gaultier and one other officer. Milton was ultimately acquitted of pointing the gun at the other officer, so the only real issue regarding the pointing of the gun related to Gaultier. It was also alleged that Milton had obstructed justice by using his gun to stop police that day. Gaultier and other officers testified that Milton had pointed a gun at him and another officer from between "40 yards and 120 yards" away, depending on whose evidence one accepts. At the same time, Doug Clark, who was beside Gaultier that morning, testified that he saw Milton point a gun upward and shoot it. In cross-examination, Clark said that at no time did he see Milton point a gun at anyone that morning.

Officer Maguire, the RCMP officer in charge of the operation, testified. He said that he tried to notify the Piikani chief of the operation on September 7, moments before it began, but he couldn't find him. As a result, Superintendent Maguire was not even on the scene when the operation happened. During her cross-examination of Maguire, Gainer asked him about negotiations between himself and the Piikani on September 7, 1990. Justice MacLean interrupted her and asked the jury to leave. He warned Gainer that if she asked Maguire about the negotiations with the Piikani, the Crown would also have that right. He added, "But, when you start getting into this, then you expose yourself, and this is what frightens me, you are going to expose yourself to something that I think may be very damaging to your client..." He gave Gainer ten minutes to consider her position.

"I have no further question of this witness," Gainer said when court resumed.

Although the prosecution's case seemed to be a straightforward one about a firearm, there was a twist: the ownership of the land. Did the Alberta government own the land where the Lonefighters were digging? Henry Thiessen, a former deputy minister for the Alberta government testified about this point. It is a rare criminal trial indeed in which a deputy minister is required to prove ownership of a piece of land. Thiessen testified that Alberta did own the land at the weir, including the weir itself, but that Alberta had also signed an agreement with the Piikani in 1981 that seemed to affirm that the Piikani owned the land. So, the issue of ownership was as clear as murky water.

Gainer and Justice MacLean had many exchanges on the

relevance of the 1981 agreement between the Piikani and Alberta, and the dispute over who owned the land. At one point, Justice MacLean asked, "How does this dispute help your client?"

"The Permit shows that the land belongs to the Peigan Nation, not the Province of Alberta. Frankly, given that the land is owned by the Peigan, when the RCMP came down the dyke that morning they were trespassing on Peigan property." Gainer said.

"That is a contradiction in terms," Justice MacLean said.

"It is not My Lord."

In a later decision on this case, the Court of Appeal made two points clear. First, the RCMP do have the right to patrol on the Piikani Reserve. Secondly, the Court criticized the trial judge's view of the RCMP. If the RCMP do not act in accordance with the law, they do become trespassers, like anyone else.

———————

When the Crown's case was finished, Gainer gave an opening statement to the jury. She said that the defence admitted that Milton fired two shots. Next, she read to the jury from Milton's statement made to the press: "We instructed them they were trespassing, that they were violating the Peigan Nation's law and that they did not adhere to it. At that time they proceeded to move. At that time I fired one warning shot, they stopped. I fired a second warning shot, and they all took off in the bushes and hid."

Gainer continued, saying, "In many respects, Ladies and Gentlemen, this really sums up the defence." She told the jury that "certain" band councillors believed that the dike was owned by the Peigan people, based in part on opinions given to them by lawyers.

Milton, who had spoken so much to the public about his love of the Oldman River valley, would be silent during his trial. He was not silenced by his lawyer but almost certainly by her fear of prejudice of a particular kind. Gainer and Milton had a problem. They knew Milton had a very serious conviction for criminal negligence causing death. If he testified on his behalf, the Crown prosecutor would be allowed to tell the jury about his conviction—not the details but that he had been convicted of a very serious charge. The jury was only supposed to use the fact of the conviction to help them decide if Milton was an honest witness; however, there was a real danger that the jury, after hearing the record, would decide that Milton was a bad man and not pay any attention to what he actually said in court: whether or not his cause was just, and if he had a valid defence in law. It is always hard for accused persons to sit silently and watch the prosecution's case unfold around them, especially if they have a story to tell. Much later, at Milton's second trial, he would speak.

Gainer called Leander Strikes With A Gun to give evidence on Milton's behalf. He was a Piikani councillor who had been supportive of the Lonefighters.

At one point, Gainer was about to file a Piikani Band Council resolution from September 7, telling police to leave the land around the weir. Justice MacLean noticed that the resolution also made reference to the "advisability of [the Lonefighters] getting arrested." He carefully edited the document to ensure that nothing prejudicial to Milton's case went before the jury.

In cross-examination, Strikes With A Gun admitted that he had spoken to Milton about the injunction, that Milton had seen the injunction and read it. And Milton's decision was, despite the injunction, "to continue."

Fraser asked, "And in spite of knowing about the injunction, and Milton knowing about the injunction, the Lonefighters, including the accused, determined and decided that you were going to violate that order by continuing to attempt to divert the river and cause damage, actual damage to that dike, right?"

"It's band land."

"Let's not argue about whose land it is, let's—"

"No, that's important."

"So you're going to continue to cause damage to that dike?"

"That's our land."

"You have to answer."

Justice MacLean intervened. "Now, just a minute, you were going to continue to work on whatever land, whoever had the land, in the same manner as you had before?"

"It's Peigan band land."

"That's not my question. I didn't ask you whose land it was. Were you going to continue working?" Justice MacLean asked.

"It's band land and I think as a band member it's what we want to do with our land."

Fraser began again, "One more time. Leander, regardless of what you think, I have the right to ask you questions and you have to answer them, so if you could help me by being responsive to the question that I ask, we'll get through this a lot faster."

"Okay, I'm being helpful."

"Let me ask you the question again, and see if you can respond to the question. Did you, the Lonefighters, knowing about this valid court injunction, take the position that you were going to ignore it and cause further damage to the dike?"

"That's band property."

"So you don't want to answer the question?"

"Signed, sealed, delivered."

"Yes, okay, whatever," Fraser said.

Moments later, during this cross-examination, the judge turned to the Crown and said, "Crown, get out of it now."

Next, Gainer called a professor of history and religion, James

Penton, as a witness (not as an expert) who could voice what he saw on September 7. Fraser complained that he could not see any relevance to Penton's evidence. Justice MacLean said, "Oh, I'm sure that we can straighten this out, you know, what can he do to you?"

"I—," Fraser began.

"What can he do?"

Gainer asked him questions. He was at the Lonefighters' camp on September 7. He saw RCMP "hiding in the bushes... There was excitement, anger, and a feeling of resignation in the camp, and, a determination to turn to higher powers, I should say to spiritual forces for comfort."

"When you talked about spiritual powers—"

"Excuse me, relevance?" Justice MacLean asked.

"My Lord, I am trying just to illicit from him what he actually saw and—"

"Well, how, how could he see them reaching out for spiritual help?"

"If I could just go on a bit?"

"Go on."

Gainer continued for a while, then finished. It was time for cross-examination.

"I have no questions of this witness," Fraser said.

Gainer then called Evelyn Kelman to testify about the significance of the Oldman River to the Piikani people. She began, "Can you tell the members of the jury about the Oldman River, the significance it has with respect to the Peigan Nation?"

"My Lord—" Fraser stood up and spoke.

"Hold it, jury out. Witness out," Justice McLean said. The jury and the witness left. "Relevance?"

Gainer said that "the jury is entitled to understand the significance of the river itself to what was happening. This will explain why the diversion was done in August."

"Now listen, I'll concede for you that this may be very, very relevant and very, very important to the members of the Peigan Reserve. Underlined, quotation marks, accentuated. But until you tell me that it is important to the accused, it has no more relevance to me than somebody telling me about Satanism that an accused has not said he agrees with. How are you going to make it relevant unless your client tells me himself if he believes this stuff?… I might be hearing about Buddhism for all it means to the accused. I don't know whether the accused is offended by Indian culture as much as he is offended by white man's culture. Until I get that, this evidence is irrelevant. In my view, the spirituality evidence is not going to come in to court in this case unless something changes in the case. It is inadmissible—got that?"

The next day, Gainer called Evelyn Kelman again to the witness box. Evidently, she had not spoken to the justice before court, because he had to ask why she wanted to call Kelman.

"Because she was at camp."

"What's the camp got to do with anything? Who cares?"

"It's immediately adjacent to the dike."

"Who cares what the dike looks like?"

"The jury cares, My Lord."

After this exchange, and many others in which Milton's lawyer had trouble explaining what she was doing, Justice McLean blurted out, "I don't care what the dike looks like. I care about whether this man had a firearm and he shot it and whether he pointed it at people." He added that the case was simple—did Milton use a firearm that day? He continued, that the case:

…has nothing to do with a sacred river or anything else because that doesn't become an issue… You haven't got anything to go on. You're attempting to attack an indefeasible title to land issued under the Land Titles Act of the Province of Alberta, and you—boy, to attack that, you got to have a lot bigger gun than some member of the Peigan Indian Reserve who says "We think we should have that land."... I don't care in the long run who ends up owning the land. For the purpose of this trial, the land is owned by the Province of Alberta. Now, have you got that? You know, you don't want me sending the jury out every time you open your mouth in questions. She can say what she saw, in relation to the incident—in the morning around 8:00 or so.

MacLean added, "She will not be giving evidence in relation to this fantasy that these people seem to have that they own this land, because the Province has the duplicate Certificate of Title, the finest possible proof that we can get, and the Torrens System is one of the greatest in the world, and that title is indefeasible. Even if the Indians claim the land is theirs, all we've got is a dispute."

Evelyn told the court about what happened the morning of September 7, 1990, the same story she told me years later. She described going to the river, to pray.

"Why did she walk to the river?" asked Justice MacLean.

"To—to offer tobacco to the spirits of the river for protection, that's what I did," Evelyn said.

"And why did you do this that morning?" Gainer asked.

"Now just a minute," said Justice MacLean. "What is—we're talking about walking to the river to offer tobacco to the river? Forget it. Irrelevant. Get on with your point, whatever it may be. What did she do that relates to the charges before the court?"

"With respect, My Lord, this does relate," Gainer said. Then she asked Evelyn Kelman, "Where did you go after the river?"

"I went back to camp. I gathered the women and the children in the camp, which was our usual time for—for smudging and our ceremony in the morning. I gathered them there because they were afraid."

"Do you want me to stop her?" Justice MacLean asked. He paused, then added, "Irrelevant."

"My Lord, with respect, this is the actual time when the incident takes place. How can it be irrelevant?"

"Jury out. Now, you still don't understand, do you? The spirituality of the situation has nothing whatsoever to do with it… She went to the river and threw some tobacco in. Who cares? Now forget it. Let me repeat: she can tell us what she saw as it relates to the charges. But the religious sacred beliefs of the Peigan Reserve have nothing whatsoever to do with it."

Gainer continued and asked how the people in camp reacted when the word came that the RCMP were coming. Evelyn said, "The reaction was excitement. There was fear. The children were crying. The women were crying. And I was afraid—something was going to happen with police. And all kinds of things went through our minds, and going through my mind was knowing what they've done."

"Hold on, Ms. Kelman. What difference does it make? Tell us what she saw," Justice MacLean said.

Gainer asked her what she saw next, and Evelyn explained that she saw Milton heading toward police with a gun. Evelyn Kelman's testimony was now over. Justice MacLean spoke to Gainer and made reference to "those pickets out front of the courthouse." It was meant to be a light-hearted moment in the midst of an increasingly difficult trial.

"Yeah, we can see a joke," someone blurted from the spectators' gallery, loud enough for the court reporter to write it down, making those words part of the official record of the trial. The judge did not acknowledge the gallery—this time.

———— ·· ————

The next day, lawyer Drew Galbraith testified. He told the court that it was his opinion, "with a substantial degree of comfort," that the Piikani own the main dike. He had given Milton and the Lonefighters "this advice just prior to their breaching the main dike with their equipment."

After Galbraith testified, the jury left, and the lawyers and judge discussed what the right law was to tell the jury. Sitting in the body of the court were protesters and other spectators. Until Evelyn testified, they had been silent. Now, like a Greek chorus, they began to speak out loudly—something unheard of in Canadian courts.

At one point Gainer said, "Well, My Lord, the evidence that the Crown led is not that they were going to carry out work that morning. They came on with a small army."

"Ah, nonsense," the judge said.

A chorus of voices, too mixed together to be separated into discrete words, erupted in the spectators' gallery. The court reporter wrote in the official transcript of the trial at this point, "Lots of noise from the gallery."

Justice MacLean addressed the gallery: "If I get any—if I need any help from the crowd, then you will help me from the street, do you understand that?"

A later comment from Justice MacLean caused a "large uproar from the audience from the gallery."

Justice MacLean spoke again to the gallery: "One more time, one more time, and don't shake your head at me, I don't need your help in the gallery. Now then, let's continue." And the lawyers continued their debate to try and decide the proper law to use to try the case.

The trial was nearly over. Now was the time for the lawyers to make their final speeches to the jury, then the justice would tell the jury about the law they had to use to decide the case. The jury was called back, Gainer rose, faced the fury, and began to tell them why Milton should be acquitted. She admitted that Milton had fired two shots that day over the heads of police but said that he was in possession of the land that day. "When he fired those shots, he was using reasonable force to defend the land. He had told them they were trespassing, and he fired warning shots when they did not leave. The two shots were in defence of property and his heritage."

She talked about the RCMP. "You don't need dozens of armed officers to repair a riverbed." The police did not need to "march in the way they did. They could have sent a single officer in and ask the people throwing stones to give themselves up. They could have gone back the next day, or the next week." She asked the jury to accept what Doug Clark had told them, that Milton did not point a gun at police but lifted the firearm up and shot it skyward.

Then she turned to the land, telling the jury, "Don't be mislead by the Certificate of Title." She explained that the deal from 1981, which seemed to confirm that the Piikani still owned the land, was signed later. "You wonder why the Peigans are so angry? Do you wonder why Leander Strikes With A Gun was so insistent that the Peigans own the land? I don't mind telling you that these actions do not just insult the Peigan people, they insult all of us. I think that this government is no different than all of us; it has to honour its commitments."

She urged the jury to try to imagine how things looked to the Lonefighters the morning of September 7. "Remember, the Peigans didn't know what was happening. All they saw, and I mean this quite seriously, was something like a small military invasion. The police testified that they had brought a helicopter, dozens of officers, dozens of vehicles, and heaven knows how many guns to enforce an injunction against six, eight, ten people? The police had no right to treat the diversion site as if it were an armed camp."

She said that the case was really about "a series of unwarranted assumptions by the RCMP. The police assumed that morning that my client and the other Peigans were going to be unreasonable. The police assumed they had to treat the Peigans like armed trespassers or some kind of rebel force. The police assumed they can do whatever they like on private property." She readily admitted that the police had every right to take reasonable precautions that morning, but "it is one thing to be prepared for trouble, and quite another to assume that it's going to happen, and more particularly, to react as if it has already happened. These kinds of assumptions invariably mean the use of power and strike at the freedom of all of us. The police have to respect the laws as much as you or I do." Then Gainer continued:

This case shows us the importance of a very important principle: Why does the rule of law exist if not to prevent those in authority from exercising their power in an arbitrary manner? The law does not exist for the benefit of those in power. It does not exist to let government or police act in any way they wish. It is for you and me and the people. It has been said for centuries that no one is above the law, and that all must respect it. No one is above the law, not the prime minister, not the government, not the RCMP.

I am now asking you to find that Indian people have the same rights as all of us. The law belongs to the Peigan people also. I suggest that Milton Born With A Tooth was doing something for all of us. He was exercising a right we all have to protect ourselves from intruders. Now, Ladies and Gentlemen, you are the judges. You are entitled to all the dignity and respect that makes the status of a judge. You have the final responsibility in this case.

When Gainer was finished, Fraser rose to address the jury. His speech to the jury was much shorter than Gainer's. He began with the following words, "When we started this trial I must tell you I didn't know what this trial would be all about. What I mean by that is that I didn't know what lawful defence would be raised. Having listened to my learned friend's submissions for the past hour or so, I have to tell you that I still don't know what the lawful defence is. So, if you are confused, don't feel badly about it."

He told the jury that Gainer's arguments were "based completely on incorrect premises of law. I will leave it to His Lordship to correct those legal premises. It is not my job. I want to deal with the evidence. I want to deal with the facts. I want to deal with the charges that are before this court so you can determine guilt or innocence. This is what you are here for. This is what we are all here for."

Fraser reminded the jurors that the court injunction stated "according to law the Lonefighters could not divert the river... nor could they interfere with the Environment people who were coming to make repairs." The police came to the camp that day to protect the Department of the Environment people and to uphold the law. Fraser continued, "You know, the accused created a very dangerous situation with that rifle. He fired that rifle. He pointed it at a number of police officers. He wanted to scare them and threaten them and keep them from the dike and from making the repairs to the damage. The accused was doing exactly what the injunction said he couldn't do."

He then commented on the Peigan Band generally, "You

know, is there any evidence before you that the Peigan Band is in any way a legal entity and capable of owning land? That permit we've been talking about is signed by the federal government. The Peigan Band signed some resolutions, but they didn't sign the permit, because they can't."

He returned to Milton, noting that not only did Milton know about the injunction but he also intended to disobey it, to carry on trying to divert the river. "Now, if the accused felt the ownership of the land was in dispute, then he shouldn't have challenged it in a court of law, not with guns. He was told this by his own lawyer."

Fraser added, "To have a defence of property, you have to have real trespassers. Who is really trespassing? The RCMP? The Environment people?" He said both were present on the reserve pursuant to a valid court order. "Police could have gone on the reserve any time to arrest the Lonefighters if they thought they had the reasonable grounds to do so…"

"…bullshit, they don't have to," said a voice from the gallery, interrupting Fraser's speech.

But, Fraser continued, saying the police "don't have to ask anyone's permission to do their police duty on the reserve. The reserve is not an entrée created to escape the criminal law or federal or provincial law. They are subject to the same prosecutions if they commit crimes as you people…"

Fraser then turned to the question of who owns the land on the weir. "We know that the land that they were on does not belong to the Indian band nor does it belong to the federal government or the Department of Indian Affairs. The land they were on belonged to the Alberta government who had access to that land by way of a permit from the federal—"

"…bunch of fuckin' bullshit," said a member of the gallery.

Here, Justice MacLean stopped proceedings and sent the jury

out. He told the gallery,

"You'd better behave out there or you're out and the next incident may well invoke some contempt proceedings. This jury has trouble enough without you people acting and reacting to it. If you can't stand it without doing that, that includes you, then you leave. Let's get the jury back."

When the jury returned, Fraser continued, "The RCMP have a right to be there regardless of who owns the land. Here, the government owned the land. The RCMP weren't trespassers. But even if they were, I can't say it strongly enough, even if they were trespassers, you're not allowed to use guns against them... Ladies and Gentlemen, it seems to me, quite frankly, a clear way, the way it's been phrased, fairly easy job, there is very little for you to decide. There is no defence available, no defence, no evidence that is capable of raising a defence." He spoke about the importance of the presumption of innocence, but he noted that in this case the Crown had discharged its burden, their duty was to convict.

With that, Fraser was finished.

Justice MacLean turned to the jury, and spoke, "Ladies and Gentlemen of the jury, it's been a long day. Let's come back tomorrow morning."

The next morning Justice MacLean told the jury that Gainer "unfairly attacked the RCMP as having ignored the rights of the accused, if not all of the Peigan Indians." He added that the police were not trespassers, as the Government of Alberta owned the land. "It is not unreasonable that the police and the Environment officials acted as if they owned it. What other way would you act? They did own it." He continued, "Which of the groups is, under these circumstances, arrogant? Which group is ignoring lawful rights of the other? That kind of an attack on the police is unfounded in law and unfounded on the evidence and totally ignores the rights of the owners."

Then, Justice MacLean reviewed Milton's defence. Since he had already decided that the land belonged to Alberta, the only question left was whether Milton honestly believed that the Piikani were the rightful owners of the land, that the RCMP were trespassers, and that he had the right to use reasonable force to eject them. If so, then firing the gun would be justifiable or excusable. He would have made an honest mistake. He would not have a guilty mind. The justice noted how Milton had told Leander Strikes With A Gun he would ignore the injunction, and ignore the courts. He continued, "What evidence have you got to show that he had any belief in his right to use force to expel and eject the RCMP? What harm was that group of five policeman and six Environment officers going to do? Sure they had guns, but the guns were a perfectly normal everyday part of their dress. Our security officers here in court are sitting here with guns. Is there anything unusual about that? The defence says these people were scared and frightened. I think the real evidence contradicts that. They stood their ground, threw rocks, shouted, right out in the open. Is that being scared?" He added that the fact that Milton stood on the CAT suggested that "Milton knew well that he was completely and totally safe from any forceful act on the part of the RCMP." He described the RCMP walking down the dike that morning as "very passive conduct."

The jury left the courtroom at 12:06 p.m.

Shortly before 3:56 p.m., the same day, the jury returned and found Milton guilty of all charges except one. He was guilty of pointing a firearm at Officer Gaultier but not the other officer. After the verdict, the jury was polled—each juror was asked if they agreed with the verdict. They all agreed. Many lawyers go their entire careers without ever hearing a juror disagree with the verdict.

As the jury's role was now finished, Justice MacLean

thanked the jury, and they left the court. The case would be adjourned to allow both lawyers to prepare for the hearing to decide what Milton's sentence would be. Justice MacLean had a choice of allowing Milton to remain on bail until his sentencing or put him in jail. He chose to put Milton in jail. Milton was handcuffed and taken into police custody.

From jail, Milton continued to speak: "The judge wasn't representing the court system, but the province, the Lethbridge Northern Irrigation District and farmers... I am sick and tired of living in a racist situation... people say that the judicial system is working fine. It isn't. It needs to be educated. We didn't write the laws, so why should we be recognizing laws that allow government to build dikes that destroy the environment and the land we live on, when we were never part of writing those laws? When Indian people use the mountains, birds and wind to describe their beliefs and concerns, white people see it as romantic, but we are actually citing our own constitution. We didn't decide one day to sit on the prairie and make it all up. We didn't need someone to come down from a mountain and give us laws. We are and always will be a part of creation."

———————

Justice MacLean decided on Milton's sentence on March 24, 1991. Four days before, the *Lethbridge Herald* ran a story about a planned "Day of Protest and Reflection" to be carried out on the day of sentencing by some professors from the University of Lethbridge and the Canadian Alliance in Solidarity with Native People. The protest would be followed by an open forum for discussion after Milton's sentencing. According to one story in the same newspaper, during the sentencing, "with clenched fists raised in solidarity, supporters

268

jeered a Court of Queen's Bench justice as Peigan activist was sent to jail." The article described Milton as a "hero among many Natives and environmentalists." As Milton entered that prisoner box, he smiled and "waved at nearly eighty supporters who had squeezed into the jammed courtroom." As he arrived, the crowd in the gallery "stood at attention—many thrusting their fists of support into the air." Dozens more stood in the hall. In effect, according to one journalist, the demonstration outside the court had spilled into the courtroom.

Bruce Fraser spoke first. He said that many innocent lives were put at risk because of the accused. He also said that the accused had shown no remorse for his actions. He said there were no positive factors that would mitigate the crime to allow the court to give the accused a shorter sentence. He then filed the accused's criminal record with the court. There were two convictions. The first was very minor. The Crown continued that Milton was convicted in 1989 in Colorado of criminally negligent homicide and spent two years in jail. The way the word "homicide" is used in Colorado seems to mean an accidental death through negligence. In Canada, "homicide" means to intend to kill. Once the Crown had finished, Gainer referred to a letter she had received from Colorado's Public Defender's office. It set out the background to the charges and the circumstances of Milton's case there. Gainer explained:

> The circumstances of the charge are as follows. In 1984 my client was working in Colorado with his wife, Leslie Yellow-horn, and their young son Shining Eagle. The event happened in a motel room. The child was in a cot next to them. They had fallen asleep. They awoke to find their son not breathing. They immediately called the emergency personnel, but they were unable to resuscitate the child. The case was investi-

gated at that time by the Lakewood Police Department. It was determined to be an accidental death. My client and his wife returned to Brocket to bury the child and to continue their lives.

Several years passed. My client and Leslie Yellowhorn became estranged and parted in a hostile manner. My client had, in fact, taken up with another woman. Years later, after the separation, Leslie Yellowhorn came forward and denied her earlier statement to police in Colorado, and suggested that my client had placed him under the bed and suffocated him. A second investigation ensued, and ultimately my client was charged with murder and child abuse. The matter finally proceeded to trial in 1989. It was before a jury. The jury acquitted my client on the murder charge and could not agree on a verdict with respect to the child-abuse charge.

In the United States they were able to poll the jury and they found that ten out of twelve jurors wished to acquit my client. There were only two who believed that my client should be punished for something. My client had been in jail by this time for over two years. Since the jury could not reach a decision, there would be a new trial. This may involve my client staying in jail many more months. The defence and district prosecutor tried to find another way to resolve the case. A deal was struck. My client would enter a plea of no contest to criminal negligent homicide. In Colorado at the time, this was not a serious charge, it was a misdemeanour.

Gainer continued that Milton maintained his innocence. He pleaded "no contest" to the charges, which allowed him to maintain his innocence, yet have a guilty plea go forward. This allowed Milton to get out of jail immediately rather than remain in jail for another year while waiting for a new trial.

Gainer then told the judge about Milton's childhood, and his growing awareness of his culture. In his twenties, he learned:

…what it meant to be Native, to acquire some self-esteem and to quit blaming himself and his people for the problems, for the destruction, for the death that he found around him. He learned that residential schools were not part of his tradition. He learned that he should be proud of, and cherish, his language and culture.

As he grew older, he better understood his father's teachings. He was raised by the Oldman River. His father taught him about the "commitment to the river and the importance of the river." That the river was really the spiritual background—the backbone, of the Peigan people. His people had lived by the river and had done so for generations, and, if they were to survive, they must continue their relationship with the river. And that is what he tried to do—to preserve the river.

Gainer listed the many people and groups across the country "who are supporting my client."

"Are they supporting the use of firearms?" asked Justice MacLean.

"They're supporting my client's protest with respect to the river, my client's defence of his people. With respect, it's not a simple issue, My Lord." Gainer closed her submissions by saying, "This is not the most serious matter to come before the criminal courts. In many ways, it's quite a minor matter dealing with the use of a firearm."

Justice MacLean then spoke to the court and gave his reasons for sentencing Milton. Then he turned to a defence of the rule of law. "If our society is to survive, then the rule of law must prevail. The rule of law—" One gallery member interrupted him, but what was said wasn't clear. Justice MacLean looked up from his notes and addressed the gallery: "Remember what I have said. It would be very unfortunate if I had to clear this courtroom, so do not do that to me. I don't want it to happen, but I must have your undivided attention and your polite quietness. Failing that, I cannot perform in your presence and I'm not bound to. Until then, you will refrain from any further comment." Then he continued with his verdict on Milton's sentence: "The rule of law applies equally and generally to everyone, without regard to race or colour or creed—"

"Horse shit," said one member of the gallery.

"One more time. One more time," Justice MacLean said, turning again to the gallery. "One of the most basic premises of the rule of law is that our differences must be settled by the courts. No one has the right to resort to the use of firearms to further their cause. Those very great rights that we enjoy in this country—"

"In our land we will," said a member of the gallery.

"—include the right to the benefit of the rule of law, and that right imposes—"

"That's how your history repeats that—"

"—upon each of us an obligation to abide by the rule of law."

"Immigrants go home. Colonists. That's how they got this land."

"The courts—"

"White man's justice—"

"—as guardians of our right, must loudly and clearly bring home to those who offend the rule of law that society will not countenance such conduct. In pursuit of protecting the rights of everyone, the police of this country, while acting in the lawful execution of their duties, must be given our respect and support."

"Bull."

"The use of firearms to obstruct the police in the lawful execution of their duty is a serious offence and invites a serious sanction. However great—"

"Where do you come from—South Africa?"

"—the accused may have believed his cause to be, he had no right to further that cause by the unlawful use of a firearm."

According to *Windspeaker*, a man from an Aboriginal group in Saskatchewan, "Kevin Daniels, wearing dark sunglasses and dressed in combat attire, approached the judge, drew an imaginary rifle and said, 'I guess I'll be next.'" The *Lethbridge Herald* has a second version of what happened at this point: "'This comes next,' blurted another Native, his hands flailing in feigned uppercut punches."

Justice MacLean tried to continue, "In this country, where the rule of law prevails, it cannot be said that there is no other remedy. The courts have the power and the ability to identify our rights when they exist and to re-address any breaches."

"Southern Alberta redneck justice."

Justice MacLean concluded that Milton knew about the injunction and that the Ministry of the Environment workers had a right to be there. He did not find Milton's criminal record to be an aggravating factor, "given the circumstances surrounding the record. I can find nothing in the conduct of the RCMP that invited or precipitated the confrontation—"

"You weren't there. You weren't there. We seen it. We were children. We were mothers." According to *Windspeaker*, it was Lorna Born With A Tooth who said these words, and she stood as she spoke them.

"The alleged spiritual and cultural background spoken to as being the impetus that brought about this confrontation does not assist the accused to any degree. He may be well-advised to direct some of his energy toward abiding by the rule of law."

"Whose law? It's not his law, it's your law and it's unjust."

Justice MacLean concluded the proceedings by sentencing Milton to a shorter sentence than many outside observers had expected: one year in jail, in addition to the four months he had already spent in jail. The judge noted that one year in jail is the minimum sentence possible where a firearm was involved. In effect, he sentenced Milton to the lowest possible sentence he could. His final words that day were, "That ends it."

In one sense, it was over; in another sense, it was just beginning.

In his report for the *Lethbridge Herald*, Mike Lamb wrote that, after the sentencing, Crown attorney Bruce Fraser left through the prisoner's elevator. He speculated that Fraser did this to "avoid national media inquiries," though he may have been concerned about his personal safety. Gainer was surprised that Milton's sentence was as short—relatively speaking—as it was. Native protesters were appalled by any sentence. One Native person, Mike Bruise Head, of the Lethbridge Native Friendship Centre, said that the judge was in a predicament. "Basically, the judge had no choice but to uphold the rule of law," he said.

That same month, March 1991, a report called by Justice Robert Cawsey on the plight of Native and Métis people within the Alberta Justice System was released. It is called "Justice on Trial." The report stated: "The Aboriginal people and all levels of government have concern about the level of justice provided by the current criminal justice system to Aboriginal people. Unless more balance is created, justice will remain elusive and discontent will be created." Justice Cawsey noted that Aboriginal persons are disproportionately represented in Alberta's correctional institutions. He added that "Aboriginals are often at the receiving end of what appears to them to be a foreign system of justice delivered to a large extent by non-Aboriginals."

On April 3, 1991, the Court of Appeal for Alberta released Milton on bail pending his appeal. Justice Roger Kerans said that "there is no harm to come from his release."

Cry for Justice

A week after Milton was sentenced to jail, Karen Gainer filed an appeal. After the trial was finished, many who had sat in on the trial expressed shock and outrage at the conduct of Justice MacLean during the trial, and at Milton's having remained so long in jail before being released on bail. Jack Glenn notes in his book that "a spokesperson for the Canadian Alliance in Solidarity with the Native Peoples said that Justice MacLean's behaviour 'from the standpoint of natural justice or even of good manners was particularly outrageous.'" This group complained to the Canadian Judicial Council about Justice MacLean's conduct. It alleged, among other things, that MacLean's comments were "gratuitously insulting to Native people." Lorraine Land, from the Alberta Citizens for Public Justice, attended the trial as an observer for the Ottawa-based Aboriginal Rights Coalition. She reported: "Born With A Tooth was by no means treated justly by the legal system. The overtly hostile judge and the all-white jury who tried the case were in the end simply accommodating players on the much larger scale of a justice system seemingly unable to deal justly with aboriginal people."

It is not considered appropriate for judges to respond in the media, so Justice MacLean said nothing. If there was to be any public explanation for this trial, the Court of Appeal for Alberta would give it.

Some said the trial denied Milton his human rights. Others called for a federal inquiry. One observer from a Native-rights

276

organization said she was "unprepared for the overt bias and racist remarks made by the trial judge." Another wrote, "Here in a nutshell is what Native people have had to face for the past 120 years." One critic of the trial wrote in a letter to the Minister of Indian Affairs that Milton Born With A Tooth had "diffused a very tense situation and performed, in a fashion, a peacekeeping role."

As these words were entering the public discourse, Milton's appeal was being prepared and, finally, heard. The hearing was adjourned the first time because, according to Justice Roger Kerans of the Appeal Court, Karen Gainer was "too personally involved" to make submissions about the trial judge. About thirty-five people protested outside the Court of Appeal.

Later, the Court of Appeal ordered a new trial because Justice MacLean had made a number of mistakes during the trial. The jury should have heard what the Piikani were doing at the site before September—including "religious and ceremonial" activity. This would have helped the jury better understand the accused and what he did. The court also said that Justice MacLean "curtailed cross-examination designed to raise a doubt about the true intentions of the police. Moreover, he told the jury that the police had behaved reasonably. He may express his views to the jury, but he must leave relevant issues of fact for them to decide." The court said the trial judge "forbade any evidence tending to show peaceable possession of the Peigan on the ground that the title to the lands held by Alberta conclusively decided all questions of the sort... In short, he had concluded the accused was a trespasser, and could not possibly invoke the defence." The Appeal Court said this was wrong in law.

The Court of Appeal ruled Alberta's title to the land did not decide the question of whether or not, in fact, the RCMP came on the land for an unlawful reason. If the police did come on the land with an illegal intent, they would be trespassers. This is a question for a jury to decide. The Appeal Court continued, "Moreover, it is not beyond argument that the settlement agreement did not 'abrogate in any way' the title of Alberta." In effect, Alberta's deal with the Piikani in 1981 may have altered whatever rights Alberta had to the land according to the title. The court noted that even if Milton had thought the injunction was illegal, "he, like other Canadians, was nonetheless bound to obey it until he succeeded in having it vacated."

The Appeal Court went on, however, to note that "it would be extremely unfair to the trial judge to speak of these or any other errors at the trial without some explanatory comment," that the defence counsel's inability to explain the defence theory of the case, despite repeated requests to do so by the trial judge, had provoked the judge to the remarks he made. On the other hand, the Court of Appeal did not comment on the rude and imperious remarks of the trial judge to Karen Gainer, which set the tone for her attitude. This was later set in relief for me by the transcript of her impeccable politeness to the trial judge at Milton's second trial.

The Court of Appeal did not mention the propriety of Justice MacLean's hearing the case when he had previously represented the LNID. Gainer told me that she did not know about Justice MacLean's past ties to the irrigation district until much later, so she did not argue this point.

Since evidence had been excluded at Milton's trial, it was impossible to assess whether or not a substantial miscarriage of justice had occurred. Therefore, the Court of Appeal decided that the wisest course was to order a new trial. Milton's conviction was overturned.

Milton was "buoyant" at the decision. "I have just had three judges tell me that they were the ones in the wrong." He added that this had "exonerated" his position; the Lonefighters "weren't just a bunch of hoodlums."

After the Court of Appeal ordered a new trial, the Judicial Council considered the complaint lodged with them by the Canadian Alliance in Solidarity with the Native Peoples, mentioned above, about Justice MacLean's conduct during the trial. This complaint related to Justice MacLean's behaviour during the trial and was a separate process from Milton's appeal of his guilty verdict. The issue before the Judicial Council would be whether or not Justice MaClean should be reprimanded, punished, or removed from his job as justice based on his behaviour during Milton's trial.

The Judicial Council is comprised of chief justices and associate chief justices of federally appointed courts all across Canada. The council assessed the complaint against Justice MacLean. It "repri-manded" him for his actions and comments voiced during Milton's trial. The council ruled that the judge had "displayed an insensitivity to cultural and religious differences, displayed discourtesy to defence counsel, characterized evidence with unnecessarily colourful epithets and, generally, did not conduct himself in an appropriate manner for a trial involving sensitive and cultural issues." MacLean admitted that his conduct had been "unacceptable... and that he was taking concrete steps" to ensure that it did not happen again. The Judicial Council noted that Justice MacLean "had responded to this complaint by unequivocally acknowledging that his conduct had been unaccept-able. He accepted full responsibility for his conduct. He expressed his regret that it had occurred." The council decided that, under the circumstances, it was not necessary to take a further step to investi-gate if Justice MacLean should be removed from the bench.

Many years later, Evelyn was working as a Native court worker at the courthouse in Lethbridge. She was called forward to help a young woman facing criminal charges. She looked up and saw Justice MacLean sitting before her on the bench. She thought, "Now what?" She was worried. He looked at her, and then he said,

"I remember you. And I respect you." After that brief reference to the past, the case continued. Evelyn told me that she felt he was sincere that day.

Back in April 2007, when I spoke to Barbara Hoyt, the wife of Martin Hoyt, we also spoke about Justice MacLean. She did not say so directly, but I could tell that she was horrified at the notion that Justice MacLean might be portrayed as very conservative in the public record. She said that in southern Alberta on the liberal side was her husband, and on the other side were a number of very conservative judges, especially with regard to First Nations issues. She then said that Justice MacLean was more moderate. He was in the middle.

I was not sure of the year Justice MacLean died until I found the "Lawrence Maclean Tribute Fund," published on the Web by the Chinook Regional Hospital. I read that he was a "beloved" husband, and a "loving" father to four children. Despite the formulaic nature of these words, they reminded me that Justice MacLean's life represented much more than this one trial. After he retired from working as a justice, he worked in a law firm. The Web article identifies him as having been "a mentor to many, and he gave freely of his time and knowledge."

While Milton Born With A Tooth was making his way through the justice system, the Alberta government continued to move ahead with both building the dam and reversing the work done by the Lonefighters. On November 30, 1990, over seventy "armed, camouflaged" RCMP officers with dogs came onto the reserve to ensure that no one was there to stop the workers who were to make repairs to the LNID Weir. No Lonefighters were left at the scene, so the

WHO SPEAKS FOR THE RIVER?

repairs were done over a few days. Piikani Chief Leonard Bastien learned of the repairs being done through reporters. He said that the government's action was "another broken promise... a total disregard and lack of respect for the Piikani people."

In February 1991, the Supreme Court of Canada heard the Alberta government's appeal of the court decision that cancelled its license to build the dam until Canada did an environmental assessment. The Canadian government and six provinces joined the Alberta government and argued against Martha Kostuch and Friends of Oldman River. Other environmental groups joined on Martha's side. Years later, Dianne Pachal remembered walking into the Supreme Court building and thinking, "Damn, you guys are going to win this, and I am not going to give up."

For Martha Kostuch, it was one of the best days of her life, one of the most memorable days. Later, she remembered, "The seating place was completely packed. There were twenty-four gowned lawyers. There were nine justices. They were fully robed. The court was packed. We had seven provinces and the federal government against us. We had our lawyers. One or two environmental groups and Native groups intervened in support." Martha did many interviews; she was literally, as she put it while laughing, "swarmed" by the media.

When we spoke, she reflected on the Supreme Court of Canada. "It is a great institution... While in our judicial system we do not always get the decisions we like, nor always the best judges, our system is so much better than those in the vast majority of the world. Here, me—basically a nobody—an individual, can form a group and take a case all the way up to the Supreme Court of Canada and be heard. And that is just incredible, and I am very proud of our judicial system, and I have a lot of respect for it.

"I am glad to be able to live in a country [where] we can speak and take government to court and challenge governments and not be thrown in jail or be shot ....hat I have done in Canada, I couldn't have done in many other places."

———— -——

Although it was not completely finished by the spring of 1991, the dam was in operation and began holding back the annual flood of water. Slowly, imperceptibly at first, the water of the Oldman River slowed then rose over the salvaged rock, blowing soil, and tree stumps, backing up and up, eventually flooding five valleys. Anything left alive in those valleys that could not swim or move fast enough to get out of the way, drowned. Or, more likely, tried to find new habitat and then died. Animals that had once used this corridor of wilderness between the mountains and the prairies now had a forty-two-kilometre water barrier to negotiate. What had once been a living ecosystem, formed over thousands of years by the power and life-giving force of flowing water, became silent, still, and sterile, more like a stagnant pond than a river or lake. The rich diversity of vibrant life became a holding tank of water. Now that there were no trees, and the habitat was flooded out, there was no shelter for anyone or anything.

Lorne Fitch explained, "If you canoe down the reservoir today, the wind is very strong. The wind howls over. It is a long reach of water. You might hear Canada geese, but I doubt that you would hear much more."

The twists and turns of the valleys themselves, the tipi rings and ancient campsites, the willows and sacred places, the power places of the Piikani First Nation and their link to their historic past went under, as the reservoir water rose. The rich legacy of the Piikani's past lay either underwater or in boxes in Edmonton. The lands and historic homesteads of settlers to Alberta also succumbed to the rising reservoir. There was no more wildlife for local people to see. There was no more valley; no more forest. That first spring, the water rose to 60 per cent of its expected height. At its full height, the water came nearly to the rim of the valleys. Looking west from the dam site, all one could see, according to Lorne, was "part of the dark green line left on the upper rims of the valleys. But you would not have seen anything else that you had seen before, just the widening band of water, and stumps of trees... When the water draws down, as the irrigators take the water, you would see these huge mudflats. Nothing can grow along those banks because they are covered for too long by the water."

Years later, in the book that Alberta issued about the project, its writer devoted one sentence to the consequences of the drowning of the five valleys: "The watchman of the Oldman Dam site spoke of the 'magic of watching a lake form in a desert.'" Many kilometres away, the beneficiaries of this dam—the suffering farmers, the many who rely on the farmers for their economic life and who rely on water for economic development—celebrated this water.

As the water rose, Milton used his one remaining weapon—the power of words. He explained, "How do you tell it to people who are no longer rightly connected? How do you explain it in layman's terms? Everything you say is watered down. Even the feelings are no longer sincere. The approach no longer seems valid. But when the right things are said in the right way, people have no choice but to feel it."

At this point, Milton was out on bail again, waiting for his second trial. He crisscrossed the country, performing his story, over and over to university radio stations, Native centres, conferences on Native people and the justice system, and journalists. In one article, called "Crossing Over," a journalist quoted Milton explaining where he got the authority to do the Lonefighter protest:

If the water had a voice it would say that same thing I said, but it doesn't, so the Creator said this is what we all must do. The Lonefighter Society, we ask for no permission, we have permission. I get permission from no one, except from nature and that's the way I live it out. I don't need human permission, all I know is: nature is really—if you want to put words in its mouth—it's screaming. There's no other way to say it. It is screaming and it is dying. Are you willing to listen? I'm willing to listen, so now it's something everyone is going to have to look at: if it's worth dying for? We're all going to die, let's set our priorities as to how we want our tombstones to read.

Milton also sat for radio interviews, one of which Jim Vella in Toronto heard. Later, a painter Jim knew, Doug Fox, also met Milton and spoke to him. Fox thought about what Milton was trying to do and his plight. He decided to do a painting depicting Milton's struggle, and that was the painting I saw in Toronto in 2004.

On May 22, 1991, as the water rose, Milton was back in the newspapers. He warned the press that he would take a "direct action" at the dam in a few days to stop its construction. He told the press: "We're at the same place we were last year. Nowhere to go, no one to go to, no one to listen. The only ones who are going to listen to us are our adversaries, and they are going to put me in a graveyard, or behind bars. We don't want a confrontation."

"Will you be armed?" someone asked Milton.

"With my heart and soul, with my life, that's what I will be armed with. If we really say we're a nation, we have a right to arm ourselves." On May 26, with the permission of dam authorities, Milton and forty other people—some from Native groups and church groups, along with environmentalists from across Canada—walked to the beat of pounding drums along a two-kilometre road to the dam site. They had been given permission to attend the dam site after promising not to cause any damage. When they arrived, Milton and the others performed a Blackfoot pipe ceremony. One man chanted. Milton and the others stood silently, with heads bowed, as the pipe was lit. Then everyone began to chant and turned roughly in unison to face the four directions. Then, as part of the ritual, Milton blew smoke toward the face of a three-and-a-half-month-old baby.

Milton told the few journalists who accompanied them, "We're here to tear the dam down spiritually. Then physically, that will come in the next little while. Today is a special day to let the river know that we haven't given up on it—to honour the river, and wish it new life."

A few days later, on May 31, the Alberta government hauled Milton back to court. This time, to the Court of Appeal. The Crown wanted to place more conditions on Milton's bail so that he could not go anywhere near the Oldman River Dam. Court of Appeal Justice Roger Kerans presided that day. He had been the Court of Appeal justice who had originally let Milton out on bail months before.

According to press reports, at the hearing the Crown prosecutor read media accounts to the court, detailing what Milton allegedly said and pointing out "veiled reports of violence." Justice Kerans "seemed unimpressed" with this evidence. He said, according to newspaper reports of the hearing, "You don't have facts, just newspaper reports?" At one point in the hearing, Justice Kerans turned to Milton and said, "You have to understand, to be released after you have been convicted is a privilege. If you abuse that privilege, you will lose that right. I appreciate that you are a political person. There is a line that you can cross between being involved in a public discussion and making threats. If you cross that line, you will be back in here and in big trouble. I don't want to gag you. Let's you and I find a middle way."

After the hearing, Milton acknowledged the line that the justice drew and said that "my intentions have never been to cross that line." He added, "If anyone has broken the law or not kept good behaviour, it is the Oldman Dam project."

Dam on Trial

Milton Born With A Tooth wasn't the only accused in the spring of 1991. Unless the governments of either Alberta or Canada could find a way to stop it, the Oldman Dam itself would face a true trial of impartial judges. Standing between Canada and Alberta and their goal was Martha Kostuch. It was an increasingly desperate struggle among equals: Martha Kostuch v. the collective might of Canada and Alberta. Back in March 1990, the Federal Court of Appeal had ruled that an environmental assessment of the dam had to be done before the project could be legal. Then, in September 1990, the Supreme Court agreed to hear Alberta's appeal of the Federal Court of Appeal decision. The Government of Canada said it would not begin the environmental assessment until after the Supreme Court had made its final ruling. However, Martha Kostuch and the environmentalists knew that by the time the Supreme Court had rendered a verdict, the dam would be done and working. So Martha went to court again to try to force Canada to follow the law and appoint commissioners.

On November 16, four days before Martha's court date and eight months after being told by a court to do so, Canada finally appointed commissioners to conduct an environmental assessment of the Oldman Dam. These "judges" had excellent credentials, and one was an Aboriginal lawyer.

In *Once Upon an Oldman,* Jack Glenn tells the story of how Alberta responded to this court-ordered assessment or "trial" of the Oldman Dam. A few days after the commissioners were appointed, the Alberta government announced that it would refuse to participate in the court-ordered assessment. Alberta went to federal court to try to have the assessment stopped until the Supreme Court of Canada decided the appeal, which would be after the dam was completed. A justice of the federal court ruled against Alberta, saying, "If I interfere with this panel, I would just further delay any good they can do." Jack Glenn adds that this "was exactly what Alberta had intended."

Experts hired by the commission said that "it was a challenge" to base their work on information provided by Alberta. Their work was "hampered by Alberta's reluctance to be forthcoming with information." Alberta had not collected some of the information the commission needed. "To further frustrate the process, some of the information that Alberta did provide 'changed over time' or 'was delivered to the reviewers too late to be incorporated' into their work." Also, Alberta refused to allow the panel's experts to speak to provincial employees or engineers under contract with Alberta about what information might have been available. The wildlife specialist, Dr. Brian Horejsi, reported that Alberta's "wildlife studies are deficient in almost every category." So little had been done, it was as if "a wildlife assessment of the Oldman River Dam project has not yet been undertaken."

Starting in November 1991, public hearings were held in areas surrounding the dam, as well as in bigger centres in Alberta. The proceedings were transcribed, as is done during trials, to keep a permanent record of what was said—or at least, to keep a record of what was said as long as such paper records are kept. There is only one record of the hearings left in existence at a library in Edmonton.

Hearings opened on November 5, in Lethbridge, at the University of Lethbridge. The dam had great support in southern Alberta. And it was important for those in favour of the dam to demonstrate the depth and breadth of this support to the panel. The first presenter was David Carpenter, the city's mayor. He told the panel: "Farming is a tradition around Lethbridge. Agricultural production is the backbone of Lethbridge's economy. We have some of Canada's finest grazing land, some of the world's best wheat, and fields that produce an abundance of crops. This is the garden of Alberta. This is why we are called the breadbasket of the world, and the importance of agriculture cannot be overestimated. Irrigation is the heart of our agricultural success. We want it to remain viable— so we have taken a strong position in support of the Oldman Dam."

He held up a photograph for the panel to see. It was a picture taken on July 31, 1988, of the Oldman River. The level of water flow "looked pretty sorry." He added that the Bow River, which flows through Calgary, and the Oldman have the same minimum flows, yet the Bow River "has seven reservoirs, and diversion points." Without these diversions and reservoirs, he explained, "Calgary, as we know it, would not exist. Like those from other communities, I am sold on water resource management." He told the panel that the decision to have the Oldman Dam wasn't so much a question of "being all right or all wrong, but a rational decision based on the fact that the benefits outweigh the detriments."

Next, a representative from the Village of Nobleford spoke: "We need water to fill our reservoirs for the winter. All of our water comes from the irrigation district. On some years there is not enough water to fill our reservoirs to full capacity for the winter. There is not enough water—it is stagnant, and stinks."

Later that morning, Lethbridge Alderman Don Lebarron spoke. He would speak again at other hearing locations. But that first morning, he said: "The dam is supported by 200,000 people. Most studies since WW2 have supported the dam, so we find it absolutely incredible that the reality of the dam be questioned. We are very frustrated that this kind of thing can be brought against a project that is totally completed. We are frustrated at the cost to the taxpayer of these hearings."

Lebarron also noted: "We have never had a greater mitigation project in this province than for the Oldman Dam." He continued that a "propaganda machine" of "anti-dam people" has "painted southern Alberta as anti-environment." He said, "We are all concerned with the environment. We live here. Why shouldn't we be?" Near the end of his speech, he spoke about the economic benefits of the dam, prefacing his remarks with the following words: "If economic activity can be used as a measure of quality of life..." he hoped that the dam would stop rural depopulation. He concluded by saying that some call the dam "evil, whereas, the facts show that it was simply necessary..."

Roy Jenson spoke at an evening session in Lethbridge on November 6. He said that he was chairman of the LNID but he was "first and foremost, a farmer." Roy explained: "The Oldman Dam is essentially complete. Three hundred and fifty-three millions has been spent. The money is sunk. There is no way to get the investment back. It is redundant to further consider at this time the economic cost benefit to build the reservoir. We must move ahead. Since the costs are sunk, the real issue is how to maximize the benefits. To tear down the dam is a frightening prospect. The costs of dismantling the dam could be as much as to build it."

The commission's third hearing was held on November 7, in Calgary, at the Travelodge Airporter Hotel. Martha Kostuch made a presentation for the Friends of Oldman River, during which she said: "The Oldman Dam is illegal." She accused the Government of Alberta of breaking the law in building the dam, and "continuing to break it every day building."

Letters and reports were also forwarded to the panel. On

November 7, the commission received a medical report from the Piikani Board of Health and Medical Services Branch, noting its concern about a possible increase of mercury in fish found in the reservoir behind the dam. The board had taken hair samples from willing Piikani to provide a history of levels of mercury in their bodies and provide a baseline to assess the rise in mercury they expected to see due to consumption of fish caught in the reservoir behind the dam. Since the farmers who would ultimately get the water stored by the Oldman River Dam did not live near the dam reservoir and likely bought their fish in stores, they were not tested to prepare for a possible spike in mercury.

The next day, November 8, at the second session in Calgary, scientists hired by the commission and unpaid environmentalists spoke or handed up letters. Wildlife expert Dr. Brian Horejsi told the panel, "I think we may be overemphasizing the strict ecological emphasis on studies while the sky is falling down around us… When the reservoir is full, I don't think it takes the proverbial rocket scientist to see that we have a significant impact here. We're not talking about moderate or minor impact, we're talking about some degree of severe." He added that viewed over the long term, "the mitigation process has almost a zero percent chance of success."

Late in the day, Milton Born With A Tooth spoke to the panel. The session had run long and he was the final speaker. In a week, the Piikani people would put forward a community presentation to the panel in Brocket, laying out a plan that included economic uses for the Oldman River valley. Instead of joining them, Milton had elected to speak in Calgary, alone. When Milton rose and approached the microphone, the chairman said, "Mr. Born With A Tooth. We are running very late, sir, so I'd appreciate it if you would be succinct."

"Don't worry, it's going to be quick," Milton replied, then he continued:

You don't understand what we mean when we talk about cottonwood trees. Destroying cottonwood trees is like removing the Mormon Tabernacle—it is a desecration. Cottonwood trees are the centre of our lifestyle. But how can we measure it in technical terms? This panel does not have the foundation to know how to measure how we perceive the environment—why it's a genocidal process.

What's going to fall first is the cottonwood trees. You are interfering into a religious ecosystem. Are you going to condone that? The ultimate price of this is going to be a way of life. All I am saying is that the only protection we have—in a moral and just way—is this process. If nothing else is left, then I myself as the leader of the Lonefighter Society, regardless of what people think or not, I got to go back and do what I think is best. Because the only thing and the only hope that we have is this process, and right now this process is forgetting one thing, and that's the main objective—you have to let people really expose this way of life that you're destroying.

"I'm afraid we're running a little late, so at this time I'd like to thank you for your advice," Chairman Ross said.

"I appreciate that."

"I would also—"

"Because I don't want to destroy this process. What I wanted to do is to at least give some hope in this process, because the thing is, you know, they're doing an illegal process by doing that dam…"

"Thank you, sir," Chairman Ross said.

"I go downstream and I do something and I get the whole system jumping all over my case, and nothing has been done on the other side. So that's all I am saying, is that there's a serious question here, and it's you people that can deal with that."

"Thank you, sir. We appreciate that."

***

On November 11, 1991, four days after that hearing in Calgary, a lawyer from the law firm Milner & Fenerty, which was representing the Alberta government, sent a letter to the commission, stating that the Oldman Dam was not illegal as a court had turned down Martha's request to halt the dam, and the Federal Court of Appeal had not ordered Alberta to stop building the dam when the court rendered Alberta's permit invalid. This position would later be answered by the Supreme Court of Canada, and Canada's leading Constitutional scholar, Peter Hogg.

***

On November 16, 1991, the commissioners travelled south again to conduct a hearing on the Piikani Reserve. Martha Kostuch's efforts to put the dam on trial, using the law, allowed this day to happen. On that day even if only briefly, the powerful had been forced by the law to listen to the dispossessed. The commission arrived at the scattering of houses and band buildings that comprise Brocket. TA commission ordered by the government came perhaps for the first time ever, to listen to Piikani Elders speak on questions of justice and fairness, on history, on their treatment by Canada and Alberta, on the river, and on the dam.

The day began with a Grand Entry—in which the Piikani Elders came into the hall in full dress, each with an eagle-feather headdress. Prior to the opening prayers, Chief Leonard Bastien spoke: "It is our traditional Native custom from years ago, our

Elders, whenever they hold an important meeting, they always have an invocation on the understanding, all the people, so we can work together in unity, sharing, cooperation, and peace." Then the "Flag Song" of the Piikani people was sung. Chief Bastien introduced others who would participate, including many Piikani Elders. He also introduced Devalon Small Legs, who "put in his own time and money" to create the presentation, and through his "vision" helped the Piikani organize their presentation to the commission on that day.

Many spoke that day, including Evelyn Kelman and Lorna Born With A Tooth. Chief Bastien spoke first. He told the panel that the Piikani have title and rights to the Oldman River "since time immemorial" and based on their treaty. He said that the Government of Alberta had built the Oldman Dam, "despite the prior and superior reserved rights of the Peigan Nation in the Oldman River." He added that Alberta built the dam and allocated water to other users in a way that "presumes that Peigan Band is without rights to the use of the Oldman River."

Following this opening, Eddy Yellowhorn spoke about the history of the Piikani and their relationship with the Canadian government. Near the end of his speech, he said, "The biggest problem we had was the interpretation in 1877 of the signing of that treaty. Just for example, one of the leaders in that Treaty 7, he talked for almost an hour, and when the interpreter interpreted his words, all he says is, 'He's damn glad.'"

Next, Joe Crowshoe spoke. He told the story of his journey along the Oldman River down to the proposed site of the dam, just after he learned it would be dammed. As he walked, he thought about the government, about his people, and:

...about my young generation today looking down on the

Oldman River seeing the beavers, seeing the fish, seeing deer, coyotes, eagles. And I thought to myself that God has provided for the people. There's no man in this world is going to create the same situation and the spiritual situation and understanding. They're spoiling our Mother Earth.

We notice downstream, some of the wildlife are not as plentiful as they used to be, not as healthy as they used to be. Also the fish. Along with the berries, all the fruit. They've been affected. We're quite scarce in our Saskatoons and chokeberries and other berries. Some of our herbs too. We feel the water is not fresh and the ground is not good... We know down on the irrigation farms, they need the water, but how are we going to share with that, without both understanding. That is a big problem to us. We're not complaining about the dam. Nature will look after its dead. What I meant to say is the Great Spirit—we know this place is our place. We don't have the runoff from the mountains like we use to have...

Joe continued. He spoke about the significance of the Blackfoot treaty with Canada. "My ancestors, they did witness the treaty, my great grandmother... Both the government people and the Peigan Nation, we all need to come together and understand each other and support each other. One man can't do nothing. We need our voice. Today our young people don't understand about the treaty. They need to be more educated from the Elders on the Indian Act. That's out of sight now. Our rights to the land, and the rivers. They're coming to the last stand now. They're coming to the last stand."

Later that day, Devalon Small Legs read from the Piikani document explaining the band's plans to develop the Oldman River for irrigation and economic uses. One of the commissioners,

Dr. Michael Healey, asked Devalon to explain whether the Piikani wanted the Oldman River "for culture, or for irrigation or some other economic use?"

Devalon replied, "There is a delicate balance between the two. I think in terms of who we are as a Peigan Nation, we are the ones that can determine what that balance is." He added that such a balance might include irrigation. Devalon concluded his presentation by saying that the Canadian department responsible for the protection of First Nations people, the Department of Indian Affairs, had "thrown the Peigan people to the wind."

———————

The commission travelled to Pincher Creek on November 19, 1991, where Kevin Van Tighem was ready to speak. He had carefully crafted an eight-page document, designed to expose and transcend the thinking that created the dam. Van Tighem began by saying, "[T] here is an ethical dimension to this question, as well as economic, environmental and social dimensions, that forbid me from simply standing back and letting special interest groups push this project through."

He noted that environmental assessments are "a logical extension of our Western cultural imperative to manage and control the context in which we live. It favours left-brain processes: rationality, data, logic. It frowns on unquantifiable inputs such as emotion and intuition." Van Tighem suggested that when we really think about it, we realize that our most profound decisions as humans involve "a lot more emotion and intuition than logic." He added that the "mess" caused by human management of the earth involves costs that go on forever.

Van Tighem explained, "A decision to build this dam in spite of common sense was a political decision—a tangible, high-profile way of spending public deficit dollars in the south while signalling a commitment to water supply... We have had too much cold-hearted pragmatism already. The results have been awful—the mitigation program, for example, that simply adds new layers of damage. You have a public trust mandate. Please, for God's sake, give us a principled decision. There have been far too few principled decisions in this dirty little squabble over an irreplaceable ecosystem and a region's future."

He seemed to taunt the experts, suggesting that the commission had perhaps already "half-written" their decision "based on logical conclusions drawn from political pragmatism." Van Tighem added "Irrigation expansion does not make economic or environmental sense. As soon as we fire God and take over the job of running the river, we will create more and more technical problems to be solved, on and on, which will cost money forever, or at least as long as there is a dam."

Van Tighem continued, "We have a water welfare state in southern Alberta masquerading as a proud, conservative, self-sufficient society..." in which farmers worked eighteen-hour days and saw no profit from their labour. He called this "state" a "sick and distorted society."

Still, Van Tighem saw a way to save the river. The ecosystem could be restored with "volunteer effort," sustainable agriculture could be "reintroduced," and "water metering and fair pricing to rationalize water demand in irrigation districts" could be implemented. He felt that "we who call ourselves Albertans and Canadians" had a chance to find a way to live within "this ecosystem, with humility, respect and restraint. We can still change course and save that which stands to be lost. Only if we make that hard, radical decision—to put principle above expedience and pragmatism—can we really begin to turn around the forces of greed, compromise and tradition that have led to this water debate."

Commissioner Tracy Anderson asked Van Tighem how we as a society could better support the human values he had spoken about. Van Tighem responded, "We consult too late. We have no conservation strategy... In the case of the Oldman Dam, there will be ill will no matter what happens. Because here we had a tyranny of experts, and a bureaucratic, political decision. The decision to build the Oldman Dam was a way of getting votes. It was at the expense of other regions, and of the environment... I could be wrong. Good people do bad things, and the point is, this is a bad thing, and it's a bad decision. In actual fact, some of the most enlightened stewards of the landscape and the things that occupy the landscape are the irrigation farmers, the dryland farmers, and the ranchers. There is no good guy-bad guy in this thing. There is no easy way out here, but I'd sure like to see us working at a slightly higher level in terms of saying what kind of Alberta and Canada we want to see in a hundred years' time."

Commissioner Anderson then suggested that, in effect, if one wanted the land in a pristine wilderness state, a great deal of development would have to stop.

Van Tighem replied, "I am not saying that all places have to stay in a pristine state. But we have lost so much wilderness already—we need this place . . ."

The final day of hearings was also in Pincher Creek. Dianne Pachal attended that day and told the panel, "The disregard for the law displayed by our Alberta government, and the failure of our federal government to implement and enforce the letter and the spirit of the law regarding this mega-project, exemplifies a root of anarchy that strikes at the very foundation of a just democracy. It perpetuates a 'just us' system, instead of justice where no one, not

WHO SPEAKS FOR THE RIVER?

even government, is above the law."

She continued: "In our wild, primeval places we can find a sense of place and time. They are our connections to the lessons of the past and our bridges to the future. It is within wild places that we, as a society, learn that we are not full masters of the earth; that there are processes at work far beyond our present grasp of knowledge. In their retention and protection we can find security from the possibility of overdevelopment, and the domestication and loss of the human spirit." She quoted writer Michael Frome: "'Alas, the analytical type of thinking of Western science has given us the power over nature yet smothered us in ignorance about ourselves as part of it.'"

Writer Andy Russell also spoke that day. "It is an ugly process involved with greed and ignorance where people with power really do not care about what happens to the land or the future generations of people who will be faced with what we have allowed to be done with it." At the bottom of his typewritten letter to the panel were the following words written in black ink: "I am angry and disgusted."

Once again, Don Lebarron spoke on behalf of the dam. He brought as a special guest of Mayor Eldred Lowe of Pincher Creek. Mayor Lowe told the commission that his town supported "the dam due to downstream needs for water... The belief that a controlled and constant supply of water was necessary for those citizens living downstream was a reasonable scenario ... We think the benefits of controlled water supply will be more valuable as time goes on."

After the mayor spoke, Lebarron filed dozens of letters of support for the dam—from Lethbridge, Medicine Hat, Drumheller, Red Deer, Taber, Cardston, various counties, irrigation districts, and chambers of commerce, and others. Then he said, "The time for discussions on whether the dam should be built is over. It is here. It is very surprising that after 400 million dollars, people are challenging the very future and survival of this dam. We want people in Alberta to benefit. We want Native people to benefit… Back in 1935, there wasn't a green blade of grass or wheat visible between Taber and Moose Jaw—a distance of nearly 400 miles. Similar conditions were present in 1982, 1987, 1988, and periodically since the 1930s in the Palliser Triangle. Why not do something to ameliorate the effects of such occurrences?"

Lebarron closed his final speech to the commission with the words of farmer Ralph Erdman: "The shortage of water is a vital concern. At the moment the dam may not be vital for the economic survival of southern Alberta, but I would hate to have our grandchildren in a few years' time point their fingers at their forebears and wonder why, when construction was underway, the dam was not completed to conserve irrigation water for future generations."

Commissioner Jim Gladstone asked Don Lebarron a question: "You mentioned at the Lethbridge Hearings the other night that the human need has not been considered with respect to the Oldman River. Maybe you can explain it to me. How do you put the human need above the loss of particular species of fish, for mercury contamination of the fish, for genocide of the river value, of the potential loss of the cottonwoods, which we know is eventually going to happen? Someone mentioned the other day—'I'd hate to tell my grandchildren that I had a chance to build a dam and benefit them.' But by the same token, I would hate to say, hey you know, to tell my grandchildren I had a chance to stop the destruction of all this and I didn't do anything. So how do you put a human need ahead of that?"

Lebarron answered, "I think that we have heard the terrible horror stories that have happened in certain cases when dams were built … we've heard other stories where proper mitigation was done, and that kind of result didn't take place. I believe with proper mitigation now and later, that these kinds of problems can be eliminated. I don't see the mercury poisoning is inevitable … my understanding is that the dam will lead to a number of enhancements. Certainly the fact that the water is even through the year is important. That doesn't mean that there's not some minuses… But in our view, there are so many more pluses."

Commissioner Gladstone then turned to Mayor Lowe and asked a final question, one of the final questions of the hearings: "You have had a chance today to hear some of the comments about the dam. I am sure that this was not available to you before. But if all the facts were put to you at that particular time, do you think you would have made the same decision to support Lethbridge, the 300 farmers, and potential new farmers, to destroy a beautiful wilderness area that was one of the best fishing areas in the world?"

"Boy, that's a tough one," Lowe replied. "Hard part for us as lay people is to try to determine where the facts are."

Gladstone said, "One of the best solutions may be to tear down the dam. I don't know. All I wanted to point out here is that had this panel, or had there been a similar process in place prior to the dam, the position of Pincher Creek might have been entirely different? Would that be fair to say?"

"Yes."

With this interchange, the panel hearings passed into history. What remained was the commission's decision.

———————

In January of 1992, the Supreme Court of Canada released its judgement proclaiming that the Federal Court of Appeal was right and the Alberta government's position was wrong. Canada did have to do an environmental assessment before Alberta could have a license to build the dam. The environmentalists were ecstatic. There is no record of Minister Jim Horseman's reaction to the confirmation by the Supreme Court of Canada that the dam was illegal. One of Canada's leading constitutional scholars, and former dean of Osgoode Hall Law School, Peter Hogg, wrote in his book *Constitutional Law of Canada*, in relation to a further decision confirming the federal court's ruling: "The ruling of the Court rendered the project illegal." Further building would also be illegal, unless a court ordered that construction could continue.

Dianne Pachal remembered speaking to Milton after hearing the news. They were both ecstatic. He told her, "The law says we won, the law says the dam is illegal." Dianne told me, "We thought, 'It's got to stop. We played by the rules that you guys set up, fair is fair, the dam has got to stop.' That is how it should have stopped. The government kept building. Their position was: Might is right."

In May 1992, the Environmental Assessment Commission concluded that the Oldman Dam was unacceptable for a number of reasons. All of the panelists, except Tracy Anderson from Lethbridge, concluded that the dam should be "decommissioned," meaning it should never be used, its tunnels should be opened and the river allowed to run freely. To those who opposed the dam, a miracle had happened: the commissioners had listened.

The commission's report elaborated that the dam could not be justified on economic grounds and resulted in "substantial environmental, social and economic costs" for fisheries, wildlife, the river-valley ecosystem, and the "Peigan Indian band." Therefore the project was "unacceptable." Critical fish habitat would be affected by the dam. There had already been a "substantial loss" of a "highly valued" cottonwood ecosystem upstream, and there was no certainty that it would not happen downstream. Such losses would be "extremely undesirable." The decline of the cottonwood forests would have an impact on fish, birds, wildlife, as well as Native and non-Native people.

The commission said that the Piikani "were not treated fairly in the decision-making, planning or implementation phases of this project." That there was no deal between the Alberta government and the Piikani was "one of the most significant and unacceptable features of the project." The commission noted other issues: "[T]he Piikani were not involved in key decisions; many resources important to their culture, such as cottonwoods, fish, game and willows, will be affected by the project; the potential for mercury contamination of fish downstream from the dam could have health consequences for the Piikani; and important culturally and spiritually valued areas within the reservoir were flooded."

As for archaeology, the panel concluded: "The existence of a record of the unique cultural achievement of the bison hunters, in situ, is important provincially, nationally and internationally. The irreversible loss of an area which contains so much historic and prehistoric information is a significant cost of the project." The panel stated that First Nations people were never interviewed: "This is an inexcusable omission, in the panel's opinion, because it overlooks a very important source of local information."

The commission concluded that the Oldman Dam would lead to more water consumption, thereby leading to "future water shortages." The report suggested that "a clamour" for further dams or diversion "is probable."

Roy Jenson called the decision "unbelievable." The Canadian government stated: "We are confident, based on the evidence presented to the panel, that the environmental impacts can be and are being mitigated effectively. Therefore, we are rejecting the option of decommissioning the dam." Alberta Environment Minister Ken Kowalski called the panel's report "technically adolescent." He added, "There is no way the dam will ever be shut down." Minister of the Environment Ralph Klein said he honestly felt that Alberta had addressed most of the concerns. Later, when asked if Alberta could operate the Oldman Dam without a federal license, Klein replied, "Of course we can … we're doing it now."

One of the commission's recommendations, which Canada had agreed to comply with, said that the Canadian government should not give Alberta license to operate the dam unless Alberta made a deal with the Piikani compensating them for their losses. In September 1993, without any agreement between the Piikani and Alberta, Canada gave Alberta all the authorizations it needed to operate the dam.

Chief Bastien wrote a letter to the Department of Indian Affairs expressing "disgust" at this, suggesting that Canada had shown "contempt for the Crown's obligations to our people."

On September 10, 1994, a *Lethbridge Herald* article read: "Reservoir Ends Summer Water Woes." Alberta Environment engineer Doug Clark was quoted as saying that "relief from the risks of summer drought comes from the Oldman Dam reservoir, which even after an unusually hot summer is still about 75% full." Yet, the man responsible for the City of Lethbridge water supply, Dalton Stafford, explained, "the increased flow has not significantly altered the city's water supply or quality. Little has changed since the dam was built."

To Redo the Past: Milton's Second Trial

The dam was official, already a familiar part of the landscape for many people and certainly not the centre of media attention, when Milton's second trial started on February 22, 1994, in Calgary. This was to be the retrial of what happened in Fort Macleod on September 7, 1990. It is impossible to be perfect in a complex trial—there is too much to know, too many implications that cannot be thought out beforehand. All lawyers are better in a second trial because they have already done it once before. In a second trial, lawyers get to do what rarely happens in life: they get to redo everything, benefitting from information that came to light only at the end the first trial. A second trial represented a second chance, not only for the lawyers and Milton, but also for the legal system itself.

Justice Willis O'Leary presided over the trial. He studied law at the University of British Columbia, where he achieved the singular distinction of winning the Gold Medal for having the highest standing in his graduating class. He later obtained a master's in law from Harvard University. He was a justice of the Court of Queen's Bench of Alberta for eleven years, then at the Court of Appeal for Alberta for twelve years.

During the trial, when Justice O'Leary asked questions, he almost always began his queries with "Please..." When someone answered him, he said, "Thank you." Karen Gainer later told me that he was a "gentleman, an excellent judge." For judges and lawyers who don't really know the law, it can seem very complicated and confusing. Justice O'Leary was able to distill the law to its essence, without sacrificing exactitude, and so when he spoke about the law it made sense and was usually clear. Justice O'Leary was also at the forefront of a new trend in Canadian courtrooms, one that allowed for a multiplicity of religions and beliefs to claim legitimacy within the courts.

In the past in Canada, witnesses had to swear on the Christian Bible or affirm that they would tell the truth. Today, it is common in large city courtrooms to have many holy books available for a person to use to promise or "swear" to tell the truth. Even as recently as 2004, however, this was much less common. During the second trial of Milton Born With A Tooth, for the first time in Alberta, a person swore to tell the truth using a Blackfoot Oath instead of the Bible. Instead of being outside the process from the very beginning— swearing, in some cases, to an alien God—the Blackfoot witness was welcome to swear to the Great Spirit.

Reg Crowshoe told me that it is vital for First Nations peoples to find parallels between their justice practices and Western practices common in Canadian courtrooms. He said it would be useful for the Canadian justice system to look to First Nations' practices for inspiration, as well. If First Nations peoples go to a court and feel that their practices are honoured, they can feel that they are part of the court process; if not, they will feel mistreated. In Milton's case, Justice O'Leary decided there was no reason why a Native witness could not promise to tell the truth by using the traditional Blackfoot pipe ceremony.

He was polite and flexible, yet he was also firm in his positions. On one occasion, he disagreed with Karen Gainer about how something should be done by saying, "I prefer the other, but I'm certainly going to abide by your wishes." At another point, the Crown objected that the defence was not doing something correctly. The judge agreed with the Crown, turned to Gainer and said, "We've all been there before. It's hard to conduct a decent examination of any kind and at the same time remember all of the little rules of procedure and evidence. So I excuse you..."

"Thank you, sir," Gainer responded.

Justice O'Leary's relationship with the court observers was also very different than Justice MacLean's was during Milton's politically charged first trial. One day, high-school students from Lester B. Pearson High School came to watch the trial. The judge welcomed them and noted their attendance. He confirmed with Gainer that another witness would be sworn in using the traditional Blackfoot Oath. When she said yes, he turned to the students and said, "Welcome, and I hope you enjoy the proceedings and get something out of it."

For this trial, Alberta's Attorney General's office had assigned a different prosecutor—William Pinckney. Gainer was, of course, back for Milton, and this time, she had another lawyer to help her— Louise Mandell. Mandell practiced in Vancouver. She is a leading Aboriginal and Treaty Rights lawyer in Canada, having not only argued key cases at all court levels in Canada but also made crucial contributions to the development of this area of law. In addition, of course, Mandell was familiar with the Piikani, as she and fellow lawyer, Thomas Berger, had launched lawsuits on behalf of the Piikani in 1986 against Alberta and Canada, regarding their treaty rights, and water and riverbed rights to the Oldman. She had also been hired by the band to commence a lawsuit claiming that the expropriation of the Piikani land in 1922 was illegal.

A jury was chosen with one Native person on it, and the trial began. The Crown put the same witnesses before the court as it had during the first trial, and they were cross-examined by Milton's lawyers. The evidence was almost identical, but now and then something new came to light.

RCMP Superintendent Maguire testified again. He told Pinckney, "In the initial plan, I, together with a couple of senior officers, would go to the Lonefighter camp and tell them what was taking place. That was eventually changed, because once again I had told chief and council that as we went in new directions and so forth, we would do our best to keep them informed." Maguire added, "In hindsight, if I had been there, no doubt I would have gone out first and tried to talk to the Lonefighters, as was our plan, but I wasn't there and that didn't happen."

———————

Later in the trial, the former deputy minister for Alberta, Henry Walter Thiessen, testified again. Again, the Crown tried to show that the land where Milton fired his gun belonged to the LNID. This time, Louise Mandell rose to cross-examine Thiessen. Thiessen had held power at the highest levels in the Alberta government. He had negotiated the water deal between Alberta and the Piikani in 1981. To do that, he had extensively studied the history of the expropriation of the land in 1922 from the Piikani. As a result, he was in a position to both explain and defend that expropriation.

Louise Mandell was equally well placed to cross-examine him. She was a good and rigorous lawyer, with sound knowledge of the past history and experience of Native people, general knowledge of Treaty 7, and the expropriation in 1922. She had represented many First Nations clients over the years, dedicating herself to ensuring that their Aboriginal and treaty rights were recognized

and respected by the Canadian and various provincial governments. It was not unusual for her to cross-examine a former senior
government official, such as Thiessen. Fighting for the rights of First
Nations peoples in court often involved her asking tough questions
of powerful government officials.

While the actions of Milton were not planned by the Piikani
council, Mandell was authorized by both band council and Milton to
cross-examine Thiessen. She knew that there was not, as she put it
to me, a "level playing field between the Piikani and the government
of Alberta" in the Piikani court actions as Alberta had the money
and power to use delaying and other tactics to stop the Piikani from
"vindicating" their rights. In this context, Mandell considered the
chance to cross-examine Thiessen, and bring these issues before the
court in a public way, to be a "gift." She explained to me how, in her
view, the legal and political aspects of the case came together: for
her, the cross-examination of Thiessen was both legal and political
at the same time. Her goal was to "make the legal the political."
Justice O'Leary's job was rather different.

Milton stood accused of a series of crimes. Mandell had her
own view of who was guilty and what their crimes were. Thiessen,
who had been called to give evidence about why the Alberta government owned the land, would have to defend, as best he could, nothing
less than the history of a nation, a province, and an irrigation district,
in relation to their treatment of the rights of First Nations.

Mandell stood up and began. Thiessen agreed that he had
worked for Alberta on treaty issues. He agreed that treaties with the
Indians covered most of the lands of Alberta and that these treaties
"were done to mark the terms by which the Indian people and
the non-Indian people would coexist on this land." Next, Mandell
reached down onto the table in front of her and picked up a few
sheets of paper. She walked over to Thiessen and handed him the

papers. She asked him, "Can you identify this document?"

"Yes. It is Treaty 7."

Up to this point, the history of Treaty 7 had been like a sleeping giant, seemingly outside of the issues discussed in Milton's trials. Mandell brought it inside the court, to the centre of the proceedings, and said: "I would ask that the treaty be marked as an exhibit."

"I would presume the relevance of this will appear," said Pinckney.

"It will. It should," said Mandell.

"I'll trust my learned friend," said the Crown. This form— "my learned friend"—reflects the attempt of the Courts themselves to keep decorum, and in so doing, to remind everyone that respect is the best way to pursue one's individual rights.

Next, Mandell said that at the back of the treaty are a series of Xs, instead of signatures, and that these Xs were there because the Native people could not understand English when the treaty was made.

"That's my understanding," Thiessen said.

A bit later, she asked, "Are you aware that an issue in Alberta raised by the First Nations is that their understanding of the spirit and intent of the treaty differs from that of the written text?"

"I have heard that," he said.

Next Mandell suggested that the Piikani own their reserve land.

Justice O'Leary politely stopped her and said, "I question the relevance of these questions. Let's keep in mind that we are not here dealing with who owns the land. That is for some other court on some other day. Today we are talking about the five criminal charges, and let's focus our attention on the law that is relevant to the criminal charges, instead of running some kind of trial here that publicizes all kind of claims and counterclaims."

Mandell returned to Treaty 7. She asked Thiessen if he was

familiar with the book *The Treaties of Canada,* by Alexander Morris. Thiessen said that he was. Mandell continued, quoting a speech from Morris's book:

When the Piikani met with the representatives of Canada to try to negotiate a treaty, the chief negotiator for Canada, Lieutenant Governor Laird, made a speech to the Indians that day:

A reserve of land will be set apart for yourself and your cattle upon which none others will be permitted to encroach. For every five persons one square mile will be allotted on this reserve on which they can cut the trees and brush for firewood and other purposes.

[And later he says:] The chiefs all here know what I said to them three years ago when the police first came to the country, that nothing would be taken away from them without their own consent. You see that I have always kept my promises. As surely as my past promises have been kept, so surely shall those made by the commissioners be carried out in the future. If they were broken, I would be ashamed to meet you or look you in the face.

"Yes, I recall reading that document," Thiessen said.

Mandell continued, "And that expropriation from 1922, while it was, as you say, an option under the Indian Act, it is an option which runs contrary to the treaty promise; is that not so?"

"He can't say that," the Crown stood up and objected.

"I think I would want to look at that for a few minutes before I would comment on that," Thiessen said.

"I think that's a legal conclusion, isn't it?" Justice O'Leary asked.

"Well," Mandell said, "it is, but—"

The Crown spoke. "I suggest that the jury can make up their own minds about whether what she is talking about is just the bare words."

Mandell quoted: "'A reserve of land will be set aside for yourself and your cattle upon which none others will be permitted to encroach.' An expropriation appears to run contrary to those words."

Justice O'Leary said, "This is a legal conclusion. First of all, it is statements by people that are not included in the treaty and the wording itself. Whether there is a conflict between the interpretation of those words and expropriation or the *Indian Act* is a legal conclusion and I don't think this witness is qualified to answer that."

"What about from a layperson's point of view. If you were listening to the word of Colonel Macleod, and you had your land expropriated, would you think that maybe there was something that was going—"

The Crown stood up and spoke. "Objection. Argumentative."

Justice O'Leary said, "The words speak for themselves. The treaty speaks for itself, the Indian Act speaks for itself, and this witness is not qualified as a legal expert and able to interpret those words."

This area of cross-examination was now closed.

Mandell, however, was just beginning. She established with Thiessen that in the 1920s First Nations people had no water rights because to be on the LNID board of directors one had to be eligible to vote. She continued, "And do you know that Indian people didn't have the vote until 1960?"

"Yes," Thiessen said.

She confirmed that the LNID had a license from Alberta to take 156,000 acre-feet of water from the Oldman River. Then, she asked, "Would you disagree with me if I said that the Peigan have never had any water protected for them by the provincial irrigation system?"

"That may be that they have never applied for it."

"I am not asking if they applied for it, I'm asking whether or not, to your knowledge, when LNID got 156,000 acre-feet of water protected, whether there was any water protected at the same time for the Peigan?"

"Based on the record of 1917, there was no water protected for the Peigan Indian Reserve."

Mandell turned to the part of the Indian Act (section 46) under which the LNID said that the expropriation of Indian land was legal. First, she showed that the expropriation of the land was against the treaty. Now, she wanted to try to show that the expropriation itself was not done properly, and therefore the Indian land had been taken illegally. She showed that many things were not done properly, which suggested that there was a live issue as to whether the land had even been expropriated legally.

Later, Thiessen explained that there were no issues raised about the validity of the expropriation until the late 1970s. Mandell confirmed with him that he found no evidence in the newspapers, for example, that the Indians back then were concerned about title. She asked if he knew that in the 1920s "the Department of Indian Affairs controlled the dealings that the Peigan Band had with government and with non-Aboriginal people?"

"Yes."

"And that they prevented the Indian people from leaving the reserve except by way of permit?"

"That was done at that time, yes."

"And that they were controlling or invasive in the life-style that the Indian people had?"

"I think I would have trouble answering with any certainty.

All I know is what I have seen in the records. To what extent it was invasive is a matter of judgement, I guess."

"I am going to ask whether you can identify this letter. It is from files you reviewed and gave to me. It is dated December 15, 1921. It is a letter from the Department of Indian Affairs sent to all directors or officials of Indian Affairs in the region. I am just going to read to you from the letter. This is around the time that the LNID was expropriated:

> Sir, it is observed with alarm that the holding of dances by the Indians on the reserve is on the increase and that these practices tend to disorganize the efforts which the department is putting forth to make themselves supporting. I have, therefore, to direct you to use your utmost endeavours to dissuade the Indians from excessive indulgence in the practice of dancing. You should suppress any dances which cause waste of time, interfere with the occupation of the Indians, settle them for serious work, injure their health, or encourage them in sloth or idleness. You should also dissuade and, if possible, prevent them from leaving their reserves for the purpose of attending fairs, exhibitions, et cetera, when their absence would result in their own farming and other interests being neglected.

Mandell continued reading: "It is realized that reasonable enjoyment and recreation should be enjoyed by Indians but they must not be allowed to dissipate their energies and abandon themselves to demoralizing amusements, but by the use of tact and firmness you can obtain and keep it, and this obstacle to continued progress would then disappear. The halls, rooms, and other places in which Indians congregate should be under constant supervision."

She stopped, looked at Thiessen, and spoke, "So the Department of Indian Affairs and their agents were inspecting the activities of the Indian people; is that your general knowledge of the period?"

"I don't know. It sounds that way from that document, but I don't have any knowledge."

She continued reading: "They should be scrubbed, fumigated, cleansed, or disinfected to prevent the dissemination of disease. The Indians should be instructed in regard to the avoidance of overcrowding rooms where public assemblies are being held, and proper arrangements should be made for the shelter of their horses and ponies…"

Mandell turned to Thiessen again, and spoke, "I'm going to suggest to you that it's not surprising that you don't find much of what the Peigan were reacting to in the papers in Lethbridge in 1922 when they were in this state, dependent and being directed by the Department of Indian Affairs in their dealings with third parties?"

"Is that a question?"

"It is a question. I'm saying are you surprised?"

"I must admit I am somewhat surprised by the tone of the letter, but I guess that's history."

"Mr. Peters, Surveyor-General for Canada, concluded that the waters of the river are subject to the jurisdiction of Alberta, but that the area of the bed of the river is included in the reserve, is that correct?"

"That is what he said in his report, yes," Thiessen agreed.

In the end, Mandell concluded this area of cross-examination with the following questions.

"Now, according to your understanding of things, who owns this land—the riverbed in the reserve—today?"

"That's probably a $64 question. I believe that depends on a variety of legal interpretations, ma'am."

"Well, that is—you have come here to say that there is a state of certainty about the title issue, and I am just wondering, who does own the river bed today?"

"You could take the position that the LNID owns that 4.1 acres."

———— • ————

On March 4, 1994, now that the case for the Crown was over, Milton walked to the witness box to testify. He had decided to testify in his own defence, unlike at his first trial. The courtroom of the Court of Queen's Bench in Calgary had few spectators. Most of the protesters from Milton's first trial had moved on to other things. Silently, the judge and jury, the lawyers, and Milton watched as the pipe ceremony, conducted by pipe carrier Devalon Small Legs, began.

Devalon explained to the judge, the jury, and the court the meaning of the pipe. "First of all, this pouch is the pipe bag. Inside we have the pipe, tobacco, and we have a stone pipe bowl. Oh, by the way, Paul Daniels here is my senior man. So if I say something wrong, he is going to correct me. So this is the pipe bowl, and this is the pipe stem.

"In the long ago time, in the time before, when grandfathers were still here, when they created us to come on this earth, we were given a way to talk to our Creator through our Grandfathers. The Creator decided that if his children wanted to talk to him, he set forth an instrument by which they could talk to him. And that instrument is the pipe. The role of the pipe is represented in different ways, in different Indian Nations. There are the Coyote stories. There are the Napi stories. But the intent is the same. The pipe bowl represents the earth and our connection to the earth. The stem represents the trees, and the Sundance tree that which we hold very sacred. The tobacco represents the offering that we use to talk to the Creator. The sweetgrass represents the way in which our prayer goes to the Creator. When we burn the sweetgrass, the smoke goes into the air. Our prayer rides the smoke as it goes up."

Devalon lit the pipe. The smell of burning sage spread throughout the court. Milton Born With A Tooth was in the witness box, ready to testify on his own behalf. Devalon walked up to Milton and stood beside him, holding the pipe in his hand. Devalon said, "When we approach this piece of pipe in Indian country in Indian life, we agree to tell the truth, not to lie, when we pick up the pipe in our traditional way. That's how we believe in the Great Spirit on this earth, to tell the truth and nothing but the truth, help God."

"I promise," said Milton. At long last, nearly three years after the day he fired his gun, Milton, who had spoken so much to the media, was finally telling his story to the court, before the power not only of the Queen but also of the Great Spirit. Gainer asked him questions, and Milton gave his testimony about what happened and why. He explained about meeting the Elder, Tiny Man Heavy Runner, the beaver, and why he did the protest. When Gainer finished asking him questions, she sat down, and Pinckney began his cross-examination.

"Sir, I understand you were out of town when the injunction was served; did you ever see a copy of it?"

"No."

"You discussed the injunction at some length, with others?"

"It was brought to my attention, but it was decided that it would be discussed with chief and council."

"Okay, you knew that according to the injunction you couldn't interfere with the Alberta Environment people coming onto the land to repair the dike—on the right-of-way; you knew that?"

"I knew that. As far as information I was given it was an

illegal injunction. But at that point in time the decision was brought to the band council."

"You knew you couldn't dig any more on that land; right?"

"I didn't know that. It was not discussed in the manner to where I understood it; it was brought up in the meeting we had early that morning. It was going to be brought to band council."

"I take it the real purpose of your digging at the dike was to draw attention to your protest against the building of the Oldman River Dam; is that fair to say?"

"No, it was to more or less uncover the wrongdoing of the— of the Oldman River Dam and the legal things around it."

"You knew the government wouldn't let you keep digging through that dike; what you wanted was them to take some action to stop you, right?"

"No, we wanted them to follow their own laws. We wanted them to follow the federal ruling that came down. For my part, I was hoping a dialogue would ensue. That's what I was hoping."

Pinckney continued, "Now on the morning of September 7, the first thing you saw was a group of men on the other side of the breach, right?"

"All I seen, the view I had when the bulldozer went up, I just seen a few RCMP moving off to the side. I guess I seen about three or four RCMP," Milton said.

"All right. It's your position that you didn't know why they were there, is it fair to say?"

"Up to that point in time it was like it was an invasion."

"Well, an invasion of four men is not much of an invasion, is it?"

"Well, you'll recall before that, so-called information had come to me that told me there had been an army coming down of RCMP."

"Well, shortly after you'd shot, you'd certainly be aware that it wasn't an army at all?"

"It was," Milton said.

"It was a very few men," Pinckney said.

"After that. After that, there was a lot of them."

"You would agree with me, that if the Environment people were going to fix the dike, they would have to come down both sides of the breach?"

"If they were. But they weren't going to do that."

"I am going to suggest you aimed the gun at a number of police officers. And when Officer Gaultier was trying to run away from you, you levelled the rifle at him and essentially frightened him into diving for cover along with Constable Whittington, didn't you?"

"No."

"Let me show you photos 14 and 15. Look at the photo: you are pointing a firearm directly at the bush that the camera is coming out of, is that fair to say?"

"Looks like it," Milton said.

"That's what you are doing."

"No, I wasn't."

"That's the rifle, and you're pointing it."

"That was within—between a motion."

"You knew there were men in those bushes?"

"Yes."

"And you felt free to point the firearm at the bushes with the men in it, is that fair to say?"

"At that time, on doing this, I was giving them equal access of me."

"You are saying when you were up there, that you weren't pointing the firearm into an area where you thought there were people?"

"No, I just—you couldn't see them anyway. You just knew they were somewhere in the vicinity."

"So, that morning, after the Lonefighters told the police they were trespassing, since they didn't march smartly away, you thought it was fair that you start firing with that rifle?"

"They were in a threatening position."

"I suggest that they weren't in a threatening position at all. What you saw was three or four men. Nobody had their guns drawn. All they were doing was walking along the gravel pile. There was nothing threatening in what you saw. There were more of you than what you could see, isn't that true?"

"There was an army there. I mean, that's a reality. That's not a myth. I mean, there was an army there. Whether I seen it or not, I knew they were coming."

As quickly as it began, the cross-examination of Milton Born With A Tooth was nearly over. Pinckney's file had a copy of Milton's criminal record. He was allowed by law to put Milton's criminal record in front of him and get Milton to confirm whatever crimes he had committed in front of the jury. The jury was allowed to use Milton's past crimes only to help them decide if he was telling the truth now. They were not allowed to use the criminal record to decide if Milton was a bad man, or if he did bad things, which made it more likely that he did these crimes, since, after all, people think that bad men do bad things. Pinckney knew that the jurors might unfairly judge Milton because of his past, even if the judge warned them not to. He left Milton's criminal record in his file and said, "No further questions." And he sat down.

Next, Devalon himself swore on the pipe and testified. He explained his opinion—and that of chief and council of the Piikani people—that the deal between the Piikani and the Alberta government signed after the 1978 Piikani water blockade "extinguishes

Alberta's title" to the weir, and the area where Milton fired his shots.

On March 11, 1994, the lawyers gave their closing arguments to the jury. Milton's trial was nearly over. The judge now had to charge the jury: tell them what the law was and how they should go about deciding the verdict in the case. Reduced to single-spaced typed print, Justice O'Leary's charge was sixty pages long. Justice O'Leary also told the jury: "Our system of law demands that cases be decided objectively on the basis of evidence presented. If we depart from that and make our decisions on the basis of other considerations, then we have betrayed the trust which society places in us. That may not be easy in given cases, but the hard cases are that much more important to our system of law... The only law which applies to this case is set out in the Criminal Code, which prescribes the criminal law in this country... The only law which we can apply is the law contained in the Criminal Code, which applies to all of us, including the accused. So you have to be bound by that law."

Later in his charge, Justice O'Leary noted that the use of force to defend oneself or one's property is, "as one might imagine, rigidly controlled and the situations in which it might be used are specifically stated; otherwise, we would have chaos in society and people would be using force for various reasons without justification." He added that the court injunction in this case, stopping the Lonefighters from digging and interfering with the Department of the Environment workers' attempts to fix the dike, was the law and had to be followed by all persons.

The judge was nearly finished. He had to mention one other matter, which probably was the most crucial issue of all. He said that even if Milton was wrong in thinking that he had a valid right to fire his gun in self-defence, the jury had to consider that he honestly thought he had the right to do what he did but was mistaken. Being honestly mistaken could be a defence to the charge, as well. Finally, Justice O'Leary added that the law cannot condone willful blindness: "A person cannot have an honest belief if they willfully refrain from considering things that are perfectly obvious to them or should be obvious to them. In other words, you can't close your eyes and not see what is obvious and then turn around and say you didn't know, I honestly believe in another set of facts. Had I looked, had I opened my eyes in the ordinary way, I would have known perfectly well what the circumstances were." In this case, the law does not allow a person to assert a belief in another set of circumstances. If a person is willfully blind to facts that are obvious, he or she is guilty.

The judge said that if the jury had any further questions, they could put them in writing. It was lunchtime when Justice O'Leary sent the jury to deliberate the fate of Milton Born With A Tooth.

———— — ————

That night the jury deliberated until 9:00 p.m. They deliberated all day on March 12 and again on March 13, until late in the evening. On the morning of March 14, the beginning of their fourth day of deliberations, the jury had a question. Lawyers try to interpret these questions the way ancient seers interpreted the entrails of animals. The question was as follows: "Can you please elaborate on honest but mistaken belief defence, as we are unclear as to the definition. Also, further define willful blindness and possibly provide some practical examples of it at your earliest convenience."

The lawyers and judge had a long discussion about the best way to answer the question fairly. Then the jury was called into court.

Justice O'Leary told the jury again about the defence, using the same words he had said the first time he explained it to them, fearing that more explanation might further confuse them.

At 4:30 p.m. , Justice O'Leary called the lawyers back into the courtroom. In such moments, during a case a lawyer thinks he or she should win, the lawyer may almost be sick to his or her stomach with worry; of course, that is nothing compared to what the accused feels, as the one who may be going to jail.

The jury entered the courtroom and slowly took their seats. The court clerk turned to the jury and spoke: "Members of the jury, have you arrived at a verdict as to the accused Milton Born With A Tooth? If so, please say so by your foreperson. Please stand." Such words are said all over Canada every day, as they have been said for decades. Milton was charged with pointing a firearm at Officer Gaultier, using a firearm to obstruct police, and dangerous use of a weapon. He was charged with doing each of these crimes more than once, so he had five charges in all.

"Yes, we have," said the foreperson.

"What is your verdict as to Count No. 1?" said the court clerk.

"We, the jury, find the defendant guilty," said the foreperson of the jury. They found Milton guilty of all charges. There is no record of whether Milton flinched. The jury was then polled by the court clerk because each juror must agree with the verdict, and say so publicly in the court. That day, something happened that "old-timers of the court" have told the media that they had never seen.

"Do you all agree?" the court clerk asked the jury.

"Yes," said Juror No 1.

"Oh, yes," said Juror No. 2.

"I don't know," said Juror No. 3. According to press reports, as the juror said these words, she "slumped forward in her seat." As the other jurors were asked, she "burst into tears." A *Calgary Herald* reporter explained, "The lone Native person on the twelve-member panel refused to make it unanimous." Justice O'Leary gave advice to the confused clerk. "Poll the rest of the jury and we will come back." The rest of the jurors simply said, "Yes."

"Do you want to ask Juror No. 3 once more, madam clerk?" Justice O'Leary asked. Instead of having the juror polled again, Justice O'Leary spoke. "I guess she's not prepared to answer." He turned to her and said, "Are you prepared to answer, ma'am?" She did not, or could not, answer. Justice O'Leary turned to all the jurors and spoke. "Well, as you know, ladies and gentlemen, your verdict has to be unanimous and it appears from what we have heard that the verdict is not at this point unanimous. I would assume that my duty now is to ask you to go back and continue deliberating."

"You don't understand," blurted out Juror No. 3.

"Pardon me?"

"You don't understand," she repeated.

"I think the best thing is to ask you to retire to the jury room and to continue your deliberations and advise the jury attendant when you are ready to come back into court again. I will speak to the lawyers. If we decide to take any other action, I will have you recalled." The jury left.

Justice O'Leary asked the defence and Crown, "Have I followed the proper procedure or should I have done something else?" He later decided that he had done the correct thing. The juror had not said that she could not decide. So, it was best to let the jury continue to deliberate. A little less than two hours later, the jury announced again that they had reached a verdict: guilty, on all counts. The jury was polled again. When Juror No. 3 was asked if she agreed, she said, "Yes." There is no record of how she looked or spoke that word. The court entered the verdict of guilty in the trial of Milton Born With A Tooth, on March 15, 1994.

Justice O'Leary let Milton stay out of jail while waiting for his sentencing. The day after the trial, Milton was photographed by a *Calgary Herald* reporter with his sister Lorna and a number of unidentified children. He was smiling, holding an eagle feather in one hand, the other hand held forward in front of him, palm out, the way a traffic cop would tell the driver of a car to stop. He looked lean and fit. Sentencing was delayed until September.

Karen Gainer asked Justice O'Leary to agree to let Milton be sentenced by a Native sentencing circle. The sentencing hearing was held at Brocket on September 9, 1994. Milton spoke to the press on the courthouse steps shortly before his sentencing hearing began. He had gained about nine kilograms since the time of his conviction. He said, "It is the provincial government that are the real criminals. Why do I have to go to jail when Ralph Klein is the real criminal? The man who administers the policies like the ones that govern the Oldman River Dam. I'm going to jail today. I've been used as a scapegoat. Who are they going to use after I'm gone? Things could have been different on September 7. To me, what they should have done in the first place is kill me and save the taxpayers a lot of money."

During the hearing, the Crown said he—on behalf of the Province of Alberta—was in favour of a sentencing circle and would not take "an adversarial" approach. A sentencing circle is a First Nations way of sentencing that would likely not involve jail.

When I spoke to Reg Crowshoe, I asked him about the Blackfoot way of dealing with justice issues. Reg told me that the Canadian way is rooted in the idea of the domination of nature, whereas, in the Blackfoot way, "everything is equal." Reg told me that the Blackfoot system is built on avoiding conflict. For example, when the Blackfoot have gathered to resolve a conflict, they leave one sitting space unoccupied. A bundle is then placed in this space to symbolize the conflict at hand. Everyone speaks to the bundle instead of the people present at the meeting, and Elders police this process. Reg explained, "I cannot look across at you, and say, 'You did this…' One cannot do that, because they are not Creator… Conflict is sickness. It is like cancer. If you are going to deal with cancer, you can't fight cancer. You have to negotiate with cancer." After he had explained all of this to me, Reg revealed that these days less than 3 per cent of problems on the reserve are settled in the Blackfoot way. He said that his people desperately needed cultural renewal to revive traditional justice practices.

Gainer agreed with the Crown that a traditional sentencing circle should be used in this case, and urged this to the court. Justice O'Leary considered this issue, and decided that a sentencing circle was not appropriate in Milton's case. He explained that a sentencing circle is "not appropriate in these circumstances. I have arrived at this conclusion with some misgivings, because I have an urge to accede with counsel's request." He explained that a sentencing circle would not be useful for a number of reasons. "The accused was motivated by what he perceives as good motives—the protection of the environment and the protection of sacred places. There is no indication that he is prepared to admit any wrongdoing or that he is remorseful for what he has done." Justice O'Leary also felt that the community would not be able to supervise Milton, though they certainly were willing. In Milton's case, there was a minimum sentence imposed by the law of twelve months in jail. It was hard to find a suitable alternative to that.

Justice O'Leary also spoke about Milton and his degree of

respect for law: "I have concern in this case for the accused's respect for law. It is quite clear from the evidence at the trial that he broke the terms of an injunction order with impunity. He also pointed a gun at and fired in the air for the purpose of intimidating law enforcement officers. Additionally, I am satisfied from the evidence that I have heard that the accused was not truthful in his evidence at trial. These matters indicate to me that the accused does not respect the law and I have not heard anything since the trial to indicate that he has changed his attitude. These are circumstances that are not conducive to a sentencing circle."

Gainer then called a number of witnesses to testify about Milton, to try to convince the court that Milton's sentence should be as low as the law would allow. Devalon told the court: "Apartheid is alive and well here in southern Alberta. We feel it every living day of our lives and I'm sure that that frustration has been with Milton for quite a number of years. I ask that you take leniency in terms of sentencing. He has been denied community activity; he has been denied a social life due to his bail conditions for all of these last four years. Thank you."

After Devalon spoke, Gainer asked Evelyn to give evidence: "I feel that as a Native person that is living in Canada, I have— we have—our culture has always been sharing with people and I believe that for Milton to go and do what he did is an act of frustration because we have always been struggling, ever since, like five hundred years ago. I have a lot of respect for Milton. I have seen Milton grow within himself. I have seen Milton humble himself. By saying he has no remorse, I think that is wrong. He does have remorse in his own way. He has remorse because the government is destroying part of our culture. I just feel that if, the way things are going, things are going out of control not from our point of view but from the other side and I feel that there is too much getting pushed around. We have our own value system that I know would also help the non-Native people… And by saying this, if Milton goes away I'll be there with him and so will other people, and when one goes away there will always be another one in their place and I am talking from my heart, saying give us back some respect because we know we have the responsibility. Thank you."

The Crown now had the chance to cross-examine Evelyn. He spoke quickly, "No questions."

Finally, Gainer called Milton to give evidence, and he spoke:

Well, it's been a long haul, you know. I have been here for a good number of years. Even though all the odds are to say that the justice system doesn't work, I felt there was a real need, on the advice of a lot of people, to be here. I know that I am going to pay a price one way or another for what happened in 1990. But I still have to say, to be honest about it, that I feel what we did in 1990 was not wrong. Yes, the methods might be questionable. Even in my mind I have had to endure a lot of things in the last four years. My life has been taken and turned upside down and torn to pieces. I can't even live like I did before; I can't ever really get back to the way I was before. You said I was unremorseful. I mean, to me that really hurts me, because I have given this court every opportunity, because the real issue was, yes, there may be a fight, but then after that you have got to sit down and you have to heal.

We have to get to the real issue and the real issue for us is who I am. It's not just an Indian issue. It is an issue of people that have been suppressed for so long that, you know, something has to change, you know, and for me to ask for any leniency from this court, you know that is not what I'm going to do. But I'm going to put my heart down like the way I know best how to do and hope that that is going to be the beginning of a process where, you know, what this justice system and the Natives are going to go into the future as.

So for me, it was real hard but I have come to the point where you know it has to end, you know, and I'm kind of glad and maybe some people will think it's not right, but I tell you I really appreciate the courts. You let the pipe in, and to me that is where my heart is. There are things I must pay for, but it makes me feel that at least I see a change and maybe I don't have to fight again, because I don't want to. It's not nice. It's been really hard. I need strength from the mountains that is my home.

So with this sentencing circle I thought, "Hey, this is a good time if everybody don't like me, they should send me into the mountains and the bears." But, you know, that is my world, you know, I'm happy there. It's just that the river called me, you know, and it's real hard to explain where Natives are in the connection to culture, but the river called us and we had no choice but to answer the call. I mean, we stumbled all the way through it—and the court has heard all the things, so you don't need to know. The morning of September 7, 1990, I live with it; it is like a flashback to me every day. I can relate to the Vietnam syndrome. It's something you really, really never want to experience again. But yet again I felt really good because if somebody was going to die that day, then let it be me. I didn't want to do it like how they were saying it was, but I think the truth was too strong. I think the RCMP felt it and we felt it and I can't say that one or the other escalated it. I think that the Oldman River taught us a lesson and it's going to continue to teach us a lesson and I want to be part of it. I have learned things these past four years and I'm really happy there is another avenue open. Like you called me an environmental activist. I mean to me this is a big move from being called a militant and I honour that role and am going to continue to do the best in what environment means, because it is the first place that I felt at home. There is no prejudice there. So, other than that, you know, that's it.

After Milton testified, Gainer argued why Milton should have a short sentence. She told the court that "the rule of law applies to all and not just to my client, and it applies to the government and I think particularly when you look at the history of the provincial government, they haven't followed their laws, so I think it is fine to say my client is guilty, but there are many circumstances where the provincial government clearly was not negotiating in good faith and constructed the dam without following their own laws."

To give concrete examples of the behaviour of the Alberta government in the Oldman Dam battle, Gainer then directed Justice O'Leary to the environmental assessment report and read all the damning words about the treatment of the Piikani. Justice O'Leary interrupted her and said, "Well, with all due respect, Ms. Gainer, this surely doesn't have much to do with what we are talking about."

"Well, it does in the sense that what motivated my client was a concern with respect to the river, construction of the dam and lack of input by the Peigan people."

"And I'm willing to accept that," Justice O'Leary said.

Had he wished, now would be the time for the Crown prosecutor to hand up a copy of Milton's criminal record to the judge. The convictions were now fairly old, but the Crown could still, in good conscience, have put them in and said they might be in a minor way relevant to sentencing. The Crown had the right to pass the record to the judge. He also had the right, due to the age of the record, to simply leave it in his file. Once again, Pinckney left it in his file.

The end of the final trial of Milton Born With A Tooth was now at hand. Justice O'Leary began his ruling on Milton's sentence. "There has been much talk of remorse. I find that there is no genuine remorse here. Mr. Born With A Tooth is quite candid and I appreciate his candour. He did not ask for leniency and he did not express any remorse or sorrow or apologize to anyone who he may have offended as a result of his activity." He continued, "I think it is fair to look at this lack of remorse as a factor which aggravates to some extent the circumstances of the case."

Justice O'Leary was obligated by law to sentence Milton to at least twelve months in jail for using a gun. In total, he sentenced Milton to sixteen months in jail. According to a press report, "wearing blue jeans and a sleeveless red T-shirt with an environmental message on it [Stop James Bay 2], Born With A Tooth showed no emotion as he was led away by court guards after his sentence was passed by Mr. Justice O'Leary, and taken into prison."

———————•———————

I asked Reg about Milton, and about Milton firing his gun. Reg said, "Well, you know, the gun was his own action, whether it was Lonefighters, or himself, or they were pushed to it—they had no regulation, society regulation or control (unless they started making their own society regulation) to shoot the gun. Maybe they made up their own regulation to shoot that gun… But they never followed our traditional regulations. And there wasn't authority by our regulations to shoot the gun at that time. Or, even a Western law to shoot the gun at that time."

When I asked Roy about Milton's prosecution, he thought that it was important. He said, "I have always felt that there should not be two sets of laws in this country. You should have equal rights and equal responsibilities."

——— —

When Milton's sentence became public, there were a variety of responses, one of which was printed in the *Globe and Mail*. Maude Barlow of the Council of Canadians said, "Milton embodies the courage of a community fighting back." She noted that Canada refused to enforce its own environmental laws, and Alberta ignored both its own laws and protests against the dam. She concluded by saying, "We are shifting our thinking in assuming governments will defend us, to saying that we have our democratic rights, and how will we assert them if your governments will not do it?"

The Council of Canadians supported a public inquiry into the handling of Milton's case and was hoping to help him if he wanted to appeal. Milton filed papers to launch a second appeal, but he did not pursue the appeal. No public inquiry into the case of Milton Born With A Tooth, or the plight of the Piikani, was ever held.

And so this story ended. But, like all events, it was both the fruit of the past and a seed for the future. Years later, Alberta and Canada, for whatever motives, did try to reconcile with the Piikani, with decidedly mixed results.

And So It Continues ...

In the years immediately following the dam's completion, and much to everyone's surprise, bull trout were found in large numbers below the dam. Experts realized that the bull trout needed many kilometres of the Oldman River in which to spawn, both above and below the dam. Now that the dam was in operation, the trout were swimming to edge of the dam, circling, and waiting until they were either caught by fishers or died. For a while, government biologists caught them and took them to the reach of river above the dam, but quickly that became too expensive. In his book, Jack Glenn quoted a 1994 report: "Alberta's last remaining population of prairie-dwelling trout now teeters on the brink of extinction below the Oldman Dam."

When I spoke to Rick Ross, I asked him if he was concerned that more dams would bring about the extinction of a species or two in Canada, such as the bull trout. He replied, "I can say, similarly, the sage plant in the state of Washington is an endangered species. Even though there are millions of acres of sage plants in the U.S.."

"Are you saying that you are not so concerned if we lose bull trout in Alberta hypothetically in a future scenario, provided there are bull trout in other places?"

"Yes, that's it in a nutshell. I would look at it differently if we did not have them in other places," Rick said.

When I spoke to Lorne Fitch, I asked him about bull trout, too. He explained that the bull trout evolved to survive in a system with a long stretch of river. Every time we block the river we "truncate" their range. He said they had tried to transplant them to other habitat, but that failed. I asked him if the bull trout were really at risk of being wiped out in Alberta.

"How much tighter can we draw the noose around them and have them survive? We continually are removing opportunities for them to spawn by blocking the river and other streams."

"What do you think it means if through human development the bull trout are wiped out of Alberta's rivers, and the Oldman basin?" I asked.

Lorne considered, and then said, "I put it in the same category as what it would mean if we lose caribou, or grizzly bears. Here we have an animal that has survived 10,000 years since glaciation, and has thrived. In fact, some of the archival photos that I was able to uncover in my research had bull trout up to twenty-five pounds in these systems. That is a testament to their skill at exploiting the resources in arguably one of the toughest environments in which to live. I suppose in some ways we might have learned something from them. That is what the loss means to me, that we could not figure out how to throttle back our own desires and allow another species that had about 9,900 and some odd years jump start on us on this landscape to live."

In the summer of 1999, the Alberta government released a glossy report called *Environmental Monitoring of the Oldman River Dam: Eight Years of Progress*. This study was prepared by technical specialists from within the Alberta Department of the Environment. This study—and all the previous studies in relation to the Oldman Dam paid for by the Alberta government—cost money to undertake. Such studies represent additional costs of the dam, yet were never considered as such in Alberta government economic studies in relation to the dam.

Under "Water Quality," the government stated that "there are no feasible means of mitigating the presence of the Oldman Dam and reservoir on downstream water quality." The report does include a detailed analysis of the dam's effects on fish, though much was not known at the time of the study. However, "70% of anglers interviewed" were "satisfied with their overall fishing experience."

The authors of the report noted that testing was done for mercury in the area of the dam, explaining that the government was obligated to test for mercury. Mercury levels rose in all species between 1991 and 1995 then began to dip in 1997. However, 22 out of 1,484 fish's body levels did exceed the Canadian guidelines. "Yearly mean mercury levels did not exceed the Canadian Guidelines for safe human consumption in any species, with the exception of two species for which only a single specimen was obtained (lake trout and turbot)."

After the Oldman Dam battle, Alberta also formed the Oldman River Dam Environmental Advisory Committee to monitor the health of the river. This committee was of local citizens with an interest or specialty related to the health of the Oldman River, and included a member of the LNID and environmental groups. In 2001 the Oldman River Dam Environmental Advisory Committee gave its final report on the health of the Oldman River. The committee stated it was "satisfied" that there had been enough water, and the "variability of flows" of the Oldman River adequately supported riparian cottonwoods. "However, the period of record since construction of the dam is short." The committee reported concern about downstream water clarity and algae growth. In the report, the lost land, river, trees, plants—in short, lost habitat for living things due to the dam—become something called "lost habitat units."

The committee was "not satisfied that the mitigation program has fully met the objectives of compensating for lost habitat," and it mentioned "strong concerns" about "blowing sediments from mud flats exposed when reservoir levels are low."

The committee said that "additional work needs to be done to meet the original targets," and that key areas "need to be managed to optimize the production of wildlife habitat units." According to this report, the prairie falcons were no longer doing well. The committee was "very concerned" that, despite extensive monitoring, it was impossible yet to "fully answer" how well the fish were doing. The committee "does not believe" that Alberta's original targets were reached.

The Piikani are mentioned in this report: "Weak regeneration of riparian habitat through the Peigan First Nation has been identified as a specific concern. It appears that a lack of overbank flooding is reducing seeding events for vegetation and eliminating the filling and scouring of oxbows. This habitat is critical to the Peigan First Nation because of the cultural significance of the willows and sweetgrass found along the floodplain." The committee said that this matter must be studied further.

After the Oldman Dam battle, there were negotiations between the Piikani, Alberta, and Canada, in relation to the issues of water and ownership of the Oldman River. The Piikani still had ongoing lawsuits on a number of issues. These negotiations proceeded with negotiators from the two levels of government and the Piikani. A draft agreement was reached between the parties. If the Piikani halted all their lawsuits, the other levels of government offered to pay the Piikani $64 million.

In 2000 Devalon had told the press that the $64 million being offered to the Piikani was "not much at all, considering the high stakes." He said to Joanne Helmer that the $64-million deal came after "14 years of government pressure tactics and an economic embargo." Devalon added that another First Nation, the Tsu Tina, near Calgary, received a "$700-million deal." The way the proposed water deal was structured, one thousand dollars was promised to each Piikani who voted yes, to be given to them immediately. Despite this, the Piikani rejected the deal when, in late November 2001, the people voted in a referendum. Five hundred thirty-three people voted against it. Five hundred eleven voted for it.

The loss invigorated those on and off the reserve who were desperate for the deal. What happened next was no surprise to those within the Piikani First Nation who remembered their own past—in particular, the second vote arranged by their Indian Agent to sell off a big chunk of their reserve in 1909.

After the first vote in 2001, the name of the people was formally changed from Peigan to Piikani. It has been alleged—by many Piikani—that the name of the people was changed to allow a second vote. Kirby Smith, the chief civil servant for the Piikani First Nation at the time, put his allegation like this in an interview I conducted with him on the reserve in 2006: "They were first called Peigan people, they lost. Then, the only way they could hold another vote was to change the name." Some also alleged that the voting age for either one or both votes was dropped from twenty-one to eighteen, so that younger Piikani, desperate for money and possibly jobs, could vote—presumably in favour of the deal. An overall assessment of these allegations would take a full investigation of all sides of this issue, which is beyond the scope of this book; it is, perhaps, a book for someone else to do. What is clear is that these are credible allegations that deserve further investigation.

The second vote took place not long after the first. In September 2002, by a narrow margin, the majority of Piikani voted in favour of an agreement that was similar but not identical to the one they had originally voted on. Piikani gained access to water from the Oldman River for irrigation. They also were promised revenues from any future power-generation plant. In return, the Piikani agreed to discontinue all ongoing lawsuits related to water rights to the Oldman River. In essence, they gave up their right to say they owned water in exchange for money. All money would be placed in trust, to be used, hopefully, for the benefit of all Piikani.

When I spoke to Evelyn, she called this deal "our sellout." When I spoke to Reg in 2006 about it, he told me the issue for him wasn't the money but how it was done. He said, "You know, in 1909, it was the concept of colonization: here is a big vehicle that is running over us, and the white people are driving it. Yeah, then we come to this last few years, to sell the water, but the whites have got out of the vehicle… saying 'we are sorry for running over you.' But who gets in? Our own people. The vehicle was never destroyed, and our own people get the steering wheel, and they are still running over us."

Devalon told me much the same thing: "The abused become the abusers."

———

In 2003 ATCO Power Ltd. had an opening ceremony at the Oldman River Dam, commemorating its new hydro-electric project using water discharged from the dam's reservoir. ATCO also operates natural gas- and coal-fired power plants. Piikani Chief Peter Strikes With A Gun conducted a traditional peace-pipe ceremony to dedicate the Oldman River plant. According to press reports, the $34-million plant would "supply enough electricity to meet the needs of 25,000 homes." Premier Ralph Klein called this a "welcome addition to Alberta's electrical needs." He said, "I can remember—not so far from this site—a protest of 10,000 people." He said that this was in "stark contrast" to the current cooperation between Native leaders, business, and government that gave the Piikani an interest in the power plant.

———•———

It turns out that, for now, during big storms, the Oldman Dam cannot hold back all the water carried in the river, so there are still floods to help young cottonwood trees survive and grow. In addition, after the dam was built, and because of consultation with cottonwood tree experts, such as Dr. Stewart Rood, those operating the Oldman Dam have instituted a system of releasing water to try to mimic the way nature floods the valley in the spring, to help the young cottonwoods. There has been no massive die-off of cottonwood trees downstream from the dam.

When we spoke about the current state of the river, Roy Jenson said, "The river is much better now that we've got the dam because it never gets to zero flow. It used to. As long as we were taking water out for off-stream storage and irrigation purposes sometimes there wasn't enough coming for it in later summer. Consequently, parts of the river were drying up. There were areas between Monarch and where the Milk River runs into the Oldman where there was nothing. Just a little hole here where some fish died. Now, because of the dam, we have guaranteed minimum flows, which is far better than you ever had before. It doesn't drop below that anymore, so now you have the water table under that for the cottonwood trees."

The population in southern Alberta continues to grow. The pressure is on for more and more water, as humans, like other animals and plants, seem inevitably to expand to the maximum carrying capacity of the land and beyond, until there is a great reckoning.

These days, the droughts experienced in the area are even longer, and the wetter periods more intense, than they have been in the past, likely because of global warming. There is talk in southern Alberta that farmers are again running out of water and that a second dam on the Oldman may be "necessary." Rick Ross told me that he believes more dams will be built on the Oldman River at some point, likely downstream from the current dam.

Cheryl Bradley told me that another dam would mean another great loss to the river valley. She explained that no more water can be allocated from the Oldman valley for new water users—the LNID takes much of the water—so there is a question of where the water will come from for new development. She added that the Alberta government has tried to form multi-stakeholder groups to debate and set priorities for water development; in her area, the group is called the Oldman Watershed Council. The utility of these committees is unknown, as the Alberta government retains the power to make final decisions.

———————

At the end of August 2005, I finally had the time to visit the Oldman River in the high country, west of Maycroft, at a place called the Gap. I had read about the Gap. It is there that the Oldman comes down from the high mountains and shoots through a narrow canyon surrounded by rock, before it turns east, toward Maycroft, out through the foothills, and onto the prairie. Roy Jenson had told me that the original idea was to put the dam in the Gap, but there had been some engineering problems with that idea. He added that people were happy that the Gap remained untouched, because it was a nice place. I wondered what would have happened if the engineers had said that it was a perfect place for a dam.

I drove up Highway 22, turned north at Maycroft, and continued up a dirt road that ran along the Oldman River. The gentle roll of the land was replaced by sharper undulations. The ridges were greener and had more trees. Two deer were also heading west—one on the road, and the other on the far side of a wire fence to my right which separated me from the river. A few pickup trucks roared by, heading in the other direction, kicking up dust. I happened to look in my rearview mirror. My car was also throwing up dust.

After going up for a while, the road turned sharply south and went down. The broad valley narrowed, hardly leaving enough space for the river and the road. Mountains rose on all sides: to the west, they were brown in the late-day sun; to the south was a mountain much taller than the rest.

I parked my car and got out. I felt as much as heard the roar— the combined force of the wind gusts in the leaves and the sound of the water going over rapids. The sun was still warm, but the breeze was cool. The river in front of me was mostly in the sun, but some of it ran through a growing patch of shade. The wind gusted again. Above the river, to the north, the sky was clear blue, with puffs of bright white clouds far in the distance.

I sat in the sun on a rock by the edge of the river for a long time. The river seemed to be in a conversation with itself, in a language beyond my understanding. There was a call. And an answer. A call from the murmuring here, an answer from the roar of the rapids. Along its edge, past the rocks with red moss on them, the river eddied flow to and fro, with and against the stream, swirling away then back—alive. Falling sunlight hit the water at just the right angle to turn sections of the river into pools of white light. Smooth stones in and alongside the river were also lit white by the sun. It is no surprise that this is a special place for the Blackfoot people.

In his book, *The Life of a River,* in a chapter titled "The Living River," Andy Russell writes about the Gap and about the "prayer stones" of the Blackfoot people. For thousands of years a path through the Gap and out to the prairies was worn smooth by the men and women who lived and died in these valleys. Russell explains that the Oldman River was so important to the First Nations peoples of the area that they left "prayer stones" beside the river, "till they were heaped up in that great pile beside the river representing the prayers of uncounted generations of their people."

During the Great Depression, Russell went up near the Gap to "build a big camp to house and feed three hundred or so unemployed men." He explains how these men, including himself, knew "real hunger and despair." They built a "narrow, twisting" road through the Gap to "accommodate wheels... It was welcome work." At one point, these men came upon "a pile of loose rocks." He continues: "What they needed was rocks to make a roadbed ... and nobody could blame them for loading up into their wheelbarrows and scattering thousands" of these rocks.

Russell later learned that these were the Blackfoot prayer stones. They had been, in the Blackfoot fashion, something holy, a "historical monument" to their relationship to the land and the river. Russell writes, "It was an omen of what was to come in our treatment of the holy river of the Blackfoot people."

Russell wrote about the Gap and the Oldman River with the intimate knowledge of one who knows the spirit of a place in all seasons. Beneath Thunder Mountain, beneath the pure limestone rock, embedded in the road, are the prayer stones, "no longer visible as a reminder of the spirit of the river." In the spring, the water is yellow-brown, filled with silt and mud. "Floods rip and tear down the twisted channel, roaring with immense power that can be heard

342

for miles on a still day." In the summer the water goes around huge boulders, "white-water rapids, and deep blue-green pools clear as crystal." Russell found the river most beautiful in autumn. The aspens, willows, and cottonwoods are brilliant patches of yellows and reds, embedded within the deep green of the evergreen trees. This was the "gentle resting-time in prelude to the harshness of winter cold."

Andy Russell did not describe the winter season in his book. I wonder: is it because the river itself seems gone, flowing silently under snow and ice, and blasting wind above? Yet, the river is there, as it has been for millennia, awaiting a new beginning, a new cycle of life, in spring.

Afterword

After the Oldman Dam battle, life on the reserve remained hard. During the years when I visited the Piikani Reserve (2005 and 2006), the Piikani were in turmoil about a new, though related, crisis. By 2006 the finances of the Piikani were so bad that the Department of Indian Affairs took over the band's finances. The problem, according to chief Piikani civil servant Kirby Smith, was that the Piikani did not have management experience and no way to get it, at least on the reserve. But the tragic part was that the people he spoke to on the phone from the Department of Indian Affairs had no management experience either. It was a case of the blind leading the blind. Kirby told me something that shocked me at first but later made sense as an intriguing possibility; his hunch was that the governments of Canada and Alberta didn't really want the Piikani to succeed. If they succeeded, the Department of Indian Affairs would not be needed anymore, and the Piikani would assert their rights against the other levels of government. This is, of course, only his guess.

Another Piikani, who was also a top civil servant who did not want to be named in this book, told me that half of the Piikani were not living on the reserve because there were no jobs to keep them there. He said, "You know, we've got Piikani doctors and lawyers, but they're not here." At this point, he waved his hand toward the wall, toward the white world off the reserve, and said, "It is easier out there. Because out there, there are rules. Rules you have to follow.

344

You have to follow the laws that are enforced."

The other problem was the $64 million from the water deal. When the Piikani received their $64-million settlement it was supposed to be held in trust for the long-term good of all Piikani. However, there were few restrictions on how the money actually got spent. There were many credible allegations of corruption—as well as outright theft—of up to millions of dollars. Devalon told me that the money is tied up in numerous court battles. He hopes the Piikani can someday renegotiate the water deal in a fair way with a fair process.

In January 2007, Reg Crowshoe became chief of the Piikani. For the first time in years political and religious power resided in one man. After he won, he showed a sound understanding of economics by suggesting that the band desperately needed a chief investment officer. Yet, the problems he inherited would have required super-human ability to address. When he was sworn in there was a proper ceremony transferring power to him. Even Devalon was happy with the ceremony. In January 2011, the Piikani had another election, and Reg was defeated by Gayle Strikes With A Gun, who became the first female chief of the Piikani Nation.

In an interview with the press, Strikes With A Gun said, "Communication with band members both on and off reserve will be a priority. Open communication is a priority, the membership need to be informed." Devalon told me that she has been true to her word. She has been stunningly transparent with the Piikani Nation's finances, which, according to Devalon, are terrible.

——— ——

From time to time, I call Evelyn. I learned that she had to have many of her teeth pulled out, and that she had lost vision in one of her eyes due to glaucoma. In early 2008, in the middle of the prairie winter, Devalon told me that the house Evelyn had been living in did not belong to her but to her nephew, who had come back to the reserve and "kicked her out" of the house. She and her husband, Bruce, bought a trailer home, but it had been too expensive to move, so they took up residence in a bus.

In the summer of 2008, I returned to Alberta and Head-Smashed-In Buffalo Jump and sought out Evelyn. Not five hundred metres from there, in the open prairie, I found Evelyn and Bruce. Their trailer and bus were huddled together with a beat-up car, making a sort of rough circle, which might shelter them from winter winds. Even on a warm summer day, the wind blew fairly hard over the land. They had no running water, but they did have a diesel generator. Bruce showed me around the trailer and the bus. They had a little TV rigged up with power from the generator. I wondered what it would be like out in those trailers at −40°C, or in a snowstorm.

We talked. Evelyn was subdued but not in bad spirits. There was no getting around the fact that her life was very, very hard. There was a housing crisis on the reserve, and many people were affected. She told me that when she called Reg he did not call her back.

As I pulled away from their circle of trailers and drove back up the dirt road, I thought that I could not feel sorry for her. In her quiet way, she was unbowed. Still, it was a hard life. She, who had told the truth, who was half-blind, now, at seventy-two, was braving the winter storms outside. It is an old story.

———— •• ————

And what of Milton? Hard facts are hard to find. In the spring of 1993, Milton made the *Calgary Herald's* business section; he had started a company, called LNCN (Lonefighters National

346

Communications Network). He told the paper he wanted to take advantage of his fame, or notoriety, and do something positive with it. His company would make products like tipis in an environmentally sustainable way. He decided to set the business in Calgary, rather than on the reserve. He said, "If you want to be serious, you can't build a business on the reserve." He said that he wanted to make the company as "big as Esso." But he also had a deeper aim than money. He explained, "I don't have to sell my rights, put on feathers and dance. We're going to show quality and professionalism here. This is going to be a model of how self-government can be a safe and not a fearful thing to Native people. It's going to show that rather than sell our land and water, there's something that we can make."

Looking at the movement for Native entrepreneurship in Canada, combined with the global movement for sustainability, one can see that Milton had a sound vision of how things should be; whether he was able to practically make things happen was another question. With his company, Milton concluded, "We're saying 'Don't be afraid.' We can tap into that anger and use it in a constructive way." When Milton said these words he did not know that in less than a year he would be convicted a second time for what happened in 1990, and would be back in jail.

As I was researching this book and trying to speak to Milton, he was crisscrossing Canada again. His protest was called "Trail of Tears 2006: Atlantic to Pacific Oceans." This time he was protesting the Department of Indian Affairs and corruption on and off the reserve. Milton held press conference after press conference, alleging that theft and fraud were widespread on the reserve and off, and he called for a federal inquiry. As usual, he was ignored, except by his enemies. I would like to have met Milton, under the right circumstances.

After the Oldman Dam battle, Martha kept working to save the planet. In her last few years, she worked on a committee with companies to improve air quality, which was something of a return to issues she had started out with years before in Alberta, with her work related to cows and sour gas. She was the chair of the Prairie Acid Rain Coalition and was on the multi-stakeholder committee looking at Alberta's oil sands development. In 2007 she and others called for a moratorium on new oil sands development due to environmental, social, and infrastructure issues. In one of our conversations, Martha told me that sour gas emissions are now 20 per cent of what they were when she arrived in Alberta. This is a direct result of her environmental efforts.

Martha told me that pessimism is useless:

Are things bad? Absolutely. Are some things getting worse? Absolutely. But we can make them a little less bad. We can make a difference… I look at it as a train going toward a brick wall. We can just say it is going to hit the wall and let's just let it go—the faster it is over with the better. Or let's try to slow it, so impacts are not as bad. Maybe we can turn the train so it glances. Possibly stop it—but I doubt that. But we can each make a difference… We can have a better quality of life, but we must change from consumers to conservers on a large scale globally ….onservation is a better, not worse, quality of life. Not to have less, but to enjoy more, to have more time and to enjoy what we have more … we have to convince people that there is a better quality of life linked to consuming less, which is more in keeping with the sustainability of [the] earth—a huge challenge, but we have to try.

In the fall of 2007, I was shocked to learn that Martha expected to be dead within a year due to a recently diagnosed brain condition called multiple system atrophy. That was not at all the narrative I had expected for her life. Patients usually suffocate or starve to death as a result of this disease. Martha had begun to use a walker. She took heavy medication four times a day. With the help of "friends and enemies" she kept building her self-sustaining house in the woods. She kept fighting for the earth. She prepared herself and her family for her death.

On February 2, 2008, when Martha was still very much alive, Cliff Wallis organized a celebration of her life at a community centre in Calgary. The sky in Calgary that day was brilliantly blue, with a temperature of -30C. There were three dozen people there. Lorne Fitch, Cheryl Bradley, and Diane Paschal were there. The ceremony began at 10:00 a.m. because afternoons were very hard for Martha. Some afternoons she could hardly function. One could see that this was a good day for her. She had the trademark smile and that sparkle in her blue eyes. Many paid tribute to Martha, including environmentalists and former-foes-turned-friends from oil companies. Martha's blind Native son John spoke and paid tribute to Martha as a mom. Her other two sons, who had found it hard to have their mother work so much, were not there. Nor was her ex-husband. Lorne Fitch spoke. Cliff Wallis spoke. This was the first time I heard Cliff speak. Watching it all, laughing and smiling, Martha sat on a couch with her walker beside her. Everyone came over and paid their respects.

Finally, Martha spoke. She was in a buoyant mood. Her blue eyes sparkled. She spoke about her battles and her love of the earth. Near the end of her speech, she said, "Don't give money in my name, but do something for the environment in my name—something that you wouldn't have done. Do something more to remember me, in keeping with what you can do. For some, they can begin to recycle. Others can do more." On the question of what to do, Martha, as usual, came prepared. She said that there were many things that she would like to do herself, but would not have the chance. As Martha neared the end of her speech, she said, "And I have made a list." Everyone laughed and listened as Martha listed the things she felt were the most important to do.

All too soon, it was done. On April 23, I learned that she had died the day before, April 22, Earth Day. I smiled, knowing this could not be a coincidence. She had said that she did not want a tombstone. Instead, she asked to be cremated and have her ashes thrown to the wind on her beloved Kootenay Plains, where they could blow wild and free.

———————

The Oldman story has stayed with me and has become part of me, as have my memories of the people I met, the places I visited, and the knowledge I gained while learning about the story. Over the years, I have stayed in touch with Devalon. He has never tired of answering my questions when I was confused about some point. He did remain true to his promise to "push me up straight" when I was leaning to one side. He still spends several months each year in Germany, teaching the First Nations' way to German people. For a long time he was doing well, then in 2010 he had two minor but very real strokes.

In 2012, I spoke to Devalon on the telephone. He was in Germany. I asked him some final questions about the story and the people involved. I found that the robust tone I had always heard in his voice had diminished. I asked if, knowing what he knows now about life, he would have done what he did again. Would he have made his protest? I wondered if I should ask the question, if perhaps he might not have the strength to give his best answer. I was wrong.

"Would I do it again? Something needed to be done. Something drastic needed to be done. It was the only opportunity to do something. If I had the chance to do it again, I would do it again, but with different people, not with Milton as the leader. We were not supposed to fight back. The worst that was supposed to happen is that we would be arrested. When he fired the gun, he threw us into a different situation. On the other hand, some good came out of his trials." When I listened to Devalon, I felt humbled. I knew a lot about the story now, but there was so much that I did not know.

Acknowledgements

First, I would like to thank the people who kindly and patiently agreed to answer my questions and in turn have their answers and lives reflected in this book. I extend special thanks to Jack Glenn for writing his book to shed light on the Oldman Dam story, and for his unceasing efforts to help me. Also, I must thank Rick Ross for his patient help whenever I needed it. I owe a special thanks to Cheryl Bradley and Lorne Fitch for all their kindness. They did all in their power to help me, honouring requests I made at the last minute. Finally, I would also like to single out Martha Kostuch, who died in 2008. I got to know her over three days in the spring of 2005. She was an original. I cannot thank her now, but I told her my opinion of her achievement before she died.

I would also like to thank my wife, Christine, and my good friends who read early drafts of this book and gave me the benefit of their insight and knowledge: Ben Hett, Mel Gardner, Jeff Miller, Stephen Ibbott, and Roy Turner. I should also thank Jim Vella for inviting me to lunch that day back in 2004. The staff members at the Alberta Court of Appeal were also very helpful and deserve my thanks.

Former Fifth House Publisher Stephanie Stewart believed in this project. I would also like to thank current Publisher Tracey Dettman. Finally, I would like to thank my editors Meaghan Craven and Penny Hozy, for their hard work. The author's name goes on the front of a book, but the reality is that the final version of a book is a product also of the craft and work of one or more editors.

Finally, I would like to thank my mother, Marianne McLean Girvan. What is best in me I owe to what is best in her, whereas my flaws come from diverse sources.

The Making of
this Book

This book is what it appears to be. It is based on my own experiences where relevant, historical sources, court transcripts, court decisions, newspaper articles, and interviews. It is a work of history not fiction. No facts have been made up. I began the process of writing this book by reading Jack Glenn's excellent *Once Upon an Oldman*. Next, I interviewed (on audio tape) key people who participated in the story. I tried to establish trust with those I interviewed. Sometimes this meant that initial meetings were without the benefit of audio tape. I told each person I interviewed that I was writing this book and wanted to represent all sides of the struggle. I told them that, where possible, rather than merge their words into one narrative line created by the author, I would try to put their perspectives in their own words, in their own sections. Readers could then form their own conclusions based on the clash of views presented. I also explained that I would provide context for the struggle, in the form of sections of narrative history. The participants in this book consented to their lives and stories being used in the book on this basis.

I decided to maintain a third-person voice throughout, but I kept as many of the words used by each person as possible within the narrative, so that I might maintain a strong feel for each of the characters' voices, even as I provided continuity in the narrative. I have tried, where possible, to ensure that each person's unique voice comes through. I make it clear both in the narrative and in the endnotes that the information I gleaned from those I interviewed provides the backbone of the story, and one should think of these parts as the words of the participants, edited and restructured by me, rather than as my "voice" as author.

When I edited the stories of any of my sources, my main concern—beyond relevance and clarity—was that I ensured the strongest position was put forward. Occasionally, and for two main reasons, I was compelled to offer my own opinion where the known material called out for comment: first, when the material under discussion required specialized knowledge to give the context necessary to fully understand the event. For example, the actions of Bruce Fraser were not wrong in the context of the law and values at the time. One is easily tempted to criticize Fraser personally for the actions of his government, or for the state of the law itself (on challenges and Native people), without understanding the context. Second, I gave my opinion where the story was contradictory or confusing.

On a more subtle level, if the writer has really thought about the material, his or her vision permeates the whole. The story is not merely the way it is "because it happened that way" but also because the writer chose to construct the book in this or that way because it seemed best—most beautiful and true. How close or far the writer's personal opinion is from that little word with a vast history—truth—is for others to say.

In short, while my hope has been to create a story with the power and complexity of a novel, I have also tried to create a sound documentary and historical record that should, if I have done my job correctly, allow the book to stand as history. I have not encumbered the text with endnote numbers, as these may not be of interest to the general reader. For those who want to assess the text as history, the endnotes are listed in the Notes section. Here, readers can discover if the quoted material in the book is from a recent interview with the author, for example, or contemporaneous with events and gleaned from a newspaper article.

Finally, the trial chapters in this book merit special mention. Let me begin with the first trial of Milton Born With A Tooth, in Fort Macleod, 1991. The narration of the trial is based on the complete court transcripts, which are in my possession. All exchanges and all dialogue, in fact, every word, is from these transcripts, with the exception of some biographical information about the key participants, and a few facts from newspaper articles. I have always noted where I have included facts from newspaper articles. I have never mixed other accounts from other times into the narrative of the trial, which is based on the trial transcripts. Had I done that, I would have destroyed the integrity of the process I have adopted. For incidents outside the trial, I have felt free to mix together different accounts from different sources to present what was as close to what it must have been like during the events as possible.

The transcripts of the first trial are approximately eight hundred pages long. My method of selecting the material for this book was as follows:

1. I read the transcripts to see if there was any unfairness or disrespect toward Native people during the trial by the judge or any other person.

2. I re-read the transcripts from the perspective of the trial judge, the prosecutor and the legal system, to ensure that evidence supporting the trial judge, the prosecutor and the fairness of the trial was also brought forward in the book. I wanted to ensure that I presented a fair and accurate picture of the trial for the reader.

3. I wanted to ensure that all necessary context was given for all quotes from the trials. I have tried never to cherry-pick an

356

incendiary remark and snip it from its context. If the judge was angry, I tried to give the context to show why he was angry. All comments have been, to the best of my ability, imbedded in a rendering of the context of a politically charged, stressful trial.

4. The trial narratives were constructed by a method of subtraction. First, I distilled the trial into key areas of narrative, such as cross-examination. Then, I tried to decide which areas could be cut, which could be summarized and which should appear verbatim. This is why I say that the actual words in the book were all said, but the narrative is more a "construction" than a "presentation" of what happened. Meaning, if there are thirty pages of cross-examination, I might have created a narrative of three pages from that thirty, trying to condense and cut to distill the material to an essence that is fair to all sides as a representation of the much longer transcript.

I have also tried to preserve my method in describing Milton's second trial before Justice O'Leary. In this case the transcripts were approximately 1,400 pages in length.

In the past, court decisions thought to be important were published in reports of criminal law. For the past decade, in the area of criminal law, legal decisions have been increasingly available through online services. As a result, a much higher percentage of legal decisions are available. However, when a legal judgement is published, only the decision of the judge is published. In most cases the transcripts of a trial are never produced. They are expensive to prepare, and, in long trials, may be one thousand pages or more. The only time transcripts of trials are prepared is if one party wants to appeal the court decision. Even where the transcripts are prepared, they are never published in a legal report, as they constitute too many pages and make for dull reading, except for a few key areas.

In the case of the two trials of Milton Born With A Tooth, both sets of transcripts were prepared. The transcripts of Milton's first trial were prepared for his appeal. At some point, Milton must have begun the process of appealing his second conviction—hence the preparation of the second trial's transcripts—but the second appeal never happened. There should be a copy in existence of each of the transcripts I used in this book at the office of the Court of Appeal for Alberta, cited under the appeal numbers I have listed in the Notes.

Finally, a note on the words "judge" and "justice." Most readers expect that the person who oversees the trial of an accused and decides upon his or her fate is called a "judge." This is for the most part correct. In most cases, and in these notes, I use the word "judge." Those who know the legal system know that there are more subtle distinctions in the naming of this role between the various levels of court. Generally, in this book I call everyone judge, unless the person is at the Court of Queen's Bench or the Court of Appeal, in which case I call him or her a justice, which is the technically correct name.

In conclusion, I feel blessed to have stumbled on this great story. As you can see, I was lucky that the transcripts of Milton's second trial were prepared at all. Though Milton was never vindicated in a new appeal, his efforts—and those of the people who helped him order and pay for transcripts—indirectly led to this story being told with the degree of accuracy that would never have been possible without transcripts.

Finally, Jack Glenn's book was the mountain on which this book was built.

–Robert Girvan, Winter 2012

Appendix

GOVERNMENT OF ALBERTA DIVERSION PLAN, OCTOBER 25, 1979

Alberta

ENVIRONMENT   ENVIRONMENTAL ENGINEERING SUPPORT SERVICES

FROM	PETER G. MELNYCHUK, P. ENG. Assistant Deputy Minister	OUR FILE REFERENCE
		YOUR FILE REFERENCE
TO	HONOURABLE H. KROEGER Minister of Transportation	DATE October 25, 1979
		TELEPHONE

**TRANSPORTATION
RECEIVED
OCT 26 1979
26-2
EDMONTON, ALBERTA**

MINISTERS OFFICE

SUBJECT   ADVISORY COMMITTEE ON WATER

Further to the October 16th meeting of the above Committee, the following information is in response to your request and may be useful to you in preparing your speech for the Water Resources Conference in Red Deer on November 15th and 16th.

As I pointed out to the Committee, the water resources in Alberta on a province-wide and annual basis are adequate, and in some areas, even abundant. However there are two major water management problems:

1. Seasonal Variations in River Flows

Alberta's rivers are heavily influenced by the fact that the headwaters are in the Rocky Mountains. The river flows vary from spring peaks to very low summer, fall and winter flows (ie. 1977 and 1979). The high flows occur for a very short period - but move enormous volumes of water causing floods and erosion. This is due to the relatively steep gradients of our riverbeds and watersheds on the eastern slopes and the climatic conditions during the short run-off period. Under this natural condition Alberta's share of the water "flashes through" Alberta, into Saskatchewan largely unused. We have a period of large consumptive use, mainly for irrigation, in summer and fall when the natural flow in the rivers is low. It is for this reason that rivers, particularly in southern Alberta (Oldman, Bow, Red Deer), require additional flow regulation by on-stream storage reservoirs. With such storage reservoirs part of the large spring flows can be captured, stored and later released when the water is needed in Alberta for a variety of uses. The key is to seasonally even out the flow of the rivers to more effectively use the water.

more effective Resource management to benefit all Alberta present & Future.

...2

As you are aware, Environment is proceeding with the Dickson Dam on the Red Deer River which will provide flow regulation for that river. The next, first priority in our view is on-stream flow regulation on the Oldman River. The Three Rivers Dam site has been recommended. The second priority would be additional flow regulation on the Bow River. The Dalmead site downstream of Calgary has been considered in a preliminary way.

The above mentioned structures would not involve inter-basin transfer of water, but would serve as a means to effective and full use of Alberta' share of the water that presently exists in the South Saskatchewan River Basin system.

2. Geographic Imbalance - Supply and Demand

In Alberta there is a geographic imbalance between the location of major water supply and the area of water demand. Southern Alberta has approximately 20% of the total water supply and 80% of the present total water demand. In Northern Alberta the reverse is true. Essentially this is a problem of water distribution throughout the province as it relates to availability and need. The logical solution to this problem of distributi is to divert northern water southward where it is more urgently needed. This is the long-term concept of inter-basin transfer of water and was previously referred to as the P.R.I.M.E. concept (Prairie River Improvemer Management and Evaluation). The concept is that as water in southern rivers becomes fully utilized which can only be achieved by proper regulation, surplus water from neighboring basins would be diverted to augment the supply in water-short rivers. As the water of these rivers in turn becomes fully committed to a variety of uses, supplementary water would be brought in from still more northerly basins. Eventually, basin by basin, a transfer of northern water to the south would be achieved. In all cases only surplus water from storage reservoirs would be diverted in order to protect downstream users in the donor river basin. This concept is presented in detail in the main report of the Saskatchewan-Nelson Basir Board published in 1972.

PRESENT POLICY

Current departmental policy in water resources management emphasizes utilizing the water of each river basin to the maximum before consideri inter-basin transfers. Planning priorities have therefore been direct to preparing plans for each basin by inventory of current water suppli documenting existing uses and forecasting levels of water requirements in the future. This planning process does not ignore the inter-basin concept, since surpluses to each river basin will be identified and this information will be applied when the time comes to implement inter-basin transfers. However, at this time, studies are not being directed specifically to updating the existing information on means of achieving inter-basin transfers of water.

In conclusion, present policy does not preclude inter-basin transfers, but does emphasize using existing supplies fully first. Further to this,

...3

It should be noted that any dams and and reservoirs being planned and built now, such as the Dickson Dam on the Red Deer River, are being located such that they will "fit," be effective and serve as part of the eventual concept of inter-basin transfers of water.

POSSIBLE SEQUENCING OF INTER-BASIN TRANSFERS OF WATER

The Saskatchewan-Nelson Basin Report presents a number of options or alternatives which can serve to achieve inter-basin transfer of water. The schemes need to be analyzed in detail in order to select the project combinations which will be in the best interest of Alberta. This has not as yet, been done. However, possible arrangement of projects could be as follows: (refer to figure 28, page 49 - SNBB Report)

Stage I   –   <u>South Saskatchewan River Basin Flow Regulation</u>

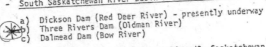

    a)   Dickson Dam (Red Deer River) - presently underway
    b)   Three Rivers Dam (Oldman River)
    c)   Dalmead Dam (Bow River)

Stage II   –   <u>Interconnection N. Saskatchewan River/S. Saskatchewan River Syste</u>

    a)   Horseguard/Rocky Mountain House Dam (*could be built sooner for power production)
    b)   N. Saskatchewan River <u>to Red Deer River Diversion Canal</u>
    c)   Red Deer River to Bow <u>River Diversion Canal</u>.
    d)   Bow River to <u>Oldman River Diversion Canal</u>

Stage III   –   <u>Athabasca River to North Saskatchewan River Diversion, Phase I</u>

    a)   Pembina Dam (Pembina River)
    b)   Pembina River to North Saskatchewan <u>River Diversion Canal</u> .

Stage IV   –   <u>N. Saskatchewan River to Battle River Diversion</u>

    a)   Carvel Dam (N. Sask. River) (*could be built sooner for pow production)
    b)   N. Saskatchewan River to Battle River <u>Diversion Canal</u>

Stage V   –   <u>Athabasca River to N. Saskatchewan Diversion, Phase II</u>

    a)   McLeod Dam
    b)   McLeod River to Pembina <u>River Diversion Canal</u>

Stage VI   –   <u>Battle River to Red Deer River Diversion</u>

    a)   Kelsey Dam
    b)   Battle River to <u>Red Deer River Diversion Canal</u>
    c)   Ardley Dam (Red Deer River)

...4

Stage VII — <u>Athabasca River to N. Saskatchewan River Diversion, Phase III</u>

    a) Oldman Dam (Athabasca River)
    b) Athabasca River <u>Diversion to McLeod River Diversion Cana</u>l

Stage VIII — <u>Athabasca River to N. Saskatchewan River Diversion, Phase IV</u>

    a) Moose Portage Dam (*could be built sooner for power production)
    b) Athabasca River to <u>North Saskatchewan Diversion Canal</u>
    c) Hairy Hill Dam (N. Saskatchewan River)

Stage IX — <u>Smoky River to Athabasca River Diversion</u>

    a) Goodwin Dam (*may be built sooner for power production)
    b) Smoky River To <u>Athabasca River Diversion Canal</u>

Stage X — <u>Peace River to Smoky River Diversion</u>

It these be 5 for -tries ?

    a) Dunvegan Dam (may be built sooner for power production)
    b) Peace River to Smoky River Diversion Canal

The above is only <u>one</u> of several options for sequencing of projects and is based on the principle that only <u>surplus</u> water from a donor basin would be diverted to a water-short basin and that such surplus water would <u>actually be diverted to a receiving basin</u> before any diversions from the water-short basin are constructed.

As future water uses continue to grow and if the water supply is not increased by regulation and inter-basin transfer there will be increasing competition between such uses for the available supply. Most of the competition between uses would be relieved if the supply could be increased. However, an increase in overall supply would not eliminate the competition completely. Different water uses require water at different times of the year. In some cases, their requirements differ so widely that a flow pattern designed for one use would cause a shortage or loss of values for another use regardless of the overall supply. The regulation studies (SSBB Report) show that the seasonal flow pattern delivered by existing and/or proposed projects, could be varied without jeopardizing the overall supply; but no attempt was made to find a flow pattern which would satisfy existing and future uses most effectively and economically. This remains to be done.

The Saskatchewan-Nelson Basin Study of water supply could be regarded as the first step in the planning of Alberta's water resources development. The second step, which is underway now, is a study <u>of current and future water demand</u>. This would be followed by a detailed assessment of the benefits and disbenefits of various project combinations <u>selected</u> to satisfy the established water needs.

Environment studying various water eds - and possible uses !

...5

I trust this information will be useful to you. You may wish to discuss this with the Honourable J.W. Cookson prior to your presentation at the Red Deer Conference. As indicated previously there are some aspects of government policy involved in the discussions the Advisory Committee has had. Please advise if I can be of any further assistance.

PETER G. MELNYCHUK, P. ENG.

cc: Hon. J.W. Cookson
    Mr. A. Hyland
    Mr. W. Solodzuk
    Mr. R. McFarlane
    Mr. C. Primus

att.

Select Bibliography

BOOKS

Bullchild, Percy. *The Sun Came Down: The History of the World as My Blackfeet Elders Told It*. New York: Harper & Row, 1985.

Crowshoe, Reg and Sybille Manneschmidt. Akak'stiman: *A Blackfoot Framework for Decision-Making and Mediation Process*. Calgary: University of Calgary Press, 2002.

Dempsey, Hugh. *Crowfoot: Chief of the Blackfeet*. Norman, OK: University of Oklahoma Press, 1972.

Ewers, John C. *The Blackfeet: Raiders on The Northwestern Plains*. Norman, OK: University of Oklahoma Press, 1958.

Glenn, Jack. *Once Upon an Oldman: Special Interest Politics and the Oldman River Dam*. Vancouver: University of British Columbia Press, 1999.

Gray, James H. *Men Against the Desert*. Calgary: Fifth House Publishers, 1996.

Gregorash, Deborah. *Just Add Water: The History of the Lethbridge Northern Irrigation District*. Lethbridge: Lethbridge Northern Irrigation District, 1996.

Johnson, Alex. *Lethbridge: From Coal Town to Commercial Centre—A Business History*. Lethbridge: Lethbridge Historical Society, 1997.

Johnson, Alex and Andy A. den Otter. *Lethbridge: A Centennial History*. Lethbridge: The City of Lethbridge and The Whoop-Up Country Chapter, Historical Society of Alberta, 1985.

Jones, David C. *Empire of Dust: Settling and Abandoning the Prairie Dry Belt*. Edmonton: University of Alberta Press, 1987.

McClintock, Walter. *The Old North Trial: Life, Legends & Religion of the Blackfeet Indians*. Lincoln, NE: Bison Books, 1999.

Morris, Alexander. *The Treaties of Canada with the Indians of Manitoba and the North-West Territories*. Toronto: Belfords, Clarke & Co., 1880.

Russell, Andy. *The Life of a River*. Toronto: McClelland and Stewart, 1987.

Ryan, Joan. *Wall of Words: The Betrayal of the Urban Indian*. Toronto: Peter Martin Associates (PMA), 1978.

Samek, Hana. *The Blackfoot Confederacy: A Comparative Study of Canadian and U.S. Indian Policy*. Albuquerque: University of New Mexico Press, 1987.

Titley, E. Brian. *A Narrow Vision: Duncan Campbell Scott and the Department of Indian Affairs in Canada.* Vancouver: University of British Columbia Press, 1986.

Treaty 7 Elders, Tribal Council, Walter Hildebrandt, Sarah Carter, and Dorothy First Rider. *The True Spirit and Original Intent of Treaty 7.* Montreal and Kingston: McGill-Queens University Press, 1996.

Tolton, George E. *The Buffalo Legacy.* Lethbridge: Fort Whoop-Up Interpretative Society, 1996.

Taylor, John Leonard. *Two Views on the Meaning of Treaties Six and Seven: The Spirit of the Alberta Indian Treaties.* Edmonton: University of Alberta Press, 1999.

Ward, Donald. *The People: A Historical Guide to the First Nations of Alberta, Saskatchewan, and Manitoba.* Calgary: Fifth House Publishers, 1995.

ARTICLES

(See also newspaper articles referenced individually in the Notes, pages 367-392.)

Dempsey, Hugh. "Treaty Research Report: Treaty Seven (1877)." Treaties and Historical Research Centre, Comprehensive Claims Branch, Self-Government, Indian and Northern Affairs Canada, 1987. www.ainc-inac.gc.ca, accessed March 13, 2012.

GOVERNMENT PUBLICATIONS

Bridges, Lois. *The Oldman River Dam: Building a Future for Southern Alberta.* Edmonton: Government of Alberta, 1992.

Canada. Alberta. Legislative Assembly. *Debates and Proceedings.* Oral Question Period, 22nd Legislature, 2nd Session, March 14, 1990, 67–68.

Canada. *House of Commons Debates.* Volume IV. 1910–11.

Government of Alberta. *Environmental Monitoring of the Oldman Dam: Eight Years of Progress.* Edmonton: Government of Alberta, 1999. (paper copies no longer available)

Government of Alberta. *Management of Water Resources Within the Oldman River Basis: Report and Recommendations.* Edmonton: Environmental Council of Alberta (ECA), 1979.

Oldman River Dam Environmental Advisory Committee, *Oldman River Dam: Environmental Advisory Committee—Final Recommendations.* Edmonton: Environmental Council of Alberta (ECA), 2001. Publication #1/906.

Oldman River Dam Environmental Assessment Panel, Transcriptions of

Public Hearings, Volumes 3–14. Edmonton: Environmental Assessment Office.

Government of Canada. *Oldman Dam Environmental Assessment Panel: Report of the Environmental Assessment Panel*. Ottawa: Federal Environmental Review Office, 1992.

Miller, Kahn-Tineta and George Lerchs. *The Historical Development of the Indian Act, Second Edition*. #QS-3292-000-EE-A2. Ottawa: Department of Indian and Northern Affairs, 1978.

R. v. Born With A Tooth, Second Trial, Calgary, February 22–March, 1994. Sentencing Hearing conducted on September 9, 1994. Court of Appeal File Number for Transcripts: 15373. Transcripts located at the Office of the Court of Appeal for Alberta, in Calgary.

R. v. Milton Born With A Tooth, Lethbridge, February 25–March 5, 1991. Sentencing conducted on March 25, 1991, Court of Appeal File Number for Transcripts: 12492. Transcripts located at the Office of Court of Appeal for Alberta, in Calgary.

UNPUBLISHED DOCUMENTS

Duncan, S.A. Inspector, Royal Canadian Mounted Police, Commercial Crime Section. *Investigation Reports Nov.4/88-July 11/90*. Located in Application Record of Applicant in the case of *Kostuch v. The Queen*; Application for Leave to Appeal to the Supreme Court of Canada, November 23, 1987. Exhibits 21–31.

Notes

Endnotes are an important part of any document that purports to call itself history. Yet, when I read narrative history, I find the endnote numbers within the text interrupt the flow of the story. A few years ago, I read the excellent book *A Team of Rivals: The Political Genius of Abraham Lincoln,* by Doris Kearns Goodwin. Instead of using endnote numbers in the text, she links the endnote citations to the text using quotations, or "text strings." I found her approach very effective and have adopted it for this book. My editor tells me that this is in fact an old style of endnotes that is making a comeback. I can see why. Quotations from interviews are self-evident in the text and are acknowledged at the beginning of each of the chapter entries below.

PART ONE: GATHERING THE EVIDENCE
THE PAINTING

"Milton Born With A Tooth vows... an economic value," "I Will be Harassing the Enemy," *Toronto Star,* June 2, 1991.

"very much... system so blatantly?" "Milton Born With A Tooth: Messenger of the River," *Nativebeat,* June 14, 1991.

"in a nutshell . . . past 120 years," Jack Glenn, *Once Upon an Oldman,* 100. Glenn is quoting an "observer" for the Mennonite Central Committee of Milton's first trial in Lethbridge.

"more rarely... capacity to live," Joseph Krutch, *The Desert Year,* 5.

THE WRITER: JACK GLENN

This chapter includes quotations from interviews the author conducted with Jack Glenn, Joanne Helmer, Leonard Hungry Wolf, Lorna Born With A Tooth, and Martha Kostuch.

THE GUARDIANS OF THE RIVER: LORNE FITCH AND CHERYL BRADLEY

This chapter contains quotations from interviews the author conducted with Cheryl Bradley, Lorne Fitch, Leonard Hungry Wolf, Evelyn Kelman, and Devalon Small Legs.

"Well, things kind of went... had been given," Percy Bullchild, *The Sun Came*

Down, 89, 90. It should be noted that in portions of the text I paraphrased the wording of Mr Bullchild, rather than using exact quotes, so there are no quotation marks for those sections.

TREATY 7: SHARING THE LAND?

The history of Treaty 7 negotiations presented in this chapter is based on Hugh Dempsey, "Treaty Negotiations – Government Perspective," 2–5; Hugh Dempsey, *Crowfoot*; and Alexander Morris, *The Treaties of Canada with the Indians of Manitoba and the North-West Territories*, 267–69. Other quotations in the chapter come from interviews the author conducted with Reg Crowshoe and Devalon Small Legs.

"had a dread... invasion of our country," Father Scollen, in Alexander Morris, *The Treaties of Canada with the Indians of Manitoba and the North-West Territories*, 247–49.

"Settlers were eyeing the rich grasslands," Hugh Dempsey, *Crowfoot*, 93.

"the interpreters... in the negative," Father Scollen, in Ibid, 106.

"wishes to allow... to encroach," David Laird, in Morris, 269.

"hereby cede, release,... to the lands," Treaty 7 Elders, *The True Spirit and Original Intent of Treaty 7*, text of treaty, 232–39.

"There was no no... land with them," Ibid, xv, 24.

"the year of the mild winter... But who would listen?" Dempsey, *Crowfoot*, 108–12, Chapter 10 ("Starvation"), and Chapter 12 ("The Long Walk Home").

Note:

What was Canada's point of view on Treaty 7 in 1877? Though he did not negotiate Treaty 7, most of the numbered treaties of Canada were negotiated by Alexander Morris, a former chief justice from Manitoba. He treated First Nations' peoples with respect, though he could not be said to transcend his time in his attitudes. While the plains tribes were starving to death in the northwest, Alexander Morris wrote a book, *The Treaties of Canada with the Indians of Manitoba and the North-West Territories*, to show the importance of the treaties, both for Canada and the First Nations. In the preface to his book he writes:

> The question of the relations of the Dominion of Canada to the Indians of the North-West, is one of great practical importance. The work, of obtaining their good will, by entering into treaties of alliance with them, has now been completed. ... As an aid to the other and equally important duty—that of carrying out, in their integrity, the

obligations of these treaties, and devising means whereby the Indian population of the Fertile Belt can be rescued from the hard fate which otherwise awaits them, owing to the speedy destruction of the buffalo, hitherto the principal food supply of the Plains Indians, and that they may be induced to become, by the adoption of agricultural and pastoral pursuits, a self-supporting community—I have prepared this collection of treaties… in the hope that I may hereby contribute to the completion of the work… that, of, by treaties, securing the good will of the Indian tribes, and by the helpful hand of the Dominion, opening up to them, a future of promise, based on the foundations of instruction and the many other advantages of civilized life.

THE FARMER: ROY JENSON

This chapter includes quotations from interviews conducted by the author with Rick Ross, Reg Crowshoe, and Roy Jenson.

PART TWO: THE PLAYERS
THE FARMERS AND LETHBRIDGE NORTHERN
IRRIGATION DISTRICT (LNID)

This chapter includes quotations from interviews the author conducted with Roy Jenson and Rick Ross, and one quote based on an interview the author conducted with farmer Leonard Haney. The information and text from the 1977 drought is very close to exactly what Rick Ross told me. He explained it very clearly, so I have put words very close to what he has said in the book

"the loneliness… trees and water," Deborah Gregorash, *Just Add Water: The History of the Lethbridge Northern Irrigation District*, 4.

"a land blessed of the Gods ….er golden horn," in David C. Jones, *Empire of Dust*, 13.

"frothy boosterism… utter miscalculation," Ibid, 3.

"Buildings and equipment were :…stop foreclosures," LNID, 14.

"several days of thunderstorms… rose quickly," Ibid, Chapters 3 and 4.

"menacing… conquest," James Gray, *Men Against the Desert*, 62.

"The Crop has failed… to my taste," Edna Jacques, in Ibid, 8.

"discovered… around abandoned buildings," Gray, 29.

"idle irrigation equipment… shout enough, we'll get rain," Jack Glenn, *Once*

Upon an Oldman, 40.

"dwindling flow of the Oldman," Lois Bridges, *The Oldman River Dam: Building a Future for Southern Alberta*, 43.

"literally running out of water... demand a commitment," Ibid, 40,41.

"instituted water restrictions on residents and businesses," LNID, 43.

CONTROVERSY AND MITIGATION

This chapter includes quotations from interviews conducted by the author with Lorne Fitch, Joanne Helmer, Louise Mandell, and Roy Jenson.

"the recreation value... very preliminary," letter from T.A. Drinkwater, Deputy Minister Alberta Parks and Recreation, to W. Solodzuk, Deputy Minister Alberta Environment, and P.G. Melnychuk, ADM, September 1976 / received October 25, 1976.

"dam is not required at this time, or in the foreseeable future," Environmental Council of Alberta, 1979 report, 196.

"indefensible," Jack Glenn, *Once Upon an Oldman*, 38.

"Alberta's studies in relation .... political decision," Ibid, 257.

"It was simply a different ....beyond a no-growth scenario," Lois Bridges, *The Oldman River Dam*, 32.

"is in response to your request," letter from Peter Melnychuk to H. Kroeger, October 25, 1979.

"create a demand," Memo from R.G. McFarlane, Chief Deputy Minister, to H. Kroeger, Minister, August 18, 1981; and Memo, from Jim Martyn, Director, Public Communications—to File—Water Advisory Committee "Confidential," July 23, 1981. Both memos refer to the use of the wording "create a demand" for water resource development at a meeting of the Water Advisory Committee executive, chaired by H. Kroeger on July 22, 1981.

"water... is controversial... because it is crucial," Peter Lougheed, in letter from Jim Martyn, Director Public Relations, to file, July 23, 1981.

"convinced me... came to fresh water," Peter Lougheed, "A Thirsty Uncle Looks North," *Globe and Mail*, November 11, 2005.

"disappointed... growth in southern Alberta... environmentally aware," "Editorial Opposition to Oldman River Dam Slammed," *Lethbridge Herald*, March 27, 1990.

"no net loss... fishing opportunities," Glenn, 53.

"When the budget is spent... made our targets," told to Lorne Fitch by a senior Alberta civil servant, Lorne Fitch, interview with author.

"Another benefit from the dam... buffalo drive sites, campsites," Bridges, 98.

"nor did they seek consultation," Glenn, 53.

"[T]he proposed dam... court battles," Ibid, 45.

"soon be cut off... slipping through our fingers," Ibid, 45.

"designated a Provincial... international," Brian Reeves, in Glenn, 52, 53.

"yet-to-be-released... report is being referred to," Ibid, 53.

THE CRUSADER: MARTHA KOSTUCH

This chapter includes quotations from interviews the author conducted with Martha Kostuch, Cliff Wallis, Cheryl Bradley, Roy Jenson, and Rick Ross.

"serves a public education... monitoring ability," Alberta Information and Privacy Commissioner, Order #99-015, October 6, 1999, Alberta Environment Review #1480.

"the Alberta government... to build the dam," Joanne Helmer, "Why Do We Need a Dam on the Oldman?" *Lethbridge Herald*, September 10, 1987.

"social anarchists... being ridiculous," Minister of the Environment Ken Kowalski, in Glenn, 51.

"clear noncompliance," *Friends of the Oldman River Society v. Alberta* (Minister of the Environment) [1987], 85 Alta. A.R. 321.

"Construction is continuing... status," *Lethbridge Herald*, December 14, 1987.

"The Court decision... surprise to anybody?" Joanne Helmer, *Lethbridge Herald*, December 10, 1987.

"keep building the dam," Glenn, 55.

"This isn't justice... should be sued," *Alberta Report*, December 21, 1987.

"Justice Ellen Picard of the Court of Queen's Bench," *Friends of Oldman River v. Alberta* (Minister of the Environment) [1988], 89 A.R. 339 (QB).

"ignited," Glenn, 56.

"chief weapon... favoured the dam or the government," Glenn, 257–60.

"I did my own research... to tell me what to think," Kevin Van Tighem, Letter to the Editor, *Alberta Report*, June 27, 1988.

"we who live... stress points are everywhere," Kevin Van Tighem, "Environmental Issues Keep Blowing Up," Letter to the Editor, *Edson Report*, undated copy.

"Environment Minister Ken Kowalski... change its name," Kevin Van

Tighem, *Lethbridge Herald,* October 14, 1987.

"told the crowd… burning the furniture to keep warm," Kevin Van Tighem, "No Consensus at Dam Forum," *Lethbridge Herald,* March 7, 1988.

MARTHA V. ALBERTA AND CANADA

This chapter includes quotations from interviews the author conducted with Martha Kostuch, Lorne Fitch, and Cheryl Bradley. Some quotes attributed to Martha are from her journals and letters written at the time of the events. Martha prosecuted Alberta under s. 35(1) of the *Canadian Fisheries Act.* Initial facts of the prosecutions and the Informations themselves are contained within the decision of Judge Fradsham in the decision at 78 Alta. L.R. (2d) 131.

"no person shall carry on… destruction of fish habitat." *Canadian Fisheries Act,* RSC 1985, c. C-46, s. 35(1) and s 35 (2).

"In December 2011, I tried to speak to Fraser ….nsuccessful." On December 2, 2011, the author left a message on Fraser's work voice-mail, explaining his book project, identifying that there were chapters in the book that related to the first trial of Milton Born With A Tooth, and the attempts of Martha Kostuch to prosecute Alberta. The author also explained that he had read all the transcripts and the case decisions related to these subject areas. The author said that he wanted to speak to Fraser to understand his point of view in these matters, as it would inform how the author told the story, even though the author knew that Fraser, as a sitting judge, could not speak to him on the record. Fraser called the author back the next day and left a message on the author's work voice-mail, explaining that he would be prepared to speak to the author, though he did not know how much he could remember after all these years, and whether he could add anything to the public record. Fraser said that he would have to speak to the author later in December as he was going on a holiday. The author called Fraser back and left a voice-mail on December 21, suggesting dates to speak and asking him to call back. Fraser did not call the author back. No negative inference should be drawn from the failure of Fraser to call the author back on this matter. A lot of trust would be required for a sitting judge to speak "off the record" with someone doing a book on potentially controversial matters. In his shoes, the author may not have spoken to the writer either, out of an abundance of caution.

"by the appropriate enforcement agency ….is Department's blessing," Decision of Judge Fradsham, 78 Alta. L.R. (2d), pages 135, 136.

372   WHO SPEAKS FOR THE RIVER?

"blanket policy... committed an offence," Decision of Justice Harvie, 75 Alta. L.R. (2d) 110, page 62.

"is fairly straightforward ....one by the society," Following are citations to all the reports prepared by Inspector Duncan: Inspector S.A. Duncan, in Applicant Brief to the Supreme Court of Canada, March 22, 1993, *Kostuch v. Alberta*, Court of Queen's Bench, Decision of Mr. Justice Power refusing to overturn. Reports dated: November 4, 1988; December 15, 1988; June 18, 1989; October 18, 1989; October 23, 1989; January 29, 1990; April 11, 1990; April 18, 1990; April 24, 1990.

"We also discussed... Fisheries Act," Ibid, January 29, 1990. In this report, Inspector Duncan records a meeting between he, Federal Crown Attorney Jim Shaw, and two high-level Alberta civil servants. The "we" in the text refers to this meeting.

"came a long time... culture that will break it," Milton Born With A Tooth, in *Nativebeat*, June 1991, 14–16.

"exploited... bunch of hippies," Al Beeber, "A Dam Blockade that Fizzled," *Lethbridge Herald*, August 11, 1988.

"a rather ludicrous situation... that body itself, cannot," In the Matter of the Criminal Code of Canada, Section 507.1 Kenneth Kowalski (Minister of Department of Public Works, Supply & Services), W.A. Stephenson Construction (Western) Limited & SCI Engineering & Constructors Inc. Transcript of Hearing before Judge Harvie, January 11 and February 28, 1990. Provincial Court #Co141983273A01, B01, CO1. Comments from Fraser are found on pages 62–63 of the transcript.

"Counsel for Mrs. Kostuch appears... an independent tribunal as required," Decision of Judge Harvie, 75 Alta. L.R. (2d), page 125.

"I do not believe... proper administration of justice," Minister of Justice Kim Campbell, press release, "No Action Planned on Alberta," *Globe and Mail*, July 11, 1990.

"Dr. Kostuch has not attempted... but a very proper use of the process," Decision of Judge Fradsham, 78 Alta. L.R. (2d), page 131.

"In most instances... on its own discretion," Associate Chief Justice Miller, Court of Queen's Bench, *Kostuch v. Kowalksi*, 81 Alta. L.R. (2d), page 221.

"We do not think... suggests the contrary," 125 Alta. L.R. (2d) 214, paragraph 19.

"simply because a crime... case I can say there is none," HMQ on the Information of *Martha Kostuch v. Her Majesty The Queen in the right of Alberta*, W.A. Stephenson Construction (Western) Ltd., SCI Engineering & Constructors Ltd. Court File #21075833-P1-0101-0102, 0201,0202,0301,0402,0502. Transcript of Proceedings Before Judge Fradsham, March 22, 1993. This hearing was to determine whether or not special prosecutor George Dangerfield would either stay the charges against Alberta or determine that they should proceed. Later, Martha Kostuch applied for leave to appeal to the Supreme Court of Canada on this issue. This transcript containing these comments is located in the Application Brief to the Supreme Court of Canada, prepared by lawyer Clayton Ruby, November 23, 1995, *Martha Kostuch v. The Attorney General For Alberta;* this application for leave to appeal was denied.

MAYCROFT: THE HAPPENING

This chapter includes quotations from interviews the author conducted with Martha Kostuch, Cliff Wallis, Lorne Fitch, Cheryl Bradley, and Dianne Pachal.

"Is this where the rally's going to be?" Wendy Dudley, "Fans of Oldman Cluster at Concert Site," *Calgary Herald*, June 10, 1989.

"doubt[ed] the men… they might lose their jobs," Sally Petrich, in Ibid.

"busy driving cattle… country is nothing," Buster Davis, in Ibid.

"There wasn't much advertising… doesn't do anybody any good," Ibid.

"It may not be Woodstock… most were pleased with the event's serious tone," Wendy Dudley, "River Rally," *Calgary Herald*, June 13, 1989.

"Reg Crowshoe, son of Piikani leader… like that happen, you know,'" Mark Lisac, "Friends of the Oldman in for the Long Haul," *Edmonton Journal*, June 14, 1989.

"There will be severe upstream… of an entire ecosystem," Dudley, "River Rally."

"agrees that such concerts… something,'" Dave Veitch, "A Dam Jam," *Calgary Sun*, June 11, 1989.

"'some concern ….nhance the environment in the area," Ibid.

"drumming and dancing took place all day," Sherri Horvat, "Throngs Gather for Legends, Lessons," *Lethbridge Herald*, June 12, 1989.

"small canopied stage… want to take our holy river," Wendy Dudley, "8000 Sing Out for Oldman," *Calgary Herald*, June 12, 1989.

"Frisbees flew with kites, and dogs played catch," Dudley, "River Rally."

"foothills ranch country... ol'camp cookie sing,'" Lisac, "Friends of the Oldman in for the Long Haul."

"timelessness... will not happen," Horvat, "Throngs Gather for Legends, Lessons."

"While fans clapped... dying," Dudley, "River Rally."

"When the canaries died... Hang in there; we've got to keep this fight up," Horvat, "Throngs Gather for Legends, Lessons."

"weathered but relaxed... gave his all," Ibid.

"Many Albertans... long way into the future," Stephen Duncan, *Financial Post*, June 19, 1989.

ALBERTA: DEFYING THE LAW

This chapter includes information from interviews the author conducted with Martha Kostuch.

"If there were any... I have faith in the courts," Ralph Klein, in Jack Glenn, *Once Upon an Oldman*, 63.

"the fish habitat issue could be dealt with by the criminal courts," Ibid, 166.

"ignoring federal law... not too much to ask," Joanne Helmer, "Respect the Law," *Lethbridge Herald*, March 27, 1990.

"We see from comments... obeying the law?" Alberta Legislative Assembly, *Debates and Proceedings* (March 14, 1990) p. 67–68.

"vital to the economic... approval of the project," Joanne Helmer, "Dam Not Vital to Survival," *Lethbridge Herald*, March 16, 1990.

"frantic... carved hillsides and stumps," Mike Lamb, "Activity Continues at Oldman Dam," *Lethbridge Herald*, March 18, 1990.

"the dam was likely . . . bigger than usual," Mike Lamb, "Dam Shutdown Inevitable," *Lethbridge Herald*, March 20, 1990.

THE WARRIOR: MILTON BORN WITH A TOOTH

This chapter includes quotations from interviews conducted by the author with Cliff Wallis, Dianne Pachal, Chuck Provost, Evelyn Kelman, Leonard Hungry Wolf, and Devalon Small Legs. Quotations from Milton explaining why and how he came to form the Lonefighters come from his testimony at his second trial: *R. v. Born With A Tooth*, Second Trial, Calgary, February 22–March,

1994. Sentencing Hearing conducted on September 9, 1994. Court of Appeal File Number for Transcripts: 15373. Transcripts located at the Office of the Court of Appeal for Alberta, in Calgary.

"We as Aboriginal people… land and resources," Elija Harper, from *As it Happens*, CBC Radio, April 12, 1990.

"rare and significant pieces… discover what went on there," Barry Dau, in "Dam History Held in Boxes," *Lethbridge Herald*, June 8, 1991.

"The cultural and ecological genocide… poorer for it," Dr. Brian Reeves, in Jack Glenn, *Once Upon an Oldman*, 205.

"outrage against the law," Nelbert Little Mustache, in *Lethbridge Herald*, "Dam History Held in Boxes."

"the white children laughed… my life miserable," Darcy Henton, "I Will Be Harassing the Enemy," *Toronto Star*, June 2, 1991.

"'Destroy the Indian to save the man… humanitarians,'" Hana Samek, *The Blackfoot Confederacy*, 123.

"conversion to Christianity… civilized," Ibid, 25.

"fair play… half-Anglicized paupers?" Ibid.

"we should be compelled to feed them . . . of the buffalo," Ibid, 40.

"marriage and divorce… and horse racing," Ibid, 128.

"Each denomination clamoured… dismal as a rule," Ibid, 139, 142.

"completely unsuitable for its purpose," Ibid, 142.

"could accommodate forty or fifty pupils," Ibid.

"As D.C. Scott pointed out… children to Catholic schools," Ibid, 143.

"chased nine runaways… 'pretended grievances,'" Ibid, 146–48.

"not unusual, since churches provided health care," Ibid, 167.

"Dr. Peter H. Bryce… his post," Ibid, 168.

"presented a damning report… Indian health care," Ibid.

"just how perilously close the… suffered from Tuberculosis," Ibid, 171.

"They were disrespecting… Wow, it can be done," the last section in this chapter is derived from the trial testimony of Milton Born With A Tooth, second trial, Calgary, 1994.

THE PIPE CARRIER: DEVALON SMALL LEGS

This chapter includes quotations from interviews conducted by the author with Devalon Small Legs, Roy Jenson, Reg Crowshoe, and Rick Ross. It also contains quotations from the second trial of Milton Born With A Tooth. For citation, see Bibliography

"It is indicative of the way the bureaucracy works… precedence," Joan Ryan, *Wall of Words*, 18.

"I give up my life… suffered," Ibid, 84.

"The very nature… problem in society," Ibid, xvii.

"How you get a pipe carrier… who has that ability," trial testimony of Milton Born With A Tooth, second trial, Calgary, 1994 .

THE PIIKANI AND THE LNID

"We had to slow down… understood better," Ibid.

"marked by a mounting interest… who favoured surrender," Hana Samek, *The Blackfoot Confederacy*, 111–15.

"While no doubt the holding… better policy to avoid it," Ibid, 117.

"The *Indian Act* is to protect… probably we are," Canada, *House of Commons Debates* (April 26, 1911).

"Jack Tully… span it," Mike Lamb, "Peigans give Conditions for Weir Use," *Lethbridge Herald*, May 1978; related articles: "Federal Official Explains Claim Probably Legitimate," *Kanai News* 1 (May 1978); "Peigans Block LNID Canal," Ibid. In the latter, "Dave Nicholson, the director general for Indian Affairs in Alberta said that the Peigan Band does in fact have a legitimate claim to the Oldman River and the waterbeds. He [Nicholson] added that the department has examined the legal documentation and found everything in order."

"riot-equipped… Peigan guarding," Mike Lamb, "LNID Will Seek to have Peigans Cited for Contempt," *Lethbridge Herald*, May 30, 1978.

"a deliberate and public… to the judicial system," Andy Ogle and Mike Lamb, "Their Point Proven, Indians End Blockade," by *Lethbridge Herald*, June 1, 1978.

"Court [was] more than fully… very sorry," "Dismissal of Contempt of Court Charges by Judge," *Lethbridge Herald*, June 7, 1978.

"all natural resources of the land ….elong to the Peigan people," Permit between the Minister of Indian Affairs and Northern Development and the Government of Alberta, June 11, 1991, Exhibit #18, second trial of Milton Born With A Tooth, Calgary, 1994. See also Jack Glenn, *Once Upon an* Oldman, 39. I am referring here to Clause #15, that Alberta must "vacate" the land once it no longer needs the land.

"I can remember… kicked around," Roger Epp, "Pincher Upbringing Gives Special Feel for the South," *Lethbridge Herald*, 1979.

THE SISTER & BROTHER: EVELYN KELMAN & REG CROWSHOE

This chapter includes quotations taken from interviews the author conducted with Evelyn Kelman and Reg Crowshoe. For more information on the traditional Lonefighters, see Rocky Woodward, "Lonefighter Roots Date Back to 1500s," *Windspeaker* 8, no. 13 (1990).

"supernatural power and strength… people and groups," Reg Crowshoe and Sybille Manneschmidt, *Akak'stiman*, 19, 22.

PART THREE: THE SHOWDOWN
THE LONEFIGHTERS: BACK TO THE LAND

This chapter includes quotations from interviews the author conducted with Devalon Small Legs, Cliff Wallis, Evelyn Kelman, and Roy Jenson. Quotations from Martha Kostuch are taken from her journals on the relevant dates. All quotations from trial transcripts are individually endnoted.

Trial testimony from Milton's first and second trials comes from the transcripts for those trials. See Bibliography for citations

"We had to get everyone understanding… about the issue," trial testimony of Milton Born With A Tooth, second trial, Calgary, 1994.

"advisability of getting arrested," evidence adduced at first trial of Milton Born With A Tooth, Lethbridge, 1991.

"because then it was a… muster supplies," trial testimony of Milton Born With A Tooth, second trial, Calgary, 1994.

"We did not want to just build… within our own way," Ibid.

"shield… It made sense," trial testimony of Milton Born With A Tooth, second trial, Calgary, 1994.

"A hole is being punched… groundbreaking ceremony," "Peigans to Punch Hole in LNID Weir," *Lethbridge Herald*, August 3, 1990.

"kind of at-the-wire feeling… forget something… awesome," trial testimony of Milton Born With A Tooth, second trial, Calgary, 1994.

"This dam is….e destroyed," "Peigan Group Wants Dam Halted: Lonefighters

Building Channel to Block Irrigation Flow," *Lethbridge Herald*, August 4, 1990.

"nor band council... river flow," Ibid.

"endorsed the action ....on-violent action," Ibid.

"It was stuck enough... We are digging it out," trial testimony of Milton Born With A Tooth, second trial, Calgary, 1994.

"Who are you... would report us," trial testimony of Doug Clark and Sgt. Mills, first trial of Milton Born With A Tooth, Lethbridge, 1991.

"damage... At that time... and the Alberta government," trial testimony of Sergeant Mills, first trial of Milton Born With A Tooth, Lethbridge, 1991.

"nothing to get excited about... sometimes swimming in the river," "RCMP Deny Action on Peigan's Threat to Reroute Oldman," *Edmonton Journal*, August 7, 1990.

"Furious southern Alberta... 48 little towns that need the water," Ibid.

"My personal observation... surveys had been done," trial testimony of Doug Clark, second trial of Milton Born With A Tooth, Lethbridge, 1991. Note: Doug Clark was cross-examined extensively during the second trial based on notes he himself created, a sort of running journal of his observations during the Lonefighter crisis. The author only includes quotes that are either directly from Clark or that he adopted in his testimony.

"I doubt the Lonefighter... somebody should do something about it," "LNID Considers Water Alternatives," *Lethbridge Herald*, August 7, 1990.

"We had our own... happened," trial testimony of Milton Born With A Tooth, second trial, Calgary, 1994.

"Milton Born With A Tooth was in charge... confrontational," trial testimony of Peter Melnychuk, first trial of Milton Born With A Tooth, Lethbridge, 1991.

"Klein and the project itself... to listen to the Peigan people?... Not one... consider that," "Klein Charged With Genocidal Act," *Kanai News*, August 8, 1990.

"We have to have law and order in this province," "Emergency Meeting Sought on Diversion," *Lethbridge Herald*, August 9, 1990.

"A dozen rough vigilantes... saboteurs," Brian Hutchinson, "Playing with Water—and Fire: The Oldman River Ecofreaks Take Up with Some Dangerous Indian Friends," *Alberta Report*, August 20, 1990.

"a lie... vanquished one," Link Byfield, Letter from the Publisher, *Alberta Report*, August 20, 1990.

A COMMUNITY DIVIDED

This chapter includes quotations from interviews the author conducted with Reg Crowshoe, Evelyn Kelman, and Cliff Wallis.

"A lot of us are… water diversion," "Lonefighters Claim Name Being Misused," *Lethbridge Herald*, August 9, 1990.

"virtually split ….ctions," Gord Smiley, "Province Won't Tolerate Bid to Divert River," *Lethbridge Herald*, August 14, 1990.

"The actions of band members… the supplying of food," "Chief Lends Moral Support," *Lethbridge Herald*, August 15, 1990.

"the police role is to… confrontation increases," "RCMP Have No Proof Yet of Any Native Illegalities," *Lethbridge Herald*, August 16, 1990.

"To me, whether… process of healing the river," Ibid.

"the attempt to divert the Oldman… Tonka toys," Mike Lamb, "Peigans Dig In to finish Channel," *Lethbridge Herald*, August 26, 1990.

"The feel of winter… stupid next week," Lamb, "Peigans Dig In to Finish Channel."

"one of the dikes… zero," trial testimony of Doug Clark testimony, second trial of Milton Born With A Tooth, Lethbridge, 1991.

THE BREAKTHROUGH: AT LAST!

This chapter includes quotations from interviews the author conducted with Devalon Small Legs and Evelyn Kelman. Quotations from Martha Kostuch are taken from her journals on the relevant dates. Other quotations, individually endnoted, come from testimony from the second trial of Milton Born With A Tooth.

"probably ….nd of the season," trial testimony of Doug Clark, second trial of Milton Born With A Tooth, Calgary, 1994.

"The camp was busier… carried out," "Breakdown Blamed for Diversion Delay," *Lethbridge Herald*, August 28, 1990.

"atop a windy hill overlooking… the river is going to flow this evening," Ibid.

"dismissed the activity… their privilege," Calgary Herald, August 28.

"a pipe ceremony ….ade to the river," Bert Crowfoot, *Windspeaker*, August 30, 1990.

"began to work on the final few feet… years before," Ibid.

"This is the first time anybody has… to be there to feel it," Garry Allison, "River Diversion Starts With a Trickle," *Lethbridge Herald*, August 30, 1990.

"aerial inspections… several days," "Peigans Initiate Diversion of Water," *Calgary Herald*, August 29, 1990.

"should be fully closed off… come to us," Allison, "River Diversion Starts with a Trickle."

"could possibly achieve… river off," Dennis McGowan, from trial testimony of Doug Clark, second trial of Milton Born With A Tooth, Calgary, 1994. Doug Clark was cross-examined at Milton's trial on information contained in his affidavit, including this information from McGowan.

"stuff they were… successful," trial testimony of Doug Clark, second trial of Milton Born With A Tooth, Calgary, 1994. Doug Clark was cross-examined at trial about the fact that his view that the Lonefighters were unlikely to achieve their goal was not in his affidavit. It should be noted that lawyers would have decided which facts were relevant to the application. One could not say that their failure to include Clark's view that the Lonefighters were unlikely to succeed that spring in Clark's affidavit for the judge was either morally wrong or dishonorable. One can say, however, that by doing so they did not reach a high standard of fairness, either deliberately, or through inadvertence.

"Until [the Lonefighters… something peacefully and without violence," Craig Albrecht, "Court Order Halts Work on Diversion," *Lethbridge Herald*, August 31, 1990.

"The laws of this country… sets of law," "Province Fights Diversion with Court Injunction," *Lethbridge Herald*, August 31, 1990.

"We despise him," "Tension Mounts as Police Advance," *Windspeaker* 8, no. 13 (1990).

"They haven't stopped us… in jail," Craig Albrecht, "Court Order Halts Work on Diversion," *Lethbridge Herald*, August 31, 1990.

"We started this… we're going to do," Ibid.

"It is my hope… they might run into," Susan Mate, "Militant Peigans Say They'll Die for Cause," *Lethbridge Herald*, August 31, 1990.

"If they come… come to us and negotiate," "Lonefighters Wait for Police Action," *Edmonton Journal*, August 30, 1990.

"communities have been… ransom here," Ibid.

"Had this occurred… screaming bloody murder," Allison, "River Diversion

Starts with a Trickle."

"Initially officials... meters high," Miro Cernetig, "Natives Make Good on Threat to Cut off Water: Peigan Lonefighters Have Begun Diverting Oldman River Flow in Bid to Halt Dam's Construction," *Globe and Mail*, August 30, 1990.

"invasion... We would put them first... Oka, Quebec," "Lonefighters Folly," *Alberta Report*, September 10, 1990.

"bright and windy... Peigan flag," Ibid.

"The backhoe clawed... stopped," "Lonefighters Wait for Police Action," *Edmonton Journal*, August 30, 1990.

"melancholy... rest of the Peigan band," *Alberta Report*, "Lonefighters Folly."

"It is my belief... I can act," "Peigans Defy Injunction: Lonefighters Warn RCMP Not to Stop Diversion," *Calgary Herald*, September 1, 1990.

"the protesters should stop ... sort out all these problems," "Peigans Halt Efforts to Divert Water Flow," *Lethbridge Herald*, September 4, 1990.

"If the band council... part of the enemy," *Edmonton Journal*, September 1, 1990.

THE RCMP: INVASION?

From the beginning of the chapter, to the awakening of the Lonefighters by the "frantic screams" of Murray Small Legs, quotations are taken from the trial testimony of RCMP Officer Raymond Gaultier from Milton's two trials. Evidence quotes from the point of view of police, except where attributed below to a newspaper article, are from the trial testimony of all RCMP officers who testified at both of Milton's trials.

Except where noted as being taken from newspaper articles, trial testimony, or other materials—noted below—all quotes in this article relating to the Lonefighters are taken from interviews conducted by the author with Devalon Small Legs, Reg Crowshoe, and Evelyn Kelman.

"I had very little... going to happen," trial testimony of Officer Gaultier, first trial of Milton Born With A Tooth, Lethbridge, 1991.

"We walked in a slow pace... marching," Ibid.

"This is going to get... Yes," Ibid.

"We're armed," Ibid.

"They were baseball-sized... head in," Ibid.

"He's got a gun!" Ibid.

"The inevitable woke me... They're almost here!" trial testimony of Milton Born With A Tooth, second trial, Calgary, 1994.

"initial brunt... way it should end," Ibid.

"Oh, no, they... embedded pretty good," Ibid.

"Stay down, here comes ....n my direction," trial testimony of Officer Gaultier, first trial of Milton Born With A Tooth, Lethbridge, 1991.

"no weapons were visible," Craig Albrecht, "RCMP, Lonefighters in Standoff," *Lethbridge Herald*, September 7, 1990.

"set up an observation post... weir area," Ibid.

"remained defiant," Ibid.

"twenty-four-hour truce," *Windspeaker*, September 7 and 8, 1990.

"close," Albrecht, "RCMP, Lonefighters in Standoff."

"full view," *Windspeaker*, September 7 and 8, 1990.

"We've given them... on them," Albrecht, "RCMP, Lonefighters in Standoff."

"Once again ....ot Milton Born With A Tooth," Ibid.

"Born With A Tooth... condemned... invasion," Ibid.

"there were reports of three... close to an officer," Ibid.

"between bites... free or dead," Susan Mate, Rick Mofina, Ashley Geddes, "Dam Standoff," *Calgary Herald*, September 8, 1990.

"'The provincial... emergency basis," Craig Albrecht, "RCMP, Lonefighters in Standoff."

"'The Lonefighters are breaking the... suffer the consequences,'" Mate, Mofina, Geddes, "Dam Standoff."

"negotiation is lost... as their partner," Garry Allison, "What Do Lonefighters Want?" *Lethbridge Herald*, September 9, 1990.

"possibility of death... lingered in the air," Rocky Woodward, "Medicine Man Prayed While Lonefighters Waited," *Windspeaker*, September 7 and 8, 1990.

"They prayed the crisis... well-being," Ibid.

THE PEACEMAKER: JOE CROWSHOE

This chapter includes quotations from interviews the author conducted with Evelyn Kelman and Reg Crowshoe.

Facts about and quotes related to Joe and Josephine Crowshoe—from when they were at home on the morning of September 8 until they went to the Lonefighters' camp later that day—and quotes regarding what was said at camp when Joe was there (unless otherwise noted below), come from: Dianne Meili, "Joe and Josephine Crowshoe," in *Those Who Know: Profiles of Alberta's Native Elders*, 97–107.

"Joe Crowshoe sat . . . prayer in the Blackfoot language," (Joe's location and actions) Rocky Woodward, "Medicine Man Prayed While Lonefighers Waited," *Windspeaker*, September 7 and 8, 1990; "Lonefighters Regrouping," *Lethbridge Herald*, September 10, 1990.

"We know how the white man has treated... and educate other people," "Lonefighters Regrouping," *Lethbridge Herald*, Ibid

"cooler heads to prevail... very seriously," Al Beeber, "Police Leave Diversion Site," *Lethbridge Herald*, September 10, 1990.

"will defy... heal... Roy Jenson's backyard," Ibid.

"In the Lonefighters camp... hugging and sobbing," Woodward, "Medicine Man Prayed While Lonefighters Waited."

"It's a blessing in disguise... Oldman River Valley," Jennifer Bain and Bob Bergen, "Peigans Happy at RCMP Retreat," *Calgary Herald*, September 9, 1990.

"It was tense this morning... maybe now." Woodward, "Medicine Man Prayed While Lonefighters Waited."

"lawful efforts to stop the Oldman Dam... or the Provincial Court," "Peigan Band Backs Lonefighters," *Lethbridge Herald*, September 11, 1990.

"the grinding track... groaning diesel engine... shortest questions," Craig Albrecht, *Lethbridge Herald*, September 11, 1990.

"the pounding of drums... singing... clashed," Jim Morris, "'Law before Land Claims,' Rostad Says," *Edmonton Journal*, September 13, 1990.

"If the people receiving water... damage and harm," Ibid.

"concerned about money... rental," *Lethbridge Herald*, September 15, 1990.

PART FOUR: CRY FOR JUSTICE
SOUTHERN TRIAL

This chapter is based primarily on the court transcripts for the first trial of Milton Born With A Tooth. How the author constructed the narrative from the transcripts of the first and second trials, and more information on the transcripts themselves, is located in The Making of This Book (page 354). Quotations from the narrative that don't appear credited to media articles below or aren't attributed to interviews in the text come from the transcripts of this trial.

This chapter also includes quotations from interviews the author conducted with Joanne Helmer, Barbara Hoyt, Karen Gainer, and former Justice MacLean.

"Given his political views... No,'" Joanne Helmer, "Milton Born With A Tooth Claims He's a Victim of Political Interference," *Lethbridge Herald*, January 6, 1994.

"He just arbitrarily... would he do that?" Ibid.

"high-level sources... different from others,'" Ibid.

"Judge Wood took over the court that day, and he presided over the bail hearing for Milton Born With A Tooth," and basic facts about the bail hearing around found in: "Lonefighters' Spokesman Ordered Detained in Custody," *Lethbridge Herald*, September 19, 1990.

"in the public interest," Phil Breeze, "Lonefighters' Spokesman Ordered Held in Custody," *Lethbridge Herald*, September 19, 1990.

"Suggestions have been made... no hope now," "Lonefighter's Bail Appeal Rejected," *Lethbridge Herald*, September 26, 1990.

"Justice and the law... experience in southern Alberta," "City Not Redneck Town, Says Spokesman," *Lethbridge Herald*, October 5, 1990.

"The fact Milton will be in jail... legacy of loneliness and bitterness," from the press conference naming Evelyn Kelman as leader, in Gord Smiley, "Leaders' Jailing 'Helping Cause,'" *Lethbridge Herald*, September 26, 1990.

"Milton Deserves Justice... needs encouragement," "Lonefighters, Supporters Demonstrate," *Lethbridge Herald*, October 12, 1990.

"being held as a political prisoner... to the public, is it denied," "Lonefighter's Release Sought," *Lethbridge Herald*, November 22, 1990.

"surprise decision... law on release," "Lonefighter Granted Release," *Lethbridge Herald*, December 20, 1990.

"one mile," (and Milton's criticism of bail conditions), "Lonefighter Leader Doubtful of Early Court Appearance," *Lethbridge Herald*, December 24, 1990.

"Therefore, there wasn't... Fort Macleod," "Lonefighter Leader Seeks to Relocate Trial," *Lethbridge Herald*, February 14, 1991; see also "Lonefighter to be Tried in Fort Macleod," *Lethbridge Herald*, February 16, 1991.

"He is being set up... support the dam," "Born With A Tooth Set Up to be Crucified," *Windspeaker* 8, no. 24 (March 1, 1991).

"A number of potential jurors... *Challenge*," information about potential jurors who were Native comes from: Delon Shurtz, "Accused Upset with Jury Choice," *Lethbridge Herald*, February 26, 1991; Jack Glenn, *Once Upon an Oldman*,

99; and "Born With a Tooth Lawyer to Appeal," *Windspeaker*, March 15, 1991. The problem of how to present the fact that the Crown "challenged" two Native jurors is no easy one. Both defence lawyers and Crown attorneys resort to every cliché in the book in trying to use their "challenges" to get the best jury from their respective points of view. It would be naive to think that both sides of any trial would not consider a person's ethnicity during selection. In Ontario, for example, the case law has developed along the lines of that in the United States. It is wrong for a Crown attorney (district attorney in the US) to challenge potential jurors on ethnic grounds to deliberately keep people off the jury who have the same ethnic background as the accused. The issue is always one of proof, since no defence lawyer or court can know what is going on in the head of the Crown, except by reasonable inferences based on conduct. There may be cases where the Crown challenges, for example, a half-dozen people: every person, in effect, who shares the ethnic background as the accused. This would strongly suggest that the Crown is in fact targeting those with the same ethnic background as the accused. In the case of Milton's first trial, to my knowledge, the law had not yet unfolded in such a manner that there was clear directive that such challenges, if based on ethnicity, were wrong. Of course, even then, one would know that in such a case there was a heightened concern, at the very least, of the perception of fairness issue. All we can say is that in Milton's first trial, two Native people were challenged. Any firm conclusion that these people were challenged because of their ethnicity is unfair to the Crown in question. I have tried to make this clear in the narrative.

"It's about to be a massacre," Shurtz, "Accused Upset with Jury Choice."

"The judge wasn't representing ....lways will be a part of creation," "Born With A Tooth Defiant," *Windspeaker* 8, no. 25 (March 15, 1991).

"Day of Protest and Reflection," "Protest Planned at Sentencing," *Lethbridge Herald*, March 20, 1991.

"with clenched fists... support into the air," Mike Lamb, "Born With A Tooth's Sentence Jeered," *Lethbridge Herald*, March 26, 1991.

"Kevin Daniels... I'll be next," Amy Santoro, "Milton Gets 18 Months," *Windspeaker*, March 1991.

"'This comes next... uppercut punches," Lamb, "Born With A Tooth's Sentence Jeered."

"You weren't there... We were mothers," Santoro, "Milton Gets 18 Months."

"avoid national... inquiries," Lamb, "Born With A Tooth's Sentence Jeered."

"Basically the judge had... rule of law," Santoro, "Milton Gets 18 Months."

"The Aboriginal people... by non-Aboriginals," Task Force on the Criminal Justice System and its Impact on the Indian and Métis People of Alberta, "Justice on Trial (Cawsey Report)," March 1991, Volume #1, Main Report, Introduction, page 1, http://justice.alberta.ca/programs_services/aboriginal/Documents/cawsey/Cawsey_I_intro.pdf, accessed February 2012.

"there is no harm to come from his release," "Lonefighter Leader Out on Bail," *Lethbridge Herald*, April 3, 1991.

Why did Justice MacLean not halt the proceedings during Milton's sentencing and order the gallery to leave the Courtroom? Was he weak? I cannot give an ultimate answer, as I was not there, and do not have some privileged access to his thoughts. However, my personal view, in light of all the material I have read, and the transcripts, is that Justice MacLean, whatever his flaws, was determined to have an open Court process as a matter of vital principle. As a result, he was obviously reluctant to essentially create a "hidden" or partially hidden trial by ordering the spectators to leave the Court. He tolerated the dissent caused in part by his own actions. I am putting my thoughts here in the notes rather than the text because I want the reader to have the chance to form their own opinions first. If they remain perplexed, they can read these notes for further thoughts from me.

CRY FOR JUSTICE

This chapter includes quotations from interviews the author conducted with Martha Kostuch, Evelyn Kelman, Lorne Fitch, Devalon Small Legs, Dianne Pachal, and Roy Jenson. Unless already noted from another source below, material related to the Court of Appeal decision comes from: *R. v. Born With A Tooth* [1992], 131 A.R. 193 (C.A.).

"a spokesperson for the Canadian... seemingly unable to deal justly with aboriginal people," Jack Glenn, *Once Upon an Oldman*, 100.

"Justice MacLean said nothing," interview with Justice MacLean, 2007.

"unprepared... peacekeeping role," Glenn, 100–103.

"too personally involved," "Peigans Appeal Adjourned," *Calgary Herald*, June 19, 1992; also see Court of Appeal decision.

"buoyant... weren't just a bunch of hoodlums," "Lonefighter Wins Appeal,"

Windspeaker, September 14, 1992.

"reprimanded," "Alberta Judge Reprimanded," *Calgary Herald*, January 25, 1995.

"displayed an insensitivity… sensitive and cultural issues," and quotes that follow on this issue are from a letter from the Judicial Council to CASNP (Canadian Alliance in Solidarity With Native people) responding to the complaint advanced by this organization against Justice MacLean. Letter from the Judicial Council, April 6, 1993, in possession of the author, from Jack Glenn files. See also: "Alberta Justice was Blasted for Actions at Activist's Trial," *Calgary Herald*, May 6, 1993; "Trial Judge Rebuked," *Windspeaker*, May 10, 1993.

"unacceptable… concrete steps," Ibid.

"had responded… occurred," Ibid.

"beloved… time and knowledge," "Lawrence MacLean Tribute Fund," www.crhfoundation.ca/caring_hearts/view, accessed January 2012.

"armed, camouflaged," Glenn, 98.

"another broken promise… Piikani people," Ibid, 98.

"The watchman of the… lake form in a desert," Lois Bridges, *The Oldman River Dam: Building a Future for Southern Alberta*, 70.

"How do you tell… but to feel it," "Milton Born With A Tooth: Messenger of the River," *Nativebeat*, June 14, 1991.

"If the water had a voice… to read," "Bridges and Barricades: Crossing Over," *Border/Lines* 23 (Winter 1991–92): 48.

"direct action… right to arm ourselves," "Lonefighter Leader Warns Loss of Life," *Lethbridge Herald*, May 22, 1991.

"We're here to tear the dam… new life," "Peigan Ceremony Held at Dam," *Lethbridge Herald*, May 27, 1991.

"veiled reports of violence… let's you and I find a middle way," "Don't Cross Line, Judge Warns Lonefighter," *Lethbridge Herald*, May 31, 1991.

"my intentions… Oldman Dam project," Ibid.

DAM ON TRIAL

This chapter includes a great many quotations from the *Oldman Dam Hearings: Federal Environmental Assessment*. I have taken quotes and information on the Federal Environmental Assessment covered in this chapter from the thirteen-volume set of *Transcripts of the Proceedings of the Federal Environmental Assessment into the Oldman Dam.* I first read photocopies of some of these transcripts when I visited Jack Glenn. Later, I read volumes three to thirteen at the Environmental Assessment Library in Toronto in the summer of 2011, where they had been sent from the Environmental Assessment Library in Edmonton, in an act of great kindness. Volumes one and two were for some reason not available. However, the hearings clearly start at volume three, so the absence of the first two volumes may not matter.

Quotations from and information about what Milton said to the panel are from the transcript I received from Jack Glenn, which notes Milton's input as being from "Volume 6 (Book 2) – Nov 8/11." When I could not find Book 2 in the materials I gleaned, I studied the transcript of Milton's words and could see that they are recorded in the same format as the other transcripts, and are clearly authentic. Following are the cities, source volumes, and dates for the quotations from people I have included in this chapter relative to the hearings conducted by the Federal Environmental Assessment. Other quotations in this chapter are included below, with citations.

"If I interfere ….ood they can do," Jack Glenn, *Once Upon an Oldman*, 104.

"was exactly what Alberta had intended," Ibid, 104.

"it was a challenge… had not yet been undertaken," Ibid, 106.

"In January of 1992…build the dam," *Oldman River Society v. Canada* (Minister of Transport), [1992], 1 S.C.R. 3.

Quotations from the Environmental Assessment Hearings as follows:

Lethbridge, November 5, 1991: Volume 3

1. City of Lethbridge Mayor David Carpenter

2. Representative of the Village of Nobleford

3. City of Lethbridge Alderman Don Lebarron

   Lethbridge, November 6, 1991: Volume 4

1. Bill Arsene

2. Roy Jenson

   Travelodge Airporter Inn, Calgary, November 7, 1991: Volume 5

1. Martha Kostuch

2. Letter dated November 11, 1991, from Barry Zalmanowitz of Milner & Fenerty to the Oldman Dam Environmental Assessment Panel.

Note: The letter I refer to in the text from the Piikani Board of Health was not filed during the hearing for this day, so it did not show up in the transcript for this day. I received that particular letter as part of Jack Glenn's research materials, and it is now in my possession.

> Travelodge Airporter Inn, Calgary, November 8, 1991: Volume 6 (Book 1)
> 1. Dr. Brian Horejsi
> Travelodge Airporter Inn, Calgary, November 8, 1991: Volume 6 (Book 2)
> 1. Milton Born With A Tooth
> Brocket Community Hall, Piikani Reserve, November 16, 1991: Volume 10
> 1. Chief Leonard Bastien
> 2. Eddy Yellowhorn
> 3. Joe Crowshoe
> 4. Devalon Small Legs
> Pincher Creek, November 19, 1991: Volume 12
> 1. Kevin Van Tighem
> Pincher Creek, November 20, 1991: Volume 13
> 1. Dianne Pachal
> 2. Copy of letter filed by Andy Russell
> 3. City of Lethbridge Alderman Don Lebarron
> 4. Town of Pincher Creek Mayor Eldred Lowe

"The ruling of the court… illegal," Peter Hogg, *Constitutional Law of Canada*, 23. This is Hogg's analysis of Supreme Court of Canada ruling *Oldman River Society v. Canada* (Minister of Transport), [1992], 1 S.C.R. 3., section 30–23. Hogg's comments are an answer to all arguments that somehow building the dam without a permit was magically not illegal. It was illegal. After a court refused to order Alberta to stop building, one could say that Alberta had an "excuse" to break the law, but not before.

"decommissioned… is probable," Canada, *Oldman Dam Environmental Assessment Panel: Report of the Environmental Assessment Panel*, 1992.

"We are confident . . . we're doing it now," Glenn, 113.

"disgust… obligations to our people," Ibid, 120.

"relief from the risks… since the dam was built," Editorial, "Reservoir Ends Summer Water Woes," *Lethbridge Herald*, September 10, 1994.

TO REDO THE PAST: MILTON'S SECOND TRIAL

The information and quotations in this chapter come from the transcripts of the second trial of Milton Born With A Tooth, as discussed in "The Making of This Book" (see page 354).

Quotations have also been taken from the transcripts of the sentencing hearing in Brocket on September 9, 1994. As with the first trial of Milton Born With A Tooth, the sentencing hearing forms part of the trial transcripts. In addition, this chapter includes quotations from interviews conducted by the author with Reg Crowshoe, Karen Gainer, and Louise Mandell.

"Silently the judge ....'I promise,' said Milton" The substance of what Milton said was located in the transcripts. The "colour" or facts surrounding the ceremony, such as the fact that one could smell the burning sage, are from the newspaper source listed below. (facts related to Blackfoot ceremony conducted in court) "Blackfoot Oath is a Court First," *Calgary Herald*, March 8, 1994.

"old-timers of the court," Gordon Jaremko, "Native Activist Found Guilty," *Calgary Herald*, March 15, 1994.

"slumped forward... make it unanimous," Ibid.

"It is the provincial... a lot of money." Ron Devitt, "Peigan Activist Sentenced," *Lethbridge Herald*, September 10, 1994.

"wearing blue jeans... and taken into prison," Ibid.

"Milton embodies... governments will not do it?" Rudy Platiel, "Jailed Peigan Dam-fighter Gains Allies," *Globe and Mail*, November 5, 1994.

AND SO IT CONTINUES ...

This chapter includes quotations and information from interviews the author conducted with Rick Ross, Lorne Fitch, Cheryl Bradley, Kirby Smith, Evelyn Kelman, Reg Crowshoe, Devalon Small Legs, Cliff Wallis, and Roy Jenson.

"Alberta's last remaining... below the Oldman Dam," Jack Glenn, *Once Upon an Oldman*, 129.

"southwestern Alberta... Operation of the Oldman River Dam," Government of Alberta, *Environmental Monitoring of the Oldman River Dam: Eight Years of Progress*, 1999.

"satisfied... along the floodplain," Oldman River Dam Environmental Advisory Committee, *Oldman River Dam: Environmental Advisory Committee— Final Recommendations*, 2001.

"not much at all, considering the high stakes... $700-million deal," Joanne Helmer, "Peigan Activist Bitter Over Offer," *Lethbridge Herald*, December 24, 2000.

"supply enough energy... stark contrast," "Oldman River Plant Opens to Great Fanfare," *Calgary Herald*, June 2003.

"prayer stones... harshness of winter cold," Andy Russell, *The Life of a River*, 120–21.

AFTERWORD

This chapter includes quotations taken from interviews the author conducted with Kirby Smith, Reg Crowshoe, Devalon Small Legs, Evelyn Kelman, Dianne Pachal, Roy Jenson, Rick Ross, Lorne Fitch, Cheryl Bradley, and Martha Kostuch.

"Communication with band... to be informed," "Piikani Chief and Council Setting New Direction," *Macleod Gazette*, January 18, 2011.

"If you want to be... in a constructive way," "He's Right at Home," *Calgary Herald*, June 7, 1993.

"proudest accomplishment... Oldman River Dam," "Tory Stalwart Kowalksi Retiring," *Edmonton Journal*, December 2012.